Douglas L. Anderson

BELMONT UNIVERSITY LIBRARY
BELMONT UNIVERSITY
1900 BELMONT BLVD.
NASHVILLE, TN 37212

This Book Belongs

in the library

of

DOUGLAS L. ANDERSON

OXFORD–WARBURG STUDIES

General Editors

T. S. R. BOASE *and* G. BING

THE
CONFLICT BETWEEN PAGANISM AND CHRISTIANITY
IN THE FOURTH CENTURY

ESSAYS EDITED BY

ARNALDO MOMIGLIANO

PROFESSOR OF ANCIENT HISTORY
IN THE UNIVERSITY OF LONDON

OXFORD
AT THE CLARENDON PRESS

Oxford University Press, Ely House, London W. 1

GLASGOW   NEW YORK   TORONTO   MELBOURNE   WELLINGTON
CAPE TOWN   SALISBURY   IBADAN   NAIROBI   DAR ES SALAAM   LUSAKA   ADDIS ABABA
BOMBAY   CALCUTTA   MADRAS   KARACHI   LAHORE   DACCA
KUALA LUMPUR   SINGAPORE   HONG KONG   TOKYO

© *Oxford University Press 1963*

FIRST PUBLISHED 1963

REPRINTED LITHOGRAPHICALLY AT THE
UNIVERSITY PRESS, OXFORD
FROM CORRECTED SHEETS OF THE FIRST EDITION
1964, 1970
PRINTED IN GREAT BRITAIN

PREFACE

THE relations between Paganism and Christianity in the fourth century seemed a suitable theme for a course of lectures at the Warburg Institute. The eight lectures here collected were delivered in the academic year 1958–9 and are published as they were delivered. It was, however, considered expedient to translate into English the two lectures which were given in French and the one which was in German. The lecturers were left free to choose their own subject and to add the notes they wanted for publication. Specialists will judge each paper on its individual merits. For the general reader I have added, by way of introduction, a few pages on the problem of Christianity and the decline of the Roman empire. They were originally part of the two Taft Lectures which I delivered in the University of Cincinnati in 1959.

A. M.

December 1960
University College London

CONTENTS

Introduction. Christianity and the Decline of the Roman Empire   1
By PROFESSOR A. MOMIGLIANO, *University College London*

I. The Social Background of the Struggle between Paganism and Christianity   17
By PROFESSOR A. H. M. JONES, *University of Cambridge*

II. Pagans and Christians in the Family of Constantine the Great   38
By PROFESSOR J. VOGT, *University of Tübingen*

III. Christianity and the Northern Barbarians   56
By PROFESSOR E. A. THOMPSON, *University of Nottingham*

IV. Pagan and Christian Historiography in the Fourth Century A.D.   79
By PROFESSOR A. MOMIGLIANO

V. The Survival of Magic Arts   100
By DR. A. A. BARB, *Warburg Institute, London*

VI. Synesius of Cyrene and Alexandrian Neoplatonism   126
By PROFESSOR H. I. MARROU, *Sorbonne*

VII. Anti-Christian Arguments and Christian Platonism: from Arnobius to St. Ambrose   151
By PROFESSOR P. COURCELLE, *Collège de France*

VIII. The Pagan Revival in the West at the End of the Fourth Century   193
By PROFESSOR H. BLOCH, *American Academy in Rome and Harvard University*

Figs. 1–16   between 218–219

Index   219

INTRODUCTION

Christianity and the Decline of the Roman Empire

ARNALDO MOMIGLIANO

I

I MAY perhaps begin with a piece of good news. In this year 1959 it can still be considered an historical truth that the Roman empire declined and fell. Nobody as yet is prepared to deny that the Roman empire has disappeared. But here the historians begin to disagree. When we ask them to tell us when the Roman empire disappeared, we collect an embarrassing variety of answers. The more so because there is a tendency to identify the beginnings of the Middle Ages with the end of the Roman empire: a tendency which would have given no little surprise to medieval men who firmly believed in the continuity of the Roman empire. There are, of course, historians who see the Middle Ages making their appearance and the Roman empire sinking into oblivion with the conversion of Constantine in 312 or with the inauguration of Constantinople in 330. And there are historians who would delay the end of the Roman empire to that year 1806—more precisely to that day 6 August 1806—in which Napoleon I compelled the Austrian emperor Francis II to underwrite the end of the Holy Roman empire. Between these two extreme dates there are plenty of intermediate choices. There are still traditionalists ready to support the once famous date of September 476, when Romulus Augustulus lost his throne; and there are more sophisticated researchers who would prefer the death of Justinian in 565 or the coronation of Charlemagne in 800—when the Roman empire was in a way replaced by two Roman empires. Another favourite date is the fall of Constantinople in 1453 as the end of the new Rome. Uninhibited by such a variety of opinions, Professor Arnold Toynbee has succeeded in adding one which at first sight seems to be of remarkable originality. He has reproached Gibbon for not understanding that the Roman empire began to decline four centuries before it was born. Indeed, Professor Toynbee maintains that the crisis of Roman civilization started in the year 431 B.C. when the Athenians and the Spartans came to grief in the Peloponnesian War.[1] But this opinion is really not original: it is in fact curiously reminiscent of an old Marxist point of view. Until recently Marxist historians have held that the crisis of classical civilization started with the Peloponnesian War or at the latest with the Gracchan movement. Only lately have Russian historians begun to realize that their position verged on absurdity. It is tempting to laugh at this game of finding a date for the end of the Roman empire, especially when the date is four centuries before the beginning of the Roman empire. But it is obvious that the game is after all not so futile as it looks. A date is only a symbol. Behind the question of dates there is the question of the continuity of European history. Can we notice a break in the development of the social and intellectual history of Europe? If we can notice it, where can we place it?

Historians, theologians, and political theorists have meditated on the decline and fall of Rome for centuries. Toynbee might defend himself by saying that the ancients pondered about the decline of Rome before Rome gave any clear sign of declining. They reflected on the causes of the fall of Rome even before Rome fell in any sense. Professor Mircea Eliade rightly observed that the Romans were 'continuously obsessed by the "end of Rome" '.[2] The problem of the decadence of Rome was already formulated by Polybius in the second century B.C. The idea that Rome was getting old is clearly expressed in Florus, an historian of the second century A.D.[3] After the sack of Rome by Alaric in 410 the decline of Rome became the subject of the most famous of all philosophic meditations on history—St. Augustine's *Civitas dei*. The Roman empire continued to survive, but people knew that something had happened. They spoke of *translatio imperii*—of the transition from the old Roman empire to the new Holy Roman empire of Charlemagne and other German emperors. Nobody doubted that the continuity of the Roman empire concealed a change. Indeed, about A.D. 1000 Otto III dreamt of reviving the old Roman empire: he spoke of *renovatio imperii Romanorum*. But the greatest of the Latin poets of the eleventh century, Hildebert of Lavardin, was under no illusion about the

[1] *A Study of History*, IV, pp. 61–63. E. Ch. Welskopf, *Die Produktionsverhältnisse im alten Orient und in der griechisch-römischen Antike* (Berlin Akad., 1957), gives some idea of Marxist historiography on the ancient world. Cf. K. F. Stroheker, *Saeculum*, i (1950), 433–65; F. Vittinghoff, ibid. xi (1960), 89–131; K. F. Stroheker, ibid. xii (1961), 140–57.
[2] M. Eliade, *Cosmos and History*, reprint (New York, 1959), p. 76.
[3] Cf. H. Werner, *Der Untergang Roms* (Stuttgart, 1939); S. Mazzarino, *La Fine del mondo antico* (Milano, 1959).

state of Rome: 'Par tibi, Roma, nihil, cum sis prope tota ruina.'[1] The thought of reviving old Rome, old classical civilization, became the inspiration of the humanistic movement in Italy in the fourteenth and fifteenth centuries. This implied the awareness that the Christian civilization of earlier centuries was something profoundly different from the classical world of Rome. Let us remind ourselves—because this is essential—that our problem of the decline of Rome is a product of Italian humanism. In that atmosphere Flavio Biondo wrote his history of Italy 'ab inclinatione Romanorum imperii' towards the middle of the fifteenth century. He dated the decline of Rome from the sack of Rome in 410. The Goths, the barbarians, started the decline of Rome.

Since Flavio Biondo each generation has produced its own theory or theories on the decline and fall of Rome.[2] Gibbon was heir to a long tradition of thought on the subject. Until the end of the eighteenth century few responsible historians followed Biondo in attributing the decline of Rome to the German invasions. Rather, causes of the decline were sought inside the empire. Machiavelli and Paruta in the sixteenth century tried to discover the cause of the decline of Rome in its constitution. In the early eighteenth century, more exactly in 1734, Montesquieu published his *Considérations sur la grandeur et la décadence des Romains*. By subtle analysis Montesquieu showed two of the main reasons for the fall of ancient Rome to be the power of the army and excess luxury. Later in the century, Christianity was made responsible for the decline of Rome. There is an anti-Christian note in Montesquieu which becomes loud in Voltaire and loudest of all in Gibbon's *Decline and Fall*. Gibbon focused attention on Christianity as the main factor of change and, as he thought, of decadence in the structure of the Roman empire. It was not until the nineteenth century that the German invasions came to be generally regarded as the key to the understanding of

---

[1] Text in *The Oxford Book of Mediaeval Latin Verse*, ed. F. J. E. Raby, 1959, p. 220. On Hildebert see W. Rehm, *Europäische Romdichtung*, 2nd ed. (München, 1960), pp. 43–61. Cf. P. Schramm, *Kaiser, Rom und Renovatio* (Leipzig, 1929; 2nd ed., Darmstadt, 1957); R. Folz, *L'Idée d'empire en occident du Ve au XIVe siècle* (Paris, 1953); E. Anagnine, *Il concetto di rinascita attraverso il medio evo* (Milano, 1958); W. Goez, *Translatio Imperii* (Tübingen, 1958).

[2] For what follows cf. W. Rehm, *Der Untergang Roms im abendländischen Denken* (Leipzig, 1930); A. Momigliano, 'La formazione della moderna storiografia sull'impero romano', *Rivista Storica Italiana*, 1936 (reprinted in *Contributo alla storia degli studi classici*, Roma, 1955, pp. 107–64); S. Mazzarino, *Storia romana e storiografia moderna* (Napoli, 1954); id., *La Fine del mondo antico*, 1959; A. Heuss, *Römische Geschichte* (Braunschweig, 1960), pp. 492–8, 591–600. On Gibbon see especially G. Giarrizzo, *E. Gibbon* (Napoli, 1954); G. J. Gruman, *History and Theory*, i (1960), 75–85.

the end of old Rome. During the nineteenth century nationalism prevailed, and historical research was mainly in German hands: it is not surprising that German scholars should believe that the German invasions sufficed to explain the birth of the Middle Ages. The most coherent alternative view was elaborated by Marx and his followers when they claimed that the Roman empire fell because its social structure, founded as it was upon slavery, was replaced by the feudal economic system.

In more recent years the picture has become more complex.

The enormous vitality of the Byzantine empire has been recognized, and it has been shown that much of its political and cultural tradition is of Greek or Roman origin. While older Byzantine scholars like Professor Charles Diehl stressed the oriental character of Byzantine civilization, a more modern school of thought has maintained, in Professor Baynes's words, that the Byzantine empire was the result of the fusion of the Hellenistic with the Roman tradition.[1] There is also an increasing realization of the part played by Islam in the social changes of the Mediterranean world during and after the seventh century. Other scholars like the Hungarian Professor A. Alföldi and the German Professor F. Altheim invite us to look beyond the borders of the empire at the nomadic tribes of non-German origins—Sarmatians, Huns, Slavs—who directly or indirectly contributed to changing the ways of life of Europe after the third century A.D.

As I have said, even the Marxists are no longer able to defend their tenet that the crisis of ancient civilization started at the end of the fifth century B.C. Recent discussions in the leading periodical of the Russian historians, the *Vestnik Drevnej Istorii*, show that they have been shifting their positions. A book published in 1957 by a very intelligent historian, Mme E. M. Štaerman, denies that there was a clear-cut struggle between slaves and slave-owners. She emphasizes the variety of social forms to be found in the Roman empire, and the need of avoiding generalizations.[2]

But the most important discussion on the topic of social

[1] N. H. Baynes, *Byzantine Studies and Other Essays* (London, 1955), p. 69 (from an essay of 1930). Cf., for instance, F. Dölger, 'Rom in der Gedankenwelt der Byzantiner', *Zeitschr. f. Kirchengeschichte*, lvi (1937), 1–42, now in *Byzanz und die europäische Staatenwelt* (Ettal, 1953), pp. 70–115.

[2] E. M. Štaerman, *Krizis Rabovladel'českogo Stroja v Zapadnych Provincijach Rimskoj Imperii* (Moskva, 1957). Cf. the discussion in *Vestnik Drevnej Istorii* (1953–5), which was provoked by an article by Mme Štaerman. Two of the contributions to this discussion are translated in the collective volume, *État et classes dans l'antiquité esclavagiste* (Paris, 1957). Cf. also E. M. Štaerman, 'Programmes politiques à l'époque de la crise du IIIe siècle', *Cahiers Hist. Mondiale*, iv (1958), 310–29. More recent discussion is summarized in *Vestnik Drevnej Istorii*, 1961, 4, 30–31.

changes in the Roman empire remains that which developed in the last forty years between the followers of the Belgian scholar H. Pirenne and the followers of the Austrian A. Dopsch.[1] As we all know, Dopsch substantially claimed that no break in continuity is noticeable in the Western world as a consequence of the German invasions. There was considerable redistribution of land, but the legal forms of ownership remained essentially Roman, city life survived, there was no return to natural economy, no interruption of the great trade-routes, and no interruption in the transmission of cultural goods. Pirenne accepted Dopsch's view that the German invasion did not put an end to the Graeco-Roman social structure, but contended that the ancient ways of life were disrupted by the Arabs: they played the part that more conventional historians used to attribute to the Germans. In Pirenne's opinion the Arabs destroyed the unity of the Mediterranean, paralysed the trade between East and West, drained the gold away from the West, and displaced the centre of civilized life from the Mediterranean to the North Sea. The West, having been cut off from Byzantium, had to look after itself. The coronation of Charlemagne was symbolically the answer given by the West to the challenge of Mohammed's followers. Thence the somewhat unexpected title of Pirenne's great book, *Mohammed et Charlemagne*.

It is perhaps right to say that Rostovtzeff was in essential agreement with Pirenne against Dopsch. Of course, he found the cause of the decline of the cities not in the intervention of the Arabs, but in the revolution of the peasantry against the city-dwellers. But Rostovtzeff, like Pirenne, was a *bourgeois* in the classical sense: he identified civilization with city life and saw the end of the classical world in the decline of the cities.

Now it is clear that all this recent research is unified by a common interest in the structural changes of the social organization of the Roman empire. It is also undeniable that researchers are less and less prepared to maintain that a simple formula can cover the enormous variety of local situations within the Roman empire. We are learning to respect regional differences as much as chronological sequences. We begin to see that what is true of France in the fourth century is not necessarily true of Spain, Africa, or Italy, not to speak of Syria or Egypt.

[1] Large bibliography in W. C. Bark, *Origins of the Medieval World* (Stanford, California, 1958). Notice on Pirenne, A. Riising, *Classica et Mediaevalia*, xiii (1952), 87–130.

But even regional studies cannot overcome what seems to me the most serious objection against both Pirenne and Dopsch, and, indeed, against Rostovtzeff. The objection is that these historians talked of social changes without even discussing the most important of all social changes—the rise of Christianity. More generally, it can be said that no interpretation of the decline of the Roman empire can be declared satisfactory if it does not also account for the triumph of Christianity. It may seem ridiculous to have to emphasize this proposition so many years after A. Harnack and E. Troeltsch. But a careful study of their works can perhaps explain why they failed to impress their fellow historians. Though both Harnack and Troeltsch were well aware that the Church was a society competing with the society of the Roman empire, they remained theologians to the end. They were more interested in the idea of Christianity than in Christians. Rostovtzeff and Pirenne, who loved the cities of men, may be excused if they remained unimpressed by theologians who talked or seemed to talk about the idea of the city of God.

It is the modest purpose of this paper to reassert the view that there is a direct relation between the triumph of Christianity and the decline of the Roman empire. But, of course, it will not be a simple return to Gibbon. What Gibbon saw as a merely destructive power must be understood on its own terms of *Civitas dei*—a new commonwealth of men for men. Christianity produced a new style of life, created new loyalties, gave people new ambitions and new satisfactions. So far nobody has written a realistic evaluation of the impact of Christianity on the structure of pagan society. I shall not attempt such a task here. I shall confine myself to a few elementary remarks on the impact of Christianity on political life between the fourth and the sixth centuries A.D. We all know the basic facts.[1]

---

[1] My point of view was already formulated in my article 'Roma: Impero' in *Enciclopedia Italiana*, xxix (1936) and 'La formazione della moderna storiografia sull'impero romano' (1936) now in *Contributo* quoted, 1955. Among the most recent contributions cf. A. H. M. Jones, 'The Decline and Fall of the Roman Empire', *History*, 1955, pp. 209–26, an admirable essay, and S. Mazzarino, *La Fine del mondo antico*, quoted, with bibliography. The new editions of E. Stein, *Histoire du Bas-Empire*, i (Paris, 1959) and, better, G. Ostrogorsky, *Geschichte des byzantinischen Staates* (München, 1952) (English translation, Oxford, 1956; French translation with additions, Paris, 1956) provide the basic facts. A controversial thesis is presented by A. E. R. Boak, *Manpower Shortage and the Fall of the Roman Empire in the West* (Univ. Michigan Press, 1955) (on which cf. M. I. Finley, *J. Rom. Studies*, xlviii (1958), 156–64). Essential also are A. Piganiol, *L'Empire Chrétien (325–395)* (Paris, 1947) and J. Gaudemet, *L'Église dans l'empire romain* (Paris, 1958). H. Dannenbauer, *Die Entstehung Europas*, i (Stuttgart, 1959), is a useful survey.

II

In the third century the Roman empire had faced disintegration. It survived thanks to the strenuous efforts at reconstruction which are connected with the names of Claudius Gothicus, Diocletian, and Constantine. The result was an organization founded upon compulsion. For reasons which have not yet been entirely explained, money economy collapsed in the third century: there were moments in which barter and taxation in kind seemed destined to replace money transactions in the empire. This crisis was overcome. Constantine introduced gold coins, the *solidi*, which remained the standard for about 800 years and served as an ultimate basis both for the fiscal system and private transactions. But there was a debased currency for everyday use, and the fluctuations in the rates of exchange between gold and debased currency were a source of uncertainty and an excuse for extortions. The middle class emerged from the crisis demoralized and impoverished. Civil servants and soldiers were paid less in the fourth century than in the third. They came to rely on fees and bribery to supplement their salaries. Whatever the explanation may be, there developed also a shortage of manpower, while ordinary activities were made more burdensome by excessive taxation and the general unpleasantness of life. Barbarian invasions and civil wars must have destroyed a great deal of wealth. People tended to drift away from their work; and the government answered by binding the peasant to the land, making compulsory and hereditary certain activities and transforming the city councils into compulsory and hereditary corporations responsible for the collection of taxes.

The army needed men. About 500,000 men seem to have been required by the army, and there were not enough volunteers to make up this number. Recruitment was no easy matter. Landed proprietors had to supply recruits from among their serfs or at least had to compound by paying money. The son of a soldier was bound, at least under certain circumstances, to follow his father's profession. But the best soldiers were recruited among the barbarians, mainly Germans and Sarmatians, who were settled within the empire either individually or in communities. The army was therefore organized on uneconomic lines. It was made even more uneconomic by the division between frontier army and central army. The frontiers were guarded by soldiers who were less well paid and less respected than their colleagues of the mobile force at the centre.

To pay such an army a prosperous empire was needed. The empire was not prosperous, and there are reasons to believe that insecurity and inflation curtailed traffic. We have not enough evidence about the volume of trade circulating in the Roman empire at any given moment. We are therefore in no position to state in figures that there was less trade in the fourth century than, for instance, in the second century. But we can infer from the decline of the *bourgeoisie* in the fourth century and from the exclusive importance of great landowners that prosperous traders were few. One has the impression that long-distance trade was increasingly in the hands of small minorities of Syrians and Jews.

Two capitals having replaced one, there were more unproductive expenses than before. Constantinople, the new Rome, grew up a marvel to see. But, as in the older Rome, the citizens of Constantinople enjoyed the privilege of a free supply of bread—the corn being provided by Egypt.

Preachers in their sermons painted in violent colours the contrast between wealth and poverty, and invariably intimated that wealth was the root of oppression. St. Ambrose in the West and St. John Chrysostom in the East attacked the rich who bought house after house and field after field, throwing out the former owners. What they say seems to be confirmed by the few data we have about individual estates in the fourth and fifth centuries. Some families had princely possessions spread over several provinces of the empire. They lived more and more, though not yet exclusively, in the country, and their estates were self-sufficient units. The wealthiest landowners were members of the senatorial class. Here again, the change from the third century is evident and important. In the third century the class of the senators was definitely declining. The senators were deprived of the command of the armies and to a certain extent of the provincial government. The conditions of the fourth century did not allow the senators to recover control of the army: professional soldiers, most frequently of German origin, took over. But the senatorial class absorbed their formal rivals, the knights, and developed into a powerful clique of great landowners who, especially in the West, monopolized what was left of civilized life outside the Church and played an increasing part in the Church itself. Senators and great landowners became almost synonymous terms. These people knew the comforts and amenities of life; they cultivated rhetoric and poetry. In Rome, under the guidance of Symmachus, they provided the last bastion of paganism. Elsewhere they turned to the Church.

III

The fact that the aristocracy played a role of increasing importance in the affairs of the Church is only one aspect of what is perhaps the central feature of the fourth century: the emergence of the Church as an organization competing with the State itself and becoming attractive to educated and influential persons. The State, though trying to regiment everything, was not able to prevent or suppress the competition of the Church. A man could in fact escape from the authority of the State if he embraced the Church. If he liked power he would soon discover that there was more power to be found in the Church than in the State. The Church attracted the most creative minds—St. Ambrose, St. Jerome, Hilarius of Poitiers, St. Augustine in the West; Athanasius, John Chrysostom, Gregory of Nazianzus, and Basil of Caesarea in the East: almost all born rulers, rulers of a type which, with the exception of the scholarly emperor Julian, it was hard to find on the imperial throne. They combined Christian theology with pagan philosophy, worldly political abilities with a secure faith in immortal values. They could tell both the learned and the unlearned how they should behave, and consequently transformed both the external features and the inner meaning of the daily existence of an increasing number of people.

Gibbon was simplifying a very complicated issue when he insinuated that Christianity was responsible for the fall of the empire. But he perceived that the Church attracted many men who in the past would have become excellent generals, governors of provinces, advisers to the emperors. Moreover, the Church made ordinary people proud, not of their old political institutions, but of their new churches, monasteries, ecclesiastical charities. Money which would have gone to the building of a theatre or of an aqueduct now went to the building of churches and monasteries. The social equilibrium changed—to the advantage of the spiritual and physical conditions of monks and priests, but to the disadvantage of the ancient institutions of the empire.

The expanding and consolidating hierarchical organization of the Church offered scope for initiative, leadership, ambition. With Theodosius' law of A.D. 392 pagan cults became illegal. Other laws were directed against heretics. Catholic priests obtained all sorts of privileges, including that of being judged by their own bishops in the case of criminal offences. This was the outcome of a century of struggles. St. Ambrose, having thrown the whole weight of his powerful and fearless personality into the struggle, compelled the aging Theodosius to yield to the demands of the Church. St. Ambrose's victory can be considered final in so far as paganism was concerned. When Alaric captured Rome in 410 many people asked themselves whether the ruin of Rome was not the sign that Christianity was bad for the empire. The Christian answer to these doubts prevailed. It opened a new epoch in the philosophy of history. The political disaster was real enough, but more real was the faith which inwardly transformed the lives of the multitudes and which was now given its intellectual justification by St. Augustine in his *City of God*.

If paganism was dying, this did not mean that the unity of the Church, willed by St. Ambrose and St. Augustine and accepted by Theodosius, was entirely safe. The great episcopal churches of Rome, Constantinople, Antioch, and Alexandria were manœuvring against each other. Nobody seriously challenged the hegemony of Rome in the West (perhaps because the claims of the Roman bishops were still vague), but even in Rome we meet rival bishops fighting each other with the support of excited crowds. And there were heresies. If Arianism was a lost cause inside the Empire, it prospered among the barbarians pressing on its borders. Other heresies, such as Priscillianism in Spain and Donatism in Africa, kept their appeal for a long time.

Much can be said about the internal conflicts, the worldly ambitions, the intolerance of the Church. Yet the conclusion remains that while the political organization of the empire became increasingly rigid, unimaginative, and unsuccessful, the Church was mobile and resilient and provided space for those whom the State was unable to absorb. The bishops were the centres of large voluntary organizations. They founded and controlled charitable institutions. They defended their flocks against the state officials. When the military situation of the empire grew worse, they often organized armed resistance against the barbarians. It seems to me impossible to deny that the prosperity of the Church was both a consequence and a cause of the decline of the state. People escaped from the state into the Church and weakened the state by giving their best to the Church. This is a situation which in its turn requires analysis and explanation. But its primary importance cannot be overlooked. The best men were working for the Church, not for the state.

Monasticism provides the most telling test of the capacities of the Church in the fourth century.[1] The first hermits of the third century were Christians who in order to live a perfect Christian life abandoned both the pagan world and the Christian communities and retired to the desert. This was no simple revolt against society. It was born out of a deep experience of struggle against the temptations of the flesh. Where there is a hermit, there is the devil. The devil was a powerful reality in late antiquity, and the hermit was both obsessed by the devil and determined to fight him. The devil pursued the hermit, but the hermit believed he had the right weapons to counter-attack. St. Anthony was the model hermit, and his biography written by St. Athanasius became the model for all lives of saints, one of the most influential books of any time. But the hermits were a clear menace to orderly Christian society. Each of them organized his life on his own lines, defying the authority of the bishops and claiming to be the embodiment of the perfect Christian. While official Christianity was now bent on organizing the world and on achieving a working compromise with worldly ambitions, the hermits expressed contempt for the world. On the other hand, as Athanasius himself recognized when he chose to write the life of St. Anthony, the hermits were the true representatives of Christian asceticism. They could not be eliminated. A solution of the dilemma was found in creating monastic orders where collective life according to strictly ascetic rules replaced the hermit's individual escape from this world. First Pachomius, then Basil laid down the rules for the monasteries they founded and controlled. St. Basil's Rule inspires Eastern monastic rules even today.

Monasticism was introduced to the West in the second part of the fourth century. St. Jerome was the popularizer of the Eastern

[1] Cf., for instance, F. Cavallera, *Saint Jérôme* (Paris, 1922); P. C. Baur, *Der heilige Johannes Chrysostomos und seine Zeit* (München, 1930); K. Heussi, *Der Ursprung des Mönchtums* (Tübingen, 1936); O. Chadwick, *John Cassian* (Cambridge, 1950); G. B. Ladner, *The Idea of Reform* (Cambridge, Mass., 1959), pp. 319–424 (with bibliography). An account of recent studies on St. Anthony is to be found in *Studia Anselmiana*, xxxviii (1956), dedicated to him. On the Augustinian Rule, Ladner, p. 356. A.-J. Festugière, *Les Moines d'Orient* (Paris, 1961). Cf. also D. Gordini, 'Origine e sviluppo del monachesimo a Roma', *Gregorianum*, xxxvii (1956), 220–60.

monastic ideals and found disciples among the most aristocratic ladies of Rome. Later St. Augustine dictated rules for people inclining to monastic life both in his *Regula ad servos dei* (the authenticity of which is disputed) and in his ascetic treatises, such as *De opere Monachorum* and *De sancta Virginitate*. So did his contemporary John Cassian in France. All these rules provided approved patterns of life and introduced manual work as a normal part of the monk's day. They also established direct or indirect control by the ecclesiastical authorities over the monasteries. This is not to say that the sting was entirely taken out of monastic life. The monks, especially in the East, proved often to be unruly, rebellious, disturbingly fanatical, and ignorant. Much social discontent contributed to their psychology. But monasticism as a whole ceased to be a danger and became a source of power and inspiration for the Church. Ultimately, monasticism became a constructive force in society: it united men in a new form of communal life and gave them a considerable amount of economic independence and political self-government. When Cassiodorus added specific cultural activities to the ordinary life of his monks, a new chapter opened in the intellectual history of Europe.[1] The monks were not helping the Empire to survive. Judged from the traditional point of view of the pagan society they were a subversive force. But they provided an alternative to pagan city life.

IV

Monasticism is the most obvious example of the way in which Christianity built something of its own which undermined the military and political structure of the Roman empire. Yet this is only part of the story.

As soon as the barbarians were let into the empire, the conflict between pagan society and Christian society changed its aspect. A new factor was introduced. It remained to be seen whether pagans or Christians would succeed better in dealing with the barbarians. From the end of the fourth century A.D. the Christian Church was asked not only to exorcise the devils, but to tame the barbarians. Next to Satan, the barbarians were the problem of the day. Like the devils, the barbarians could be found everywhere, but unlike the devils no simple formula could chase them away.

---

[1] Bibliography on Cassiodorus in my *Secondo Contributo alla storia degli studi classici* (Roma, 1960), pp. 219-29.

Here the Church had to operate with subtlety in a variety of situations: it had to prove itself superior to the pagans.

It was soon evident that the East was safer than the West. The main German pressure was on the Rhine and on the Danube. Asia was fairly secure. The military reservoir of Asia Minor provided enough soldiers for the emperors of Constantinople to counterbalance the influence of the German mercenaries and to help to keep them in their place. Constantinople itself proved to be an impregnable fortress. But the military aspects of the situation cannot be separated from the social ones. The East was safer not only because it was stronger, but also because it was less dissatisfied with the Roman administration. The concentration of wealth in a few hands did not go quite as far as in the West. City life survived better in the East, and consequently the peasants there were less hard pressed. If we except Egypt, the East has no parallel to the endemic revolts of the Bagaudae and the *circumcelliones* of Gaul, Spain, and Africa. In the West there were people wondering whether their lot would not be better under the barbarians. St. Augustine himself is not invariably certain that the empire was a good thing. His disciple Orosius has a telling passage about people who would have preferred to live among barbarians. The French priest Salvianus, the author of the *De gubernatione dei*, written about 450, was deeply impressed by the quality of the Germans; and there is the famous story of a Roman who lived among the Huns and explained why he was better off with them.[1]

This evidence does not of course mean that the barbarians were greeted as liberators in any part of the empire. The slaves and the serfs were not freed by the barbarians. They simply changed masters and had to bear the consequences of all the destructions and revolutions. It is true that the *curiales* were progressively relieved of their burdens and that the corporate system of the late Roman empire fell into desuetude. But the *curiales* disappeared only because city life disappeared. The picture of the barbarians arriving as a liberation army is a fantastic travesty of the facts. What must be taken into account, however,

---

[1] Priscus fr. 8 (Müller, *Fragm. Hist. Graec.* iv. 87; Dindorf, *Hist. Graeci Minores*, i. 305). In general see P. Courcelle, *Hist. littér. des grandes invasions germaniques* (Paris, 1948); J. Straub, *Philologus*, xcv (1943), 255–86; id., *Historia*, i (1950), 52–81; H. Helbling, *Goten und Wandalen* (Zürich, 1954); J. Fischer, *Die Völkerwanderung im Urteil der zeitgenössischen kirchlichen Schriftsteller Galliens* (Heidelberg, 1948); F. G. Meier, *Augustin und das antike Rom* (Stuttgart, 1955) (with ample bibliography).

is that in the West the psychological resistance to the barbarians was less strong than in the East. Not only military weakness, but defeatism paved the way for the German invasion of Italy and the western provinces.

We badly need systematic research on regional differences in the attitude of the Church towards the Roman state. Generalizations are premature. But some facts are apparent. The Greek Fathers never produced searching criticisms of the Roman State comparable with those of St. Augustine and Salvian. On the contrary, St. John Chrysostom supported the anti-German party in Constantinople, and Synesius became a convert and a bishop after having outlined the programme of that party. It would seem that in the West, after having contributed to the weakening of the empire, the Church inclined to accept collaboration with the barbarians and even replacement of the Roman authorities by barbarian leaders. In the East (with the partial exception of Alexandria) the Church appreciated the military strength of the Roman state and the loyalties it commanded. No doubt the Eastern churches, too, did not hesitate to deprive the Roman administration of the best men and of the best revenues whenever they could, but, at least from the second part of the fourth century, they threw in their weight with the new Rome.

Looking at both sides of the empire, one conclusion seems inescapable. The Church managed to have it both ways. It could help the ordinary man either in his fight against the barbarians or in his compromise with them. It succeeded where pagan society had little to offer either way. The educated pagan was by definition afraid of barbarians. There was no bridge between the aristocratic ideals of a pagan and the primitive violence of a German invader. In theory the barbarians could be idealized. Primitivism has always had its devotees. Alternatively, a few select barbarians could be redeemed by proper education and philosophic training. There was no objection to barbarians on racial grounds. But the ordinary barbarian as such was nothing more than a nightmare to the educated pagan.

The Christians had a different attitude and other possibilities. They could convert the barbarians and make them members of the Church. They had discovered a bridge between barbarism and civilization. Alternatively, the Church could give its moral support to the struggle against the barbarians: the defence of the empire could be presented as the defence of the Church. It is obvious that if we had to analyse the process in detail we should have to take into account the complications caused by the existence of doctrinal differences within the Church. It was commonly felt that an heretic was worse than a pagan. Thus the fight against German Arians was even more meritorious than the fight against German pagans. What really matters to us is that in the West the Church gradually replaced the dying State in dealing with the barbarians. In the East, on the other hand, the Church realized that the Roman state was much more vital and supported it in its fight against the barbarians. In the West, after having weakened the Roman state, the Church accepted its demise and acted independently in taming them. In the East, the Church almost identified itself with the Roman State of Constantinople.

In both cases, ordinary people needed protection and guidance. The wealthy classes were capable of looking after themselves either under the Roman emperor or under the barbarian kings. But ordinary people wanted leaders. They found them in their bishops.

Above all, something had to be done in order to establish a communal life which both Romans and barbarians could share. A glance at the life of St. Severinus by Eugippius is enough to give an impression of what a courageous and imaginative Christian leader could do in difficult circumstances. In the fourth and fifth centuries the bishops did not make much of an effort to convert the barbarians who were living outside the borders of the Roman empire. But they were deeply concerned with the religion of those barbarians who settled in the empire. In other words, the conversion to Christianity was part of the process whereby the Germans were, at least to a certain extent, romanized and made capable of living together with the citizens of the Roman empire. The process of romanizing the barbarians by christianizing them is an essential feature of the history of the Roman empire between Constantine and Justinian. If it did not save the empire, at least in the West, it saved many features of Roman civilization.

The superiority of Christianity over paganism in dynamism and efficiency was already evident in the fourth century. The Christians could adapt themselves better to the new political and social situation and deal more efficiently with the barbarians. A closer analysis of the relations between pagans and Christians in the fourth century is therefore the necessary presupposition for any further study of the decline of the Roman empire. Such analysis may show that in this field as well as in other fields the solitary Jacob Burckhardt was nearer the truth than any other historian of the nineteenth century. His book on Constantine (1852) was inspired by Gibbon and merciless in its judgement of the emperor who christianized the empire, but was very careful to avoid any confusion between Constantine and the cause he embraced. Burckhardt tried to understand what the Church had to give to a declining empire and under what conditions it was prepared to do so. We are still wrestling with the same problem.[1]

[1] On Burckhardt's *Die Zeit Constantins des Grossen* see W. Kaegi, *J. Burckhardt*, iii (1956), 377–421. The bibliographical references in the preceding notes are merely meant to help first orientation in recent literature. Further information to be found in S. Mazzarino, *Trattato di storia romana*, ii: *L'Impero Romano* (Roma, 1956). On Christian thought the above-quoted G. B. Ladner, *The Idea of Reform. Its Impact on Christian Thought and Action in the Age of the Fathers* (Cambridge, Mass., 1959). On political thought J. A. Straub, *Vom Herrscherideal in der Spätantike* (Stuttgart, 1939); O. Treitinger, *Die oströmische Kaiser- und Reichsidee* (Jena, 1938; reprint Darmstadt, 1956) are most helpful guides. On social and intellectual trends see S. Mazzarino, 'La democratizzazione della cultura nel Basso Impero', *Rapports XI Congrès Intern. Sciences Historiques* (Stockholm, 1960), ii, 35–54. On heresies A. H. M. Jones, 'Were Ancient Heresies National or Social Movements in Disguise?', *J. Theol. Studies*, x (1959), 280–98; P. R. L. Brown, 'Religious Dissent in the Later Roman Empire', *History*, xlvi (1961), 83–101. On law J. Gaudemet, *La Formation du droit séculier et du droit de l'église aux IVe et Ve siècles* (Paris, 1957); L. Harmand, *Le Patronat sur les collectivités publiques* (Paris, 1957), p. 421. On the Roman aristocracy, P. R. L. Brown, 'Aspects of the Christianization of the Roman Aristocracy', *J. Rom. Studies*, li (1961), 1–11. There is much of general interest in L. Ruggini, *Economia e società nell'Italia annonaria* (Milan, 1962).

I

The Social Background of the Struggle between Paganism and Christianity

A. H. M. JONES

CHRISTIANITY has always had its appeal for all sorts and conditions of men. Long before the conversion of Constantine made it politic for the ambitious to profess the emperor's religion, there were Christian senators and soldiers, and even Christian professors. But it remains true that for one reason or another Christianity was at the end of the third century more widely diffused in some areas and classes of society than in others. This fact makes a study of the social background against which Christianity fought its battle with paganism essential for a proper understanding of that struggle.

Christianity was at this date far stronger in the Greek-speaking provinces of the empire than in the Latin-speaking areas. This was, of course, mainly due to the fact that it had originated in an eastern province, and that its earlier missionaries were Greek-speaking. Missionary activity, it is true, was at a very early date extended to the West, but it was at first confined to the colonies of Greek-speaking immigrants in Rome and other large towns. Latin-speaking Christianity first emerges at Carthage towards the end of the second century, but at this period the Church at Lyons was still mainly composed of Greek-speaking orientals,[1] and the Roman Church continued to use Greek down to the third century, and perhaps even later.[2] Even in the fourth century, to judge by the density of bishoprics, the western provinces lagged far behind the eastern. There were areas, such as peninsular Italy and Africa, where Christianity was widely diffused, but in northern Italy, and still more in Gaul, Spain, and Illyricum, many quite important towns still lacked a bishop in the early fourth century.

In the second place Christianity was still in the fourth century

---

[1] Eusebius, *H.E.* v. 1–4.
[2] Hippolytus, who flourished under Alexander Severus, still wrote in Greek, and the epitaphs of third-century popes are in Greek.

a mainly urban religion. This was partly due to the methods whereby Christianity was diffused. The early missionaries moved from city to city and rapidly spread the gospel over a very wide area, but at the expense of leaving the intervening countryside untouched. The early churches were thus urban communities, and they tended to remain so. There was in most parts of the empire a sharp cleavage between town and country: in many areas the peasants did not speak either of the two dominant languages of the empire, but still used their old Coptic, Syriac, Thracian, Celtic, or Berber tongues.[1] Communication must then have been difficult even if urban Christians had taken more interest in their rural neighbours.

But the slow progress of Christianity in the rural areas is also to be attributed to the inherent conservatism of the peasantry. Peasants have at all times and in all places resisted change and clung stubbornly to their traditional way of life. Even in the sixth and seventh centuries, when they had for the most part long been converted, the Church in Gaul and Spain, as repeated canons of the contemporary councils show,[2] had great difficulty in suppressing the old rites whereby they had from time immemorial warded off pests and promoted the fertility of their flocks and fields.

There are, of course, exceptions to this generalization. As early as the reign of Trajan Pliny notes, with some surprise, it would seem, that 'the contagion of this superstition has permeated not only the cities but also the villages and countryside'.[3] It would appear that during the latter part of the third century Christianity became dominant in the rural areas of Africa and Egypt. It has been pointed out that in both countries pagan dedications at rural shrines come to an abrupt end in the middle of the third century.[4] This in itself is not very good evidence, for at that troubled period inscriptions in general became very sparse. But it is perhaps permissible to argue back from later conditions. The story of the Donatist controversy makes it plain that by the 340's Christianity was dominant in rural Africa: the Circum-

---

[1] For the eastern languages see my *Greek City*, pp. 288 ff. For Celtic, Jerome, *Comm. in Ep. Gal.* ii, Sulp. Sev. *Dial.* i. 27. For Berber (and Punic), Frend, *The Donatist Church*, pp. 51–58.
[2] *Conc. Aurel.* II (533), *can.* 20, *Conc. Aurel.* IV (541), *can.* 15, *Conc. Turon.* II (567), *can.* 22, *Conc. Autisiod.* (c. 585), *can.* 1, 3, 4, *Conc. Tolet.* III (589), *can.* 16, *Conc. Rem.* (624–5), *can.* 14.
[3] Pliny, *Ep.* x. 96, § 9. Nevertheless, S. Hypatius found flourishing rural pagan groups in Bithynia in the early fifth century (Callinicus, *Vita Hypatii*, 103, 124–5, 129–30).
[4] Frend, *The Donatist Church*, pp. 83–86.

between Paganism and Christianity

cellions, who were certainly peasants, were already by this period a power in the land.[1] In Egypt the scandal of the broken chalice reveals that at a slightly earlier date there was a well-established system of rural parishes in Mareotes.[2] If one goes back a generation to the time of the Great Persecution, Africa and Egypt stand out sharply in our record for the number of their martyrs and confessors, and it might be inferred that the exceptional stubbornness of the Christian resistance in these areas was due to the fact that the peasant masses, who were made of tougher stuff than the townsmen, had adopted the new faith.

The evidence that the African and Egyptian peasantry were already predominantly Christian by the beginning of the fourth century, is admittedly tenuous. By contrast there is in other areas strong evidence that at much later dates paganism was still strong in the countryside. The Life of Martin of Tours reveals that in the later decades of the fourth century rural temples and festivals were flourishing in Gaul.[3] Rather later John Chrysostom appealed to the Christian landlords of Constantinople to take some interest in the spiritual welfare of their tenants, and to win them to the faith by endowing priests and building churches on their estates.[4] Even in the age of Justinian John of Ephesus, as the result of a prolonged missionary campaign in the rural areas of Asia, Caria, Lydia, and Phrygia—districts among the first to be evangelized—found 80,000 pagans to baptize.[5] In the West, at the end of the sixth century, Pope Gregory the Great found that in Sardinia there was a substantial number of peasants, including tenants of the church, who paid the governor of the island a regular *douceur* to secure his connivance for their pagan worship.[6]

In the third place Christianity had made relatively little progress among the aristocracy, or indeed among the educated upper classes in general. This was not for want of trying, for the Church early appreciated the importance of winning converts in governing circles. But among the upper classes the education which they had received created a strong resistance to the new faith. It must be remembered that in its early days Christianity was a more uncompromising faith than it later became, and had not yet

---

[1] Op. cit., pp. 171 ff.
[2] Athanasius, *Apol. c. Ar.* lxxv, cf. lxiii–lxiv.
[3] Sulp. Sev., *Vita Martini*, xii–xv, *Dial.* i (ii). 4, ii (iii). 8.
[4] Joh. Chrys., *Hom. in Act.* xviii. 4.
[5] Joh. Eph. H.E. 36, *Lives of the Eastern Saints*, xliii, xlvii.
[6] Gregory, *Ep.* iv. 23, 25–27, 29, v. 38, ix. 204; cf. iii. 59 (Sicily).

acquired that wide variety of appeal which made it all things to all men. Christians regarded the old gods with fear and aversion: they were evil and active demons and any contact with them was dangerous. This being so, many believers felt that classical culture, permeated as it was with paganism, was to be rejected *in toto*: to study it was, if not sinful, playing with fire.

There was, it is true, in the third and even in the second century, a number of cultivated Christians who managed to accommodate their faith to classical culture, but the feeling long lingered that the two were incompatible. In Jerome's famous dream the Heavenly Judge answered his plea 'Christianus sum' by the stern retort 'Ciceronianus es, non Christianus',[1] and even at the end of the sixth century Pope Gregory the Great severely reproved the Bishop of Vienna for teaching grammar: 'one mouth cannot contain the praises of Christ with the praises of Jupiter.'[2] This feeling must have been far stronger in the early fourth century, when the synthesis of Christianity and classical culture was still in its infancy, and it formed a very real stumbling-block to men who had been brought up to reverence the poets, philosophers, and orators of Greece and Rome.

In the second place we must not forget that Christianity was in its early days a vulgar religion. Not only were most of its adherents persons of low degree and little or no education, but its holy books were uncouth and barbaric, written in a Greek or Latin which grated on the sensibilities of any educated man, bred up on Menander and Demosthenes, or Terence and Cicero. It is difficult for us to appreciate how serious an obstacle this was. On the one hand, we are accustomed to Biblical language, and venerate the Authorized Version as among the noblest monuments of English prose. And in the second place we find it hard to realize the immense importance attached in antiquity to verbal form. But under the Roman empire higher education was almost exclusively devoted to rhetoric, the art of correct and elegant speech, and the men who were the products of that education naturally tended to attach more importance to the form than to the content of what they read. Jerome himself confesses that when he weakly indulged himself by reading Plautus he found the Hebrew prophets very unpalatable.[1] When Julian forbade Christians to teach the classics, and contemptuously ordered them 'to go to the churches of the Galileans and expound Matthew and

---

[1] Jerome, *Ep.* xxii, § 30.   [2] Gregory, *Ep.* xi. 34.

Luke',[1] only two Christian professors took up his challenge. But even they felt that the Christian scriptures were in their crude form impossible as a vehicle of education and proceeded to rewrite them as epic poems, Attic tragedies, and Platonic dialogues.[2] In this mental climate it was difficult for any educated man to accept the new faith.

For members of the senatorial aristocracy there was yet another obstacle. Senators, believing themselves to be descendants of the republican nobility, and holding the republican magistracies and priesthoods, felt themselves to be the inheritors and guardians of the ancient traditions of Rome. Rome had grown to greatness under the protection of the old gods whom she so piously cherished: 'this worship brought the world under my sway', Symmachus pictures her pleading, 'these rites repelled Hannibal from the walls and the Senones from the Capitol'.[3] It was difficult for men bred in these traditions to believe that Jupiter Optimus Maximus was a malignant demon.

It is very difficult to estimate how far, despite these adverse factors, Christianity had by the beginning of the fourth century penetrated into the upper classes. The edict of Valerian, laying down special penalties for senators and *equites Romani* who refused to conform, suggests that as early as 257 there were some Christians in these classes.[4] The canons of the council of Iliberris, probably held shortly before the Great Persecution, lay down penances for Christians who as provincial *sacerdotes* or municipal *duoviri* or *flamines* take part in pagan rites or celebrate games.[5] This would imply that there were not a few Christians among the curial class in Spain, and, indeed, among its richest and most prominent members, who held not only the highest municipal offices and priesthoods, but even the supreme honour of the provincial high priesthood. But it would seem likely that in the upper strata of society Christians were in a very small minority. The old senatorial families certainly remained predominantly pagan down to the latter part of the fourth century.

The main strength of Christianity lay in the lower and middle classes of the towns, the manual workers and clerks, the shopkeepers and merchants. It is significant that the city of Cyzicus (that is its council) sent an official delegation to Julian to ask for

---

[1] Julian, *Ep.* xlii.
[2] Socrates, iii. 16, Sozomen, v. 18.
[3] Symmachus, *Rel.* iii, § 9.
[4] Cyprian, *Ep.* lxxxi.
[5] *Conc. Ilib. can.* 2-4, 55, 56.

the restoration of its temples, while Eleusius, the bishop who had destroyed them, was supported by the workers in the local mint and government clothing factory.[1] There were also Christians among the humbler decurions. The social range of the curial class was very wide, and while leading decurions of the great cities ranked not far below senators in birth, wealth, and culture, many humbler members of the council, especially in the smaller towns, were modest farmers or craftsmen with no pretention to culture. Diocletian even ruled that illiteracy was no bar to curial status.[2]

But here again it is impossible to generalize, for there were sharp local variations whose reasons we often cannot fathom. There were some towns where the bulk of the population was early Christian, but there were others which long remained solidly pagan. In Mesopotamia Edessa was Christian even in the third century,[3] but at Carrhae paganism was still dominant long after the Arab conquest.[4] In Syria Antioch was strongly Christian in Julian's day, but the Apamenes defended their temples with spirit in the reign of Theodosius the Great.[5] Palestine was in general a Christian province in the fourth century, but at Gaza the Christian community was still only a handful when Porphyry became their bishop in 395, and the temples, despite Theodosius' penal laws, were still open and the pagan cult overtly celebrated.[6]

Let us now consider the bearing of these facts on the conflict of religions in the fourth century. The economy of the Roman empire was to an overwhelming extent agricultural. The vast majority of its inhabitants were peasants, and its wealth was almost entirely derived from their labours. The state drew, it would seem, over 90 per cent. of its revenue from taxes levied on land and on the agricultural population.[7] The upper classes derived almost all their wealth from rents paid by peasant tenants. Despite their immense numerical preponderance, however, and their vital economic importance, the opinions of the peasantry did not count for anything. They were merely a vast inert and passive, if stubborn, mass. This is demonstrated by their passive attitude when in the course of the fourth century pagan rites were banned and the temples closed or destroyed. Very occasionally they might lynch a tactless missionary or offer resistance

[1] Sozomen, v. 15.   [2] *Cod. Just.* x. xxxi. 6.
[3] *C.A.H.* xii. 439 ff.   [4] *Encycl. Brit.*, s.v. Sabians.
[5] Sozomen, vii. 15.   [6] Marcus Diaconus, *Vita Porphyrii*.
[7] *Recueils de la Société Jean Bodin*, vii (1955), 161 ff.

to the destruction of their shrines.[1] But recorded instances of violence are very rare, and pagan townsmen seem to have been far more active in defending their temples. This was no doubt partly because the laws against paganism were even more laxly enforced in the countryside than in the towns, but on the whole the peasantry seem to have submitted quietly to authority. This is not to say that they readily abandoned their ancestral rites and beliefs. Christianity gradually conquered the countryside, it is true, but it was a very slow process, by no means complete even in the sixth century. But the peasantry offered a passive resistance only, stubbornly carrying on their ancient worship, overtly if, as often was the case, the authorities did not bother to interfere, or could be bribed to turn a blind eye, or surreptitiously if the law was enforced.

It follows from what I have said that the proletariat of the towns, and the shop-keeping and mercantile class, were numerically and economically insignificant. They were far outnumbered by the peasantry, and the only tax which they paid, the *collatio lustralis*, was a very small item in the budget. Except for the workers in the mints and the arms and clothing factories, they were not essential to the state. On the other hand, they had greater opportunities for expressing their views and making them felt. They could and did shout slogans in the theatre and at other public gatherings, and if such demonstrations did not produce the desired result, they could riot. In the absence of any adequate police, riots, especially in the larger cities, often assumed dangerous proportions, and troops had to be used to quell them. In this way the urban poor exercised an influence which was not justified by their numbers and economic importance. But they were not more than a nuisance, and could be suppressed whenever the government chose by a relatively small display of force.

An obviously much more important element was the army. The army was in the fourth century recruited, in what proportions we do not know, from three main sources—the sons of serving soldiers and veterans, peasants conscripted from the countryside, and barbarians from beyond the frontiers of the empire. Prima facie, then, it should at the beginning of the century have been overwhelmingly pagan. There were, of course, some Christian soldiers even in the third century. There are a few

---

[1] As in the story recounted by Vigilius of Tridentum, *Ep.* i and ii (Migne, P.L. xiii. 449–58).

genuine acts of military martyrs, and in 298 the proconsul of Africa could retort to a Christian conscientious objector: 'There are Christian soldiers who serve in the armies of our lords Diocletian and Maximian, Constantius and Maximian.'[1] But this, it may be noted, was said in Africa, where, as we have seen, the peasantry were probably already converted to the new faith. The famous Theban legion, if it is not a myth, will also have come from an exceptional area, Egypt. But by and large there must have been very few Christians in the army when Constantine decided to paint the ☧ monogram on the shields of his soldiers before the battle of the Milvian Bridge. The barbarians were still pagan, and so were the bulk of the peasantry, especially in the favourite recruiting grounds of the army, Gaul and Illyricum. We have, in fact, a little piece of evidence that the army which two years later, under the protection of the labarum, fought and won the war against Licinius, which was in Constantine's propaganda a crusade against a pagan tyrant, was still pagan. A curious law in the Theodosian Code has preserved the acclamations of the veterans discharged after the victory. 'Auguste Constantine, dei te nobis servent' is what they shouted, and the offensive words were not emended to 'Deus te nobis servet' until Justinian re-edited the law for insertion in his Code.[2]

How far the army became christianized as the fourth century progressed it is very difficult to say. Its intake must have remained predominantly pagan. Christianity, as we have seen, made slow progress in the countryside, and the bulk of the peasant conscripts must have continued to belong to the old faith. With the conversion of the Goths and other east German tribes, some of the barbarian recruits will have been Christians, but the bulk of the barbarians in the fourth century seem to have come from the Franks and Alamans, who were still and long remained heathens. The army might have been expected to be a powerful force on the pagan side of the struggle.

Actually it played a purely passive role. It obeyed with equal loyalty Constantine and his sons, Julian the Apostate, and his Christian successors. It may be that military discipline and the habit of obedience were stronger forces than religious conviction. But what little evidence there is suggests rather that soldiers conformed more or less passively to the prevailing religion of the

---

[1] *Acta Maximiliani* in Ruinart, *Acta Sincera*, pp. 340–2.
[2] *Cod. Theod.* VII. xx. 2 (= *Cod. Just.* XII. xlvi. 1); for the date see Seeck, *Regesten*, p. 176.

state whatever it might be for the time being. Julian seems to have inherited from Constantius II an army which was superficially at any rate largely Christian. His statement in his letter to Maximus[1] that the bulk of the Gallic army, which he was leading against Constantius, worshipped the gods, reads like a boast of the achievement and implies that in the brief period since his proclamation he had changed the religious tone of the troops. Gregory Nazianzen's description of his insidious propaganda once again implies that Julian found the army of the East full of Christians, and its tone suggests that his success in winning the troops back to the old religion was considerable.[2] Yet when Julian was dead the army accepted the Christian Jovian without ado, if without enthusiasm, and acclaimed Valentinian, who had publicly demonstrated his devotion to the new religion by resigning his commission under Julian.

The religious indifference of the army in an age when religious passions ran so high is a curious phenomenon. The explanation would seem to be that the army consisted of men torn from their normal environment and plunged into a new world where everything was unfamiliar. In his own village the peasant clung stubbornly to the immemorial beliefs and customs of his community, but when he was delivered over to the recruiting officers and marched to a distant province and posted among a heterogeneous crowd of strangers, he lost his bearings. His old gods were far away, and bewildered he accepted the prevailing worship of the army. The situation of barbarian recruits was similar. They too were plunged into an alien environment, and the majority seem to have been assimilated to it, losing touch with their tribesmen at home, and adopting Roman ways, and with them the prevailing Roman religion.

There were still at the end of the fourth century and at the beginning of the fifth some high-ranking German officers who retained their pagan faith despite many years in the Roman service—the Frank Arbogast and the Goths Fravitta and Generid:[3] but the two last are noted as exceptional. Under a succession of Christian emperors the general tone of the army must have become more and more Christian. The sons of soldiers and veterans would have been normally brought up in the new

[1] Julian, *Ep.* xxxviii.
[2] Greg. Naz. *Or.* iv (*Contra Julianum*, i), 64 ff., 82 ff.
[3] Paulinus, *Vita Ambrosii*, xxvi, xxxi; Zosimus, v. 20, 46.

religion, and barbarian and peasant recruits would have been quickly assimilated. It is noteworthy that when Arcadius had to employ military force to effect the arrest of John Chrysostom, he used a regiment of newly recruited Thracians.[1] He may have feared that his more seasoned troops might have had scruples about dragging a bishop from the altar, and therefore have employed new recruits who were still pagans.

To turn to the upper classes, the old senatorial order, though it retained immense wealth and social prestige, had ceased in the latter part of the third century to possess much political influence. Under Gallienus, if we are to believe Aurelius Victor, senators had been excluded from military commands,[2] and Diocletian, in his reorganization of the empire, relegated them to a very minor role. The prefecture of the city and the two proconsulates of Africa and Asia were still reserved for senators, and they could serve as *correctores* of the Italian provinces and of Achaea, but apart from these dignified but practically unimportant posts they took no part in the administration of the empire, which was entrusted to men of equestrian rank.[3] The equestrian order thus became in effect the official aristocracy of the empire, and it was greatly increased in numbers. For not only did Diocletian's reforms involve the creation of many new posts, military and administrative, but many who aspired to the social prestige and legal privileges of the order secured admission to it by the grant of honorary offices or of the titular ranks of *egregius*, *centenarius*, *ducenarius*, or *perfectissimus*.

Constantine was less hostile to the senate, increasing the number of posts reserved for senators, admitting them to other high administrative offices, and enrolling them among his *comites*. At the same time he began to expand the order, granting senatorial rank to many of his higher equestrian officers, and to others whom he favoured. His policy was carried on by his sons, and gained momentum, so that by the middle of the fourth century it had become normal for all the higher civilian offices to carry senatorial rank: that is, on the one hand, senators by birth were eligible for them, and, on the other hand, men of lower degree appointed to them thereby became senators. The same policy was under Valentinian and Valens applied to the higher military offices. The result was that the equestrian order, limited to a

---

[1] Palladius, *Dialogus*, ix (p. 57, ed. Colman-Norton).
[2] Aurelius Victor, *De Caesaribus*, xxxiii. 34.
[3] *J.R.S.*, 1954, pp. 26 ff.

decreasing number of lower-grade posts, waned in power and prestige, and the socially ambitious no longer aspired to be enrolled in it. The senatorial order, on the other hand, became once more the official aristocracy of the empire, but it was at the same time vastly inflated in numbers and profoundly modified in character. Not only was it swelled by those who entered it by tenure of civilian, and later military, offices. Those who had previously aspired to the equestrian order now strove by the tenure of honorary senatorial offices or the grant of the clarissimate to make their way into the senate. This influx into the senate threatened to deplete the municipal aristocracy of the empire, the curial order, and the imperial government made periodic efforts to check it. But its efforts were not very whole-hearted, and no regulations were proof against interest and bribery. The senatorial order continued to expand, particularly in the eastern half of the empire, where Constantius II, in his efforts to build up his own senate in Constantinople to parity with that of Rome, enrolled thousands of new members.[1]

The new senators were drawn from very various origins. A very large number, as was only natural, came from the upper ranks of the curial class, the old families of the provincial and municipal aristocracy. According to the prevailing standards of the day such men were in virtue of their birth, wealth, and education fitted to hold the civilian offices and eminently eligible for admission to the senatorial aristocracy. Moreover, they possessed the social connexions and the money to press their claims effectively. Both official posts and senatorial rank were normally obtained by the interest of great men about the court, and this interest had often to be bought by hard cash. Men of position and wealth obviously had advantage in making the necessary contacts, and recompensing their patrons adequately for their services.

But a considerable number of the new senators, including many who rose to the highest rank, came from lower in the social scale. There were those who rose through the army by the tenure of the office of *magister militum, comes rei militaris,* or *dux*. Many of these military men were barbarians, but there were not a few Romans, and as the army in the fourth century offered a *carrière ouverte aux talents*, some of these were of quite humble origins. We happen to know of two peasants who rose from the ranks to

[1] See my *Greek City*, pp. 193 ff.

high commands, Arbetio, who as *magister peditum* was long one of the most influential men in the court of Constantius II, and the elder Gratian, the father of Valentinian and Valens, who achieved the rank of *comes rei militaris*.[1] Such cases were relatively rare, but there must have been a considerable number of senators whose fathers had started life as simple peasants.

The bar was also an avenue whereby able and ambitious men of humble origin could rise. It was the practice for the military and civilian administrators to select rising young barristers to serve as their judicial assessors, and after tenure of two or three such posts they were normally appointed to a provincial governorship, and might rise to the praetorian prefecture. Libanius laments that the law had become such a popular profession that humane studies were falling into neglect. Men of liberal education no longer got the jobs, they all went to barristers; and as a result the young men despised rhetoric and flocked to Berytus to the law schools.[2] Not all barristers, of course, were men of humble origin: wealthy *curiales* and even senators did not disdain the profession. But it was possible for men of very modest status to climb to the top of the tree. Maximinus, who ultimately became praetorian prefect of the Gauls and one of Valentinian's right-hand men, was the son of a very low-grade civil servant, a financial clerk in the provincial office of Valeria.[3]

If the promotion of barristers provoked Libanius' indignation, the rise to power of palatine civil servants, in particular of imperial notaries, roused him to a white heat of fury. What an age, he exclaims more than once, when a shorthand clerk becomes praetorian prefect.[4] It was the function of the imperial notaries to keep the minutes of the consistory, and they were in the early fourth century simple clerks, whose only qualification was a knowledge of shorthand, and were normally men of very humble status. But from their intimate association with the emperor and his ministers they had great opportunities for advancement. They were employed for confidential missions, were appointed to the palatine ministries, and sometimes rose to the highest office of state. In one of his speeches Libanius gives a list of men who had thus risen from stenographers to senators. It includes many of the great names of the eastern half of the empire during the

[1] Ammianus Marcellinus, xv. ii. 4, xxx, vii. 2–3.
[2] Libanius, *Or.* ii. 43–44, xlvii. 22, xliv. 27–28.
[3] Ammianus Marcellinus, xxviii. i. 3–6.
[4] Libanius, *Or.* ii. 44, 46, 58 ff., xviii. 131–4, xxxi. 3, xlii, 25.

middle fourth century: Ablabius, Constantine's great praetorian prefect, consul in 331; Datianus, consul in 358; and four of Constantius II's praetorian prefects—Philippus, consul in 348, Taurus, consul in 361, Elpidius, and Domitianus. And of these, he declares, Datianus was the son of a cloakroom attendant in a bath, and Philippus of a sausage-maker, while Ablabius started as a clerk in a provincial office, and Domitianus' father was a manual worker.[1]

The senatorial order thus became during the course of the fourth century a very mixed body. Its composition and structure differed in East and West. At Rome there was a strong nucleus of ancient families which claimed descent from the Gracchi and the Scipios. Tenuous as these claims might be, their members regarded themselves and were accepted as aristocrats of the bluest blood, and enjoyed immense inherited wealth. Many of them were content to hold the ornamental offices which they regarded as their due, and took no active part in the government of the empire. But some, like the great Petronius Probus, played an active part in politics. In the West the senatorial order had two main foci. Rome was the titular capital of the empire and the official seat of the senate. Here the old families reigned supreme. But the administrative capital of the emperor was no longer Rome but the imperial *comitatus*, wherever the emperor might be for the time being, at Milan, Paris, or Sirmium. Here members of the old families were less at home, and were outnumbered by new men who had risen in the emperor's service.

In the East there was no such division. Constantinople was both the centre of government and the seat of the senate, and the *comitatus* and the senatorial order were closely intertwined, with the result that the court dominated the senate. Moreover, at Constantinople there was no hard core of ancient families. As Libanius with rather heavy irony puts it: 'the whole senate does not consist of nobles whose ancestors for four generations back and more have held offices and served on embassies and devoted themselves to the public service.'[2] Constantius II no doubt enrolled all senators who were already domiciled in his dominions, but they can have been few and undistinguished. The *élite* of the Constantinopolitan senate was formed of men like Philippus and Taurus who had risen to high office from quite humble origins: it was the descendants of such men who

[1] Ibid. xlii. 23–24.   [2] Ibid. xlii. 22.

in the fifth and sixth centuries were the aristocracy of the eastern empire.

These facts have their bearing on the religious struggle, for the religion of senators was to some extent determined by their social origins. In the eastern parts the upper layer of the order was mainly composed of men who had risen from the strata of society most strongly impregnated by Christianity, the lower middle class and even, if Libanius is to be believed, the proletariat of the towns. In fact most of the leading men in the East in the fourth century were so far as we know Christians; the two principal exceptions were Themistius, who owed his advancement to his repute as a philosopher, and Tatian, a barrister, who after a long administrative career rose to be praetorian prefect. Many of them were no doubt Christians before their rise to power, and those who were not had not been conditioned against Christianity by a rhetorical education, and found little difficulty in accepting the faith of the court.

The great bulk of the eastern senators, who came from the upper layer of the curial order, would have been more divided in their allegiance. They came from families which cherished their Hellenic heritage, and higher education for long retained a strongly pagan colour in the East. Most of the great rhetoricians and philosophers were pagans in the fourth century, and even in the fifth and sixth centuries many remained so. Zacharias of Mytilene in his life of Severus of Antioch gives a striking picture of university life at Alexandria, where he and Severus were students, in the last quarter of the fifth century. Not only, it seems, were most of the professors pagans, but so were a large proportion of the students, and he tells lurid tales of the hidden temple where they conducted their secret rites.[1] Even in the sixth century Athens, which remained the leading university town of the East, was still strongly pagan in tone until Justinian expelled the philosophers.

The persistence of paganism among the cultured classes of the East must not then be underestimated. Even in the second half of the sixth century a purge conducted by Tiberius Constantine revealed the existence of many crypto-pagans among the aristocracy.[2] But the furious outcry raised by Julian's law against Christian professors shows how deeply Christianity had penetrated among the educated classes by the middle of the fourth century,

---

[1] Zach. Mit. *Vita Severi*, Patr. Or. ii. i, 14 ff.   [2] John Eph. H.E. ii, 30 ff.

especially in the eastern half of the empire. It was not only that there were many Christian teachers, including so celebrated a figure as Prohaeresius,[1] who lost their posts. There were evidently a vast number of Christian parents who regarded a rhetorical education as essential for their sons, but feared that under Julian's régime the schools would become militantly pagan. It is probable that by this time only rather old-fashioned and puritanical Christians felt any objection to a classical education as such, and many pious parents did not even scruple to send their sons to professors who were well known to be pagan; John Chrysostom was sent to Libanius by his mother, a devout Christian.[2] In these circumstances many of the *curiales* promoted to the senate of Constantinople may have been Christians and the influence of the court and of the higher aristocracy must have converted many waverers. On the whole, the senate of Constantinople was probably from its origin a predominantly Christian body.

In the West, on the other hand, the old families remained on the whole faithful to their traditional religion down to the end of the fourth century, and since they dominated Roman society, the senate at Rome was strongly pagan. This is amply demonstrated by the petitions which it officially presented to Gratian and Valentinian II for the restoration of the altar of Victory and of the Roman priesthoods.

How far the senatorial order as a whole was predominantly pagan or Christian it is more difficult to say. Ambrose in 384 claimed that 'the *curia* is crowded with a majority of Christians', and in 382 Pope Damasus, as a counterblast to the official request of the senate for the restoration of the altar of Victory, was able to organize a monster petition of Christian senators, who protested that they had given no such mandate, did not agree with such requests of the pagans, and did not give their consent to them.[3] It is obviously impossible at this distance of time to discover the truth behind the rival propaganda of the two sides. From the fact that only two years after Damasus had got up his petition the senate again sent an official request to the emperor it is clear that at Rome the Christian opposition was weak, whether because Christian senators resident in the city were actually in a minority or because they were for the most part relatively humble

---

[1] Eunapius, *Vit. soph.* ccccxciii, cf. Simplicianus in Augustine, *Conf.* viii. 5.
[2] Socrates, vi. 3; Sozomen, viii. 2.   [3] Ambrose, *Ep.* xvii. 9-11.

members of the order, who dared not stand up to the great aristocrats. From the language of the petition it would appear that its signatories had not attended the meeting at which the resolution was voted. This may mean that they had not dared to voice their opposition openly. But it is more likely that Damasus obtained his 'innumerable' signatures by sending a round robin to non-resident senators. These would have been for the most part new men, and among them the proportion of Christians would have actually been higher.

At the court at Milan the balance, as the rejection of the senate's pleas showed, inclined to the Christian side. But the decision was by no means a foregone conclusion, and it needed all Ambrose's zeal and eloquence to sway the consistory.

These facts account in a large measure for the very different course which the struggle took in East and West. In the East the pagan opposition was never a serious political force. It was in both senses of the word academic. The leaders of paganism were almost all professors, Maximus, Themistius, Libanius, and the rest. The strongholds of paganism were the university towns, foremost among them Athens. It survived longest among students and intellectuals. Moreover, in the pejorative sense of the word the pagan opposition was academic. It was unorganized and ineffectual, finding expression only in speeches and pamphlets. When Theodosius the Great closed the temples and banned pagan cult, there was no serious opposition apart from the heroic but futile attempt of the philosopher Olympius to hold the Serapeum at Alexandria with a band of enthusiasts.[1] Pagans thereafter contented themselves with furtively practising their rites in secret and nourishing apocalyptic dreams of the return of the old gods. As late as the reign of Zeno great excitement was caused among the pagan intellectuals of Asia Minor when the Neoplatonist philosopher Pamprepius became master of the offices to the pretender Leontius. They began to offer sacrifice openly on his behalf and an oracle was circulated that the span allotted by fate for Christianity had come to an end and that the old gods would come into their own again.[2] Needless to say, their hopes were quite unfounded. Leontius, or rather his patron, the Isaurian general Illus, made no move in favour of paganism.

This weakness of paganism is partly accounted for by their numerical inferiority in the East. More important, however, than

---

[1] Sozomen, vii. 15.　　　　[2] Zach. Mit. *Vita Severi, Patr. Or.* 11. i. 40.

the question of mere numbers was that of political leadership. There was in the East no hereditary aristocracy bred up in the old ways to lead the opposition. The governing class at Constantinople was largely composed of parvenus drawn from the classes where Christianity was strongest, and the senate was from its first formation predominantly Christian in tone.

It cannot be claimed that the pagan opposition was very much more effective in the West, but here the Roman aristocracy did at least make an official stand for the old religion, and its representations, though rejected, were taken into serious consideration. What is more significant, a pretender at the end of the fourth century thought it worth while to make concessions to the pagan sentiments of the senate. Eugenius, though himself a Christian, if not a very fervent one, restored the altar of Victory and handed over the endowments of the Roman priesthood to pagan senators.[1] This rather half-hearted gesture met with a vigorous response, and the Roman aristocracy, led by Flavian, the praetorian prefect of Italy, threw themselves wholeheartedly into the struggle on Eugenius' behalf. They, too, dreamed of a pagan restoration,[2] but their dreams had rather more substance than those of their eastern fellow believers.

It may be claimed that the social changes of the third and fourth centuries were an important factor in the triumph of Christianity in the empire as a whole. When Constantine staked his faith on the god of the Christians in 312, he was on all human calculations making a very rash venture. Christians were on any reckoning a small minority, particularly in the West, where the struggle with Maxentius was to take place, and they mostly belonged to classes which were politically and militarily negligible, the manual workers, shopkeepers, merchants, and lesser decurions of the towns and the clerks of the civil service. The army was overwhelmingly pagan. The senate was pagan. So too in all probability was the bulk of the provincial and municipal aristocracy, and the majority of higher administration, drawn as they were from the army and the curial class. By making himself the champion of Christianity, Constantine can hardly have hoped to win for himself any useful support, and might reasonably have feared to provoke antagonism in many important quarters; and this is incidentally to my mind an important piece of

---

[1] Ambrose, *Ep.* lvii. 6; Paulinus, *Vita Ambrosii*, xxvi.
[2] Paulinus, *Vita Ambrosii*, xxxi.

circumstantial evidence in favour of the view that Constantine's conversion was not a calculated political move, but, as he himself consistently proclaimed in his public pronouncements, the fruit of a genuine if crude religious conviction that the Highest Divinity, who had chosen him as his servant, was a more potent giver of victory than the old gods.

The situation was not, however, as unfavourable as it appeared. For at the time when Constantine made his fateful decision Roman society was in a state of flux. The late Roman empire is often conceived as a rigid hierarchical society, in which every man was tied to the station in life to which he was born. The long series of laws on which this view is based seem to me to reveal a very different picture. They show that the imperial government was struggling to impose a rigid hereditary class system, but such legislation would not have been called for had not the familiar structure of society been shaken; and the constant re-enactment of the rules, and the periodical concessions made, show that the government was very imperfectly successful in checking the movements which it regarded as dangerous. There is much evidence which suggests that society was static in the second and early third centuries. The army was to an increasing degree recruited from the sons of soldiers and veterans. The peasants tilled the same farms, whether they were freeholders or tenants, from generation to generation. The decurions were a mainly hereditary class, where son succeeded father to the ancestral estates. The aristocracy of the empire, the senate, and the equestrian order, failed it is true to maintain its numbers and was constantly supplemented from below; but the rate of recruitment was slow, and the new members, who mainly came from the provincial aristocracy, were readily assimilated.

Under the impact of the prolonged crisis of the mid-third century this stable society was profoundly shaken. For a variety of reasons men of all classes became dissatisfied with their hereditary position in life, and the conditions of the time gave opportunities for change. The population had probably shrunk as a result of the wars, famines, and plagues of the years of anarchy, and at the same time the army was making increasing demands for men. The consequence was an acute shortage of manpower, which made itself particularly felt in the empire's major industry, agriculture. Landlords could not find enough tenants to cultivate their lands, and welcomed newcomers to their estates. As a result dissatisfied tenants found themselves able to throw up their farms and move elsewhere with the certainty that another landlord would offer them a home. This restlessness among the peasantry caused grave concern to the government, which saw the basis of its fiscal system imperilled. The poll-tax was based on the assumption that the peasants registered under each village or farm would remain there and in due course be succeeded by their sons. The land-tax too seemed to be threatened, since landlords everywhere complained that their estates had been abandoned by their cultivators. This would seem to be the situation which provoked the legislation tying the agricultural population to the land on which they were registered on the census.[1]

The manpower shortage gave rise to a similar restlessness in other classes of society and provoked similar legislation where, as in the mining industry, the government felt that the interests of the state were threatened. Another disturbing factor was the vast expansion of the administrative services entailed by Diocletian's reorganization of the empire. More and more clerks were required in the growing government offices, and many sons of soldiers and veterans, instead of enlisting in the army as hitherto, preferred a more comfortable and lucrative career as officials; *curiales* of the humbler sort likewise flocked into the ministries. Once again the government, finding the intake of the army reduced and the city councils, on which the administration of the empire and the collection of the taxes ultimately depended, dangerously depleted, endeavoured to tie the sons of soldiers and decurions to their respective hereditary roles.[2]

But the most revolutionary change brought about by Diocletian was the formation of the new imperial nobility of service which I have outlined earlier in this lecture. This change was of crucial importance for the future of Christianity. For it meant that Constantine and his successors did not have to face a firmly entrenched hereditary aristocracy hostile to their religious innovation, but were able to build up and mould a new nobility more subservient to their wishes.

The senate had, it is true, under the principate been powerless to resist a resolute and ruthless emperor. But an emperor could only impose his will by a reign of terror, and while emperors came and went, the senate remained. Through the generations the senatorial order preserved to a remarkable degree a corporate

[1] *Past and Present*, 1958, 1 ff.   [2] See my *Greek City*, pp. 196–7.

sense of its dignity, and a spirit of independence and even of opposition to the imperial office. The great aristocratic families regarded themselves as superior to jumped-up emperors, and their birth and wealth made them independent of imperial patronage. Such a body might be bullied into submission, but its sentiments could not be easily influenced.

The new nobility of service was a very different body. A heterogeneous collection of individuals, drawn from all ranks of society, it inevitably lacked any corporate sense. And since its members were dependent on imperial patronage for their advancement, it was as inevitably subservient to the emperor's will and took its tone from him. Constantine and his Christian successors were thus able to build up an aristocracy in sympathy with their religious policy.

In the first place they were in a position to show direct favour to Christians. They could choose their ministers and advisers with a free hand from all classes of society, and bestow rank and dignity on whomsoever they wished to favour. They certainly used this opportunity to promote Christians of low degree. Constantine himself, according to Eusebius, was lavish in bestowing codicils of equestrian rank, and even senatorial dignity, on the adherents of his religion.[1] But such a policy had its limits. The number of qualified Christians was too few to fill the posts, and any systematic exclusion of pagans would have provoked dangerous discontent: it was not in fact until the early years of the fifth century that the imperial service was formally debarred to pagans.[2] But it soon became obvious to the ambitious that their chances of promotion would be greatly enhanced if they adopted the emperor's religion, and Eusebius himself deplores that Constantine's open-handed favour to Christians resulted in a large crop of interested conversions.[3]

But it would be a grave injustice to the many upper-class converts of the fourth century to assume that they were all hypocritical opportunists. A more potent cause of conversion than calculations of material gain was the fact that Christianity became respectable and indeed fashionable in high society; and this change of tone came about the more easily because high society was in a state of flux. The old senatorial aristocracy had a strong conservative tradition, and clung firmly to the old religion, even when it was on the wane, from a sense of *noblesse*

---

[1] Eusebius, *Vita Const.* iv. 54, cf. 37–39. [2] *Cod. Theod.* xvi. x. 21, Zosimus, v. 46.
[3] Eusebius, *Vita Const.* iv. 54.

oblige. They still had great social prestige, and to some extent set the tone of society in the West, but in the East their position was usurped by the new senate of Constantinople, and even in the West it was disputed by the new nobility which clustered around the *comitatus*. In the new aristocracy of service Christians were not perhaps at first very numerous, but enjoying exceptional imperial favour and achieving the highest honours, they set the tone of the whole. The lesser members tended to follow their lead, and the fashion spread in ever-widening circles through the lower ranks of the social order.

Christianity had made great progress during the first three centuries, but it still remained a minority sect: it was still largely confined to the middle and lower classes and had made of little impression on the aristocracy. Within a few generations of the conversion of Constantine it had become the dominant religion of the empire. In this revolution the support given to Christianity by the imperial government was without doubt a major factor. But it is significant that the religious change coincided with a social change, which brought to the front men from the middle and lower classes.

BIBLIOGRAPHY

G. Boissier, *Fin du paganisme* (Paris, 1891).
S. Dill, *Roman Society in the Last Century of the Western Empire* (2nd ed., London, 1910).
J. Geffcken, *Ausgang des griechisch-römischen Heidentums* (Heidelberg, 2nd ed., 1929).
A. Harnack, *Mission und Ausbreitung des Christentums in den ersten drei Jahrhunderten* (4th ed., Leipzig, 1924).
P. de Labriolle, *La Réaction païenne, étude sur la polémique antichrétienne du Ier au VIe siècle* (Paris, 1934).
H. I. Marrou, *Saint Augustin et la fin de la culture antique* (Paris, 2nd ed., 1949).
A. Piganiol, *L'Empire chrétien (325-95)* (Paris, 1947).
E. Stein, *Geschichte des spätrömischen Reiches*, i (284-476) (Vienna, 1928). French translation with additional notes by J.-R. Palanque, *Histoire du Bas-Empire* (Paris, 1959).

II

*Pagans and Christians in the Family of Constantine the Great**

JOSEPH VOGT

In the researches of the last few decades, the conflict between paganism and Christianity in the fourth century has been represented to a large extent in terms of the transitions and contacts between the two sides; it has been looked upon as a process of give and take rather than a struggle. Historians of religion have pointed out that the solar religion, current mainly among the ruling class and the learned, had given rise to the idea of a supreme god, ruler of the universe; and that Christianity in its turn had absorbed certain features of the sun-god; we have visual evidence of this amalgamation in the representation of Christ as Helios in the mosaic discovered in the vault of the Julii when the necropolis under St. Peter's in Rome was opened.[1] Pagan philosophy had prepared the way for a monotheistic trend of thought which had found an ally in astrology and in the general acceptance of monarchy as the only effective form of government. The cult of the Exsuperantissimus, greater than all the gods, had embraced notions familiar to Jewish faith and to Christian theology alike.[2] Neoplatonists had spoken of *divinitas*, the divine essence, more powerful even than the sun-god. Sol himself had become an image of this sovereign being, and a mediator between him and the other gods with their more particularized tasks—an idea again related to notions held on the Christian side by certain gnostic sects.[3]

These observations, though valuable, should not be overrated.

---

* This article is dedicated to my dear colleague Hildebrecht Hommel on the occasion of his sixtieth birthday.

[1] O. Perler, *Die Mosaiken der Juliergruft im Vatikan* (Rektoratsrede, Freiburg, Switzerland, 1953); J. Toynbee–J. Ward Perkins, *The Shrine of St. Peter and the Vatican Excavations* (London, 1956); Th. Klauser, *Die römische Petrustradition im Lichte der neuen Ausgrabungen unter der Peterskirche* (Arbeitsgemeinschaft für Forschung des Landes Nordrhein-Westfalen, xxiv, 1956).

[2] H. Mattingly, 'The Later Paganism', *Harv. Theol. Rev.* xxxv (1942), 171 ff.

[3] F. Altheim, *Aus Spätantike und Christentum* (Tübingen, 1951), pp. 45 ff.

The common ground shared by the two positions did nothing to resolve the tension between them, or even to reduce it. In anti-Christian polemics, the sharpest note of implacability came from the Neoplatonic philosophers; and the worshippers of the sun-god were the most zealous persecutors of the Christians. Men and women who had lived through twelve years of persecution under the Tetrarchy knew that there could be no question of compromise. Pagans and Christians shared the feeling that they were faced with a final decision, however closely related their tenets might seem on the rational level and in points of detail. Both sides lived in a state of religious panic. Both were convinced that in human affairs success and failure were demonstrably and directly dependent on divine action, and that heaven's blessing could without fail be forced down upon the individual, the family, the whole Roman empire, by religious worship. The inscription of Arykanda, which contains an appeal to the emperors from the last phase of the Tetrarchy, makes this clear: ἔργοις ἀπο[δεδειγμένων ἀεὶ τ]ῶν θεῶν τῶν ὁμογενῶν ὑμῶν φιλανθρωπίας [πᾶσιν, ὦ ἐπιφανέσ]τατοι βασιλεῖς, οἷς ἡ θρησκεία μεμέληται [σπουδαίως ὑπὲρ τῆ]ς ὑμῶν τῶν πάντα νικώντων δεσποτῶν [ἡμῶν αἰωνίου σω]τηρίας . . . Lactantius, at the beginning of his book *De mortibus persecutorum*, writes: qui insultaverant deo, iacent, qui templum sanctum everterant, ruina maiore ceciderunt, qui iustos excarnificaverant, caelestibus plagis et cruciatibus meritis nocentes animas profuderunt.[1]

It was in this climate of religious ferment that Constantine the Great lived. In an act of personal decision he summed up his generation's experience, led monotheism to victory, and won the Christian Church for the state. We may, I think, credit the controversies of the last thirty years with having shown that, in terms of the emperor's personal life, the battle of the Milvian Bridge was a turning-point.[2] There are, it is true, some dissenting voices. Henri Grégoire, for example, alleges that the emperor, who like all other rulers was apt to subordinate matters of religion to political considerations, did not turn to Christianity until after

---

[1] The inscription from Arykanda in E. Preuschen, *Analecta*, i (2nd ed., 1909), 100: cf. Dittenberger, *OGIS*, 569; Lactantius, *De mortibus persecutorum*, i. 5.

[2] The sources are given in my report on the Constantinian question in *Relazioni X Congresso internaz. di scienze storiche*, vi (1955), 733 ff. and in my article 'Constantinus' in *Reallexikon für Antike und Christentum*, iii (1956), 306 ff. Cf. M. Guarducci, *I graffiti sotto la Confessione di S. Pietro in Vaticano*, ii. 16 ff., iii, pls. 12 f. (1958), and A. Alföldi, *Dumbarton Oaks Papers*, xiii (1959), 171 ff. For the beginning of these new controversies cf. N. H. Baynes, 'Constantine the Great and the Christian Church', *Proc. Brit. Acad.* xv (1929), 341 ff.

his conquest of the East. This has been disproved by documents from the early phase of the Donatist quarrel; it can also be refuted on the ground that in the East, where religious convictions were more strongly opposed and economic interests more deeply affected than in the West, the emperor's siding with the Christians would have involved him in even greater political risks.[1] Nor has it been possible for Grégoire and his pupils to explain away the Christian tradition according to which Constantine's conversion took place in 312 as a later invention or misinterpretation. No evidence has been found either of a re-working of Lactantius' *De mortibus* or of a late date of composition of Eusebius' *Vita Constantini*.[2] On the contrary, it has become clear that the two texts, one describing the shield badges, the other the vision in the sky, agree on an essential point: both proceed from the vision of the cross, but stress that it was the emperor himself who formed the monogram with the name of Christ and thus gave it the distinct character of a watchword. It should, incidentally, be noted that this monogram appears as early as 315 on a medallion on the emperor's helmet. Another critic, Franz Altheim, interprets Constantine's action as that of a new Aurelian who had replaced Helios by Christ while maintaining his own position as the sun-like divine ruler. This theory, too, is unconvincing, for we know now that the statue in Constantinople said to have represented Constantine as Helios was not that of a solar ruler at all. We prefer to trust the emperor Julian's bitter reproach to his uncle of having deserted Helios.[3] Certainly, many riddles of Constantine's political and religious tenets still remain unsolved; in particular, certain Neoplatonic and gnostic traits in him deserve a closer examination. But I think it can be regarded as established that in his time and place Constantine decided the religious conflict in favour of Christian monotheism.

[1] K. Kraft, 'Das Silbermedaillon Constantins des Grossen mit dem Christusmonogramm auf dem Helm', *Jahrbuch für Numismatik und Geldgeschichte*, v–vi (1954–5), 161 ff.

[2] Edition with translation and commentary of Lactantius' book by J. Moreau, Lactance, *De la mort des persécuteurs* (2 vols., Sources chrétiennes, xxxix, i, 1954); in the introduction, pp. 33 ff., no evidence that the book was re-edited is advanced. For the *Vita Constantini* cf. F. Vittinghoff, 'Euseb als Verfasser der "Vita Constantini"', *Rhein. Mus.* xcvi (1953), 330 ff., and K. Aland, 'Die religiöse Haltung Konstantins', *Studia Patristica*, i (Texte und Untersuchungen zur Geschichte der altchristlichen Literatur, lxiii, 1957), 549 ff. New arguments in favour of authenticity in F. W. Winkelmann, *Die Vita Constantini des Euseb. Ihre Authentizität, ihre Textbezeugung* (Diss. Halle, 1959).

[3] For the column of Constantine in Constantinople see J. Karayannopulos, 'Konstantin der Grosse und der Kaiserkult', *Historia*, v (1956), 341 ff. The testimony of Julian *or.* vii. 228D (Hertlein), cf. J. Vogt, 'Kaiser Julian über seinen Oheim Constantin den Grossen', *Historia*, iv (1955), 345.

This decision involved him in risks and sacrifices; he had to stoop to seduction and violence; he also learned to renounce and to deny. To treat his theology in isolation, as has recently been done in the otherwise remarkable German books by Hermann Dörries and Heinz Kraft,[1] is not, to my mind, the best way; I prefer to consider his religious decision in the light of his achievement as a ruler. Three outstanding points immediately come to mind: the renouncement of the Tetrarchy, the establishment of himself as sole ruler, and the founding of a dynasty on the inheritance from father to son. It has been strongly emphasized that the dynastic idea had been kept alive in the Principate from Augustus' time onward;[2] during the Tetrarchy of Diocletian, however, it had given place to the choice of the ablest. But from the moment of his elevation Constantine—and this is typical of him—had upheld his claims in virtue of his birthright, and won his way by playing on the advantages of the dynastic principle which had its firmest stronghold in the army. How, then, can we define the connexion between religion and hereditary succession? Did Constantine bring about his family's conversion? Was there a religious significance in the marriages which he caused to be concluded? And how did the religious decisions among his family affect his dynastic policy?

If we use the term 'family' here we do not understand it merely in the sense of a domestic community held together by paternal authority; nor do we mean by it that wider clan in which personal names, male and female, so often allude to the military virtue of *constantia*; we look even beyond the limits of the *gens Flavia* which in pagan eyes reflected the assembly of the gods of the Tetrarchy with its temples and organizations of priests.[3] We intend by family rather the whole circle of the *domus divina*, the sovereign with his wives and children as well as all those whom he made his near relatives.[4] At the secular games Augustus, the founder of the first dynasty, had implored divine help not only for the *populus Romanus* and the *Latinum nomen* but also *mihi*

---

[1] H. Dörries, *Das Selbstzeugnis Kaisers Konstantins* (Abh. Gött. Ak. xxxiv; 1954); H. Kraft, *Kaiser Konstantins religiöse Entwicklung* (Beiträge zur historischen Theologie, xx); 1955. Critical review of these two books by H. U. Instinsky, *Gnomon*, xxx (1958), 125 ff.
[2] L. Wickert, *Realencyclopädie*, s.v. 'Princeps' (xxii. 2137 ff.).
[3] For the cult of the *gens Flavia* E. Kornemann, 'Zur Geschichte der antiken Herrscherkulte', *Klio*, i (1901), 136 ff.; W. Hartke, *Römische Kinderkaiser* (Berlin, 1951), pp. 170 f. For the inscription from Hispellum, A. Alföldi, *The Conversion of Constantine and Pagan Rome* (Oxford, 1948), pp. 105 f.
[4] Mommsen, *Röm. Staatsrecht*, ii (4th ed.), 818 ff.

domo familiae;[1] the founder of the *genus Constantinianum*[2] may equally well have felt entitled—indeed bound—to think of his whole house when addressing the deity.

The comparison with Augustus should not blind us to the changes in the religious situation that had occurred since his time. The ties of family and kinship, so binding for pagans brought up in a strict tradition, appeared in a different light to Christians. In Graeco-Roman society the family was held together not merely by the interests of labour and reward; it was a community united by cult and celebrations. The stability of the house and the survival of the clan were guaranteed by the *sacra familiae* and *sacra gentilicia*. Even in the later empire, when in general spiritual ties became less stringent, family cults remained deeply rooted in the sanctity of tradition; they were the strongest supports of the ancestral religion which had largely become the concern of the family, particularly in senatorial circles. Christianity, on the other hand, required, like Judaism, a personal avowal of faith from its converts; they had to turn their back on tradition in a conscious resolve. The words of the Master: 'For I am come to set a man at variance against his father, and the daughter against her mother, and the daughter-in-law against her mother-in-law. And a man's foes shall be they of his own household' (Matt. x. 35, 36)—those words alone demanded that every individual should go on his own way regardless of his kith and kin. We know for instance from the Acts of the martyrs Perpetua and Felicitas how often family ties were broken by the Christian mission throughout the empire; and the legend of St. Martin tells us that he won his mother for the new faith while his father remained true to the tradition of his ancestors.[3] In pagan polemics the Christian mission has often been blamed for this breaking up of the domestic community. The gentler way of introducing Christianity into pagan families, through marriages between Christian girls and pagan men, has sometimes roused the protest of Christian writers, and in the early fourth century some synods made mixed marriages an offence. However, they were never formally forbidden, and it is not surprising to find them on the increase towards the end of the century.[4]

---

[1] Dessau, *Inscript. Lat. sel.* 5050, 97, 99.   [2] Ammianus Marcellinus, XXVII. v. 1.
[3] Sulpic. Sev. *Vita S. Mart.* vi. 3 (Halm).
[4] J. Köhne, 'Über die Mischehen in den ersten christlichen Jahrhunderten', *Theologie und Glaube*, xxxiii (1931), 333 ff.; G. Bardy, 'La Conversion au christianisme durant les premiers siècles', *Théologie*, xv (1949), pp. 220 ff. Cf. also G. Delling, 'Ehehindernisse', *R.A.C.* iv. 689 f.

the Family of Constantine the Great 43

None the less, a Christian ruler who aimed at founding a dynasty, securing his line of succession and marrying his children in a world still largely pagan, must have faced more formidable obstacles than those which Augustus had encountered; and we know that even Augustus, the good *pater patriae*, had been a hard and sorely tried *pater familias*.

The clearest and also the most attractive evidence we have of Constantine's family feelings regards his reverence for his parents: the elevation of his father Constantius (a loyal member of the Tetrarchy) to the status of an imperial exemplar, and his devotion to his mother Helena, who had had to surrender her place next to Constantius to her aristocratic rival Theodora soon after Constantine's birth, but later resumed her rank with consummate dignity as the companion of her son. The beginnings of Constantine's reign present themselves as a careful attempt at founding his succession on the right of inheritance. From 307 on, panegyric speeches glorified the young ruler as the likeness of *divus Constantius*; in deference to designs issuing from highest quarters they invented an ancestor in Claudius Gothicus, thus making the emperor third of his line; and they declared him to be the noblest of the emperors because emperor by birth.[1] As regards Constantius, the same panegyrics, as well as the coins, lead one to suspect that he was not over-particular about the theology of the Tetrarchy. We have reason to believe that he tended towards monotheism without departing from pagan traditions.[2] This would explain why he called his daughter Anastasia, a name which otherwise occurs only in Jewish and Christian surroundings. Christian reports on Constantius are not consistent, and have been interpreted in divers ways by modern scholars. Eusebius, in the 315 edition of his *Ecclesiastical History*, calls Constantius a friend of the Divine Logos and maintains that he had refrained from taking part in the wars against the Christians, leaving their churches intact. Nevertheless, he admits in his book on the Palestinian martyrs that in Constantius' own domain, Gaul, there had been a persecution of the Christians lasting almost two years.[3] Finally, in his biography of the blessed

[1] Evidence in Wickert, loc. cit., pp. 2174 ff.; E. Galletier, *Panégyriques latins*, ii (1952), 5 f., 41 ff., 111 f.
[2] R. Andreotti, 'Costanzo Cloro', *Didaskaleion*, ix (1930), fasc. 2, pp. 25 ff.; H. von Schoenebeck, *Beiträge zur Religionspolitik des Maxentius und Constantin* (Klio, Beiheft xxx; 1939), p. 31 f.; J. Moreau, *Jahrbuch für Antike und Christentum*, ii (1959), 159.
[3] For this J. Moreau, *Lactance*, ii. 290 f.

Constantine, the same Eusebius prefaces the glorification of his hero with praise of the latter's father (*Vita Constantini*, i. 13 ff.) on the grounds that he had kept his hands clean of Christian blood, rejected polytheism, and protected his house, which was dedicated to the only king and God, by the prayers of holy men. On the other hand, there is Lactantius' precise statement on the destruction of churches by Constantius (*De mort. pers.* xv. 7): it reads: 'conventicula, id est parietes, qui restitui poterant, dirui passus est, verum autem dei templum, quod est in hominibus, incolume servavit.' André Piganiol concluded from these testimonies that Constantius had been no friend of the Christians.[1] Heinz Kraft, however, follows on the whole Eusebius' report, and tries to discount Lactantius' contradictory assertion;[2] he wants to understand the term *conventicula* as meaning 'meetings' or 'assemblies', averring that Lactantius had misunderstood his source, interpreting it as a reference to assembly halls when in fact it had spoken of Constantius' ban on Christian meetings. I cannot agree with this interpretation. Lactantius uses the term *conventicula* unambiguously for assembly houses wherever it occurs in connexion with the persecutions,[3] and since his book was published in Gaul he is unlikely to have overlooked the stark evidence of the destroyed churches.[4]

Constantius, therefore, was not a Christian, though conciliatory enough to have avoided bloodshed and allowed Christians access to the court. But even assuming that his attitude had sheltered a secret amity, it in no way accounts for the conversion of his son. It would be a mistake to suppose that the order of events, from Constantius to Constantine and his sons, had followed the usual pattern of a Roman family's conversion in the course of several generations.[5] The reverse is true: it was Constantine who, after his own conversion, wanted the memory of his father to be that of a Christian. He had been prompted by a similar line of thought when he invented a founder for his house in the figure of Claudius Gothicus. It was after his victory over

---

[1] A. Piganiol, *L'Empereur Constantin* (Paris, 1932), pp. 31 ff.
[2] H. Kraft, *Kaiser Konstantins religiöse Entwicklung*, pp. 2 ff.
[3] Cf. *De mort. pers.* xxxiv. 4; xxxvi. 3; further evidence in Moreau, *Lactance*, ii. 290.
[4] The clear statement of Lactantius is not refuted by the letter of the Donatist bishops to Constantine which says: 'cuius pater inter ceteros persecutionem non exercuit' (Optatus, i. 22 = H. von Soden, *Urkunden zur Entstehungsgeschichte des Donatismus*, 2nd ed., 1950, no. 11). This can only mean that Constantius avoided any bloodshed. So, too, K. Aland, loc. cit., p. 576, n. 6.
[5] H. Kraft, loc. cit., p. 6.

Licinius that he proclaimed the great experience of his life in his letter to the pagan peoples of the East: the impious persecutors had suffered severe penalty and miserable death while the just worshippers of the sacred laws had gained riches, power, and success (*Vita Const.* ii. 24 ff.). This proposition of the violent end of the enemies of God was also the thesis of Lactantius' book; it had been generally accepted in pagan antiquity and was now being translated into Christian terms.[1] For Lactantius (l. 1) the destruction of the race is part of the punishment of the *Theomachos*; Constantine makes the same point with greater emphasis in his letter to the Provincials (of nearly the same date as the one just mentioned). Here he praises the clemency of his father, who in all his deeds had invoked the Saviour God—and in its context this can only mean the Christian God; those others who had instigated persecutions had found a shameful end 'without passing on their name and race'.[2] Eusebius does no more than point the moral when he says of the emperor: εὐτεκνίᾳ μόνος παρὰ τοὺς λοιποὺς αὐτοκράτορας διήνεγκεν, παίδων ἀρρένων καὶ θηλειῶν μέγιστον χορὸν συστησάμενος (*Vita Const.* I. x. 2). The argument therefore follows very simple lines: the persecutors have perished with their descendants; Constantius lives in his sons; he has passed the power on to the eldest; he was not party to the persecutions; he was himself a Christian. It is a strange sequence of associations, reminding one of primitive forms of belief, which thus connected the existence of heirs—the first condition for the founding of a dynasty—with the blessing of the Christian god.

Constantine's relations with his mother are equally blameless. We do not know which faith she followed prior to Constantine's elevation and her own ascent. We hear from the legend of St. Sylvester that when she heard of her son's conversion she expressed regret that he had become a Christian rather than a Jew; but according to the same legend she was herself won over to baptism by a miracle which happened before her eyes. A memory of the considerable Jewish influence prevailing in the Constantinian era may still linger on in this story.[3] Eusebius

---

[1] W. Nestle, 'Legenden vom Tod der Gottesverächter', *Griechische Studien* (Stuttgart, 1948), pp. 567 ff.; J. Moreau, *Lactance*, i. 55 ff.

[2] *Vita Const.* II. xlix. 54; cf. also *Laus Constantini*, ix. 13. The authenticity of the letters of Constantine which are mentioned here is now supported by P. Lond. 878 which contains a fragment of the letter to the pagans in the Orient; cf. A. H. M. Jones, *Journ. Eccles. Hist.* v (1954), 196 ff.

[3] *Actus Silvestri*, Latin version in B. Mombritius, *Sanctuarium*, ii (2nd ed., 1910), 508 ff., also *Reallexikon f. Antike und Christentum*, iii (1956), 374 f. For the position of the Jews in

(*Vit. Const.* iii. 47) assures us explicitly that her conversion was due to her son. It is not clear when this happened; that it could happen is proof of the affectionate relations between mother and son; it also speaks of the attractive personality of the emperor, which never failed to have its effect. It was his declared desire to win people for his faith; and at his court Helena's conversion must have been the finest reward of his missionary zeal. Helena, as is well known, made a pilgrimage to the Holy Land in her later years, and seems to have shared her son's propensity for the visible signs of worship in her devotion to the cult of relics and the building of churches. Moreover, she was an important figure in family politics. On the occasion of the Vicennalia in 325/6 she alone, with Fausta, was raised to the rank of Augusta; she alone was crowned with the diadem in token of majesty. We receive a clear picture of the position of the two Augustae next to the emperor through the cameo in The Hague, which belongs in all probability to the year 325. Constantine appears there on a triumphal chariot, together with Fausta and his son Constantius, who had been proclaimed Caesar a few years earlier. Behind the emperor stands Helena, her hair-style modelled on that of Livia, the holder of the highest rank at the court of Augustus.[1] When she died, probably in 329, she was the first member of the imperial family to be given a truly regal burial in a mausoleum adjoining a church in the Via Labicana outside Rome.[2]

In these different ways Constantine secured the connexion of his parents with the Christian Church and the rise of the dynasty. As long as Galerius watched over the Tetrarchy and he himself had only his illegitimate son Crispus and no children by his young consort Fausta, he made little of his dreams of hereditary succession. At his mother's wish, he kept his half-brothers Dalmatius, Julius Constantius, and Hannibalianus away from court and army, in order to silence their pretensions. When he had become sole master of the West after his triumph over Maxentius, he heaped personal favours on his co-regent Licinius in order to

---

the Roman empire of the fourth century J. Vogt, *Kaiser Julian und das Judentum* (Morgenland, xxx, 1939).

[1] G. Bruns, *Staatskameen des 4. Jahrhunderts n. Chr.* (104. Winckelmannsprogramm der Archäologischen Gesellschaft zu Berlin, 1948), pp. 8 ff., Abb. 5 and 6.

[2] For the honours conferred on Helena and for her funeral L. Voelkl, *Der Kaiser Konstantin* (Munich, 1957), pp. 132 f., 177 f.; F. W. Deichmann, *Frühchristliche Kirchen in Rom* (1948), pp. 19 ff.; in the light of new excavations F. W. Deichmann–A. Tschira, 'Das Mausoleum der Kaiserin Helena und die Basilika der Heiligen Marcellinus und Petrus an der Via Labicana vor Rom', *Jahrbuch d. Dt. Archäol. Inst.* lxxii (1957), 44 ff.

the Family of Constantine the Great

put him under an obligation; he also tried to strengthen the position of his house by making friends of persons in high places. He married his half-sister Constantia to Licinius and, shortly afterwards, Anastasia to Bassanius, who was then under consideration for the co-regency; at about the same time Eutropia became the wife of Nepotianus, whose father had been consul in 301.[1] We know little about the religious convictions of these half-brothers and half-sisters; but what records there are make it likely that they were Christians. Julian's silence on the subject of the religious adherence of his father Julius Constantius is so deliberate as to be virtual proof that the latter was a Christian.[2] We know that Constantia immediately sought contact with the bishops in her husband Licinius' neighbourhood; afterwards she came out so strongly in support of Arius and his followers that there is no doubt of where she stood. Anastasia was in all probability the founder of the Roman Church that bears her name.[3] Altogether we gain the impression that the descendants of Constantius Chlorus and Theodora had followed the lead given by Constantine, the oldest member of the house.

Then Crispus grew up, and Fausta presented her husband with three sons, Constantine in 316, Constantius in 317, and Constans in 320.[4] The dates of birth of the two daughters Constantina and Helena are unknown. We may see a hint of plans for the succession in the proclamation of Crispus and Constantine as Caesars in 317.[5] About the same time Lactantius, an avowed and decided Christian, was called to Treves to become the tutor of Crispus[6]—a sign that the emperor was omitting nothing to

[1] The marriage of Constantia is dated with certainty by the Milan conference of Constantine and Licinius. For Bassianus the date results from the date of the first war between Constantine and Licinius. P. Bruun, *The Constantinian Coinage of Arelate* (Helsinki, 1953), pp. 15 ff., and C. Habicht, 'Zur Geschichte des Kaisers Konstantin', *Hermes*, lxxxvi (1958), 360 ff. said that this war which had been placed by previous research in the year 314 had taken place in the winter of 316–17. R. Andreotti, *Diz. epigr. antich. Rom.* iv (1958), 1002 ff., attempts to prove a campaign in 314 and new hostilities in 316–17. For Nepotianus and Eutropia see W. Ensslin, *Realencyclopädie*, xvi. 2512.

[2] H. Kraft, loc. cit., p. 6, n. 1.

[3] H. von Schoenebeck, loc. cit., pp. 12, 88.

[4] For the dates given J.-R. Palanque, 'Chronologie constantinienne', *L'Antiquité Classique*, xl (1938), 248 ff., and the genealogical tables in J. Lafaurie, 'Médaillon constantinien', *Rev. numism.* xvii (1955), 234 f. Recently J. Moreau in his articles on the sons of Constantine, *Jahrbuch für Antike und Christentum*, ii (1959), 160, 164, 179.

[5] Licinius the younger was the third Caesar. According to the reckoning of C. Habicht, loc. cit., pp. 364 ff., the nomination of the three Caesars followed the treaty after the first war; cf. Andreotti, loc. cit., pp. 1014 f.

[6] J. Moreau, *Lactance*, i. 15; J. Stevenson, 'Life and Literary Activity of Lactantius', *Studia Patristica*, i (Texte und Untersuchungen zur Geschichte der altchristlichen Literatur, lxiii, 1957), 665 f.

strengthen his family's adherence to Christianity. Indeed, when Fausta's sons followed their father as emperors they remained Christians and were given Christian burial at the end of their chequered lives: Constantius in his father's mausoleum in Constantinople, Constans probably in the centralized building still preserved at Centcelles near Tarragona and now being systematically examined.[1] We do not wish to imply that Constantine's sons were pious Christians; nor can this be said of the daughters, who were to be laid to rest in a sepulchre adjoining a church in Via Nomentana in Rome.[2] But they remained within the Church, and Christianity had become the creed of the court and the foundation of the monarchy.

Constantine himself continued his efforts to stabilize and preserve the imperial house. A prayer which he wrote for his pagan soldiers ends with a supplication for the safety of the sovereign and his divinely loved sons (*Vit. Const.* iv. 20). When in 322 a child was born to Crispus, who had married young, the delighted emperor proclaimed a universal amnesty.[3] We can therefore imagine the shock only a few years later when he saw himself compelled to proceed against his eldest son, who had given a splendid account of himself as commander of the fleet in the campaign against Licinius. Our records of the dark events of 326 are scanty,[4] but they are significant in that they all name Fausta, the imperial consort, as the driving force. She had accused her stepson Crispus of illicit relations with herself—she must have been a person of great vitality, physiognomically not unlike her father Maximianus Herculius[5]—and thus forced the emperor to condemn his own son to death. Was this the deed of an unfortunate new Phaedra, or did she fear that Crispus would deprive her own sons of the succession? We are ignorant of her motives, as also of the reason why the emperor, a little later, pronounced the death sentence on his wife, whom the coins had just been celebrating as *Spes rei publicae*, the mother of many

[1] H. Schlunk, 'Untersuchungen im frühchristlichen Mausoleum von Centcelles', *Neue deutsche Ausgrabungen im Mittelmeergebiet und im Vorderen Orient* (Berlin, 1959), pp. 344 ff.

[2] J. Bidez, *Julian der Abtrünnige* (Munich, 1940), pp. 109 f., 203; F. W. Deichmann, *Frühchristliche Kirchen in Rom*, pp. 25 f.; W. N. Schumacher, 'Eine römische Apsiskomposition', *Röm. Quartalschriften*, liv (1959), 137 ff.

[3] *Cod. Theod.* ix. xxxviii. 1.

[4] Sources given in O. Seeck, 'Die Verwandtenmorde Constantins des Grossen', *Zeitschr. f. wiss. Theologie*, xxxiii (1890), 63 ff., and A. Piganiol, *L'Empire chrétien* (= G. Glotz, *Histoire générale*, iv. ii) (1947), pp. 34 ff.

[5] R. Delbrück, *Spätantike Kaiserporträts* (Studien zur spätantiken Kunstgeschichte, viii; 1933), pp. 18 f.

children.[1] It is not likely that Helena's excessive grief at the death of her beloved grandson should alone have driven the emperor to impose such a sanguinary sentence. In touching on this family tragedy we must mention a solitary piece of evidence, because it singles out Fausta from among the Christian women of the court. Speaking of the time before the campaign against Maxentius, Zonaras (*Ep*. XIII. i. 5 Bonn.) reports that Fausta had urged her husband to take part in pagan worship. It is hard to believe that Fausta had played this part when she was no more than a child; but there is no evidence to disprove the incident, which might have happened later. The religious gulf, if it existed, does not account for Crispus' and Fausta's guilt; but it might help to explain why Constantine, after the pronouncement of such terrible sentences, devoted himself with increased fervour to works of Christian piety. The great double church at Treves, the ground plan of which was discovered not long ago, was probably built at that time. It arose on the remains of a former palace of Helena's; and the richly framed portraits of her and Fausta adorning the ceiling of the central hall[2] may have been a sight which seemed no longer bearable. Finally, the much discussed passage in Zosimus (II. xxix. 2) to the effect that Constantine had not found his way to Christianity until he was in dire need of expiation may reflect the impression which the emperor's obvious and extended endeavours in the cause of the Church made at that time. The pagans must have looked upon his pious works as the offerings of a man seeking to make amends. The emperor himself may have felt secure in the knowledge of having obeyed the commands of the law; more, he may have felt himself the prisoner of his own laws against adultery promulgated only a little while before.[3] And many who had regarded the rise of the Christian dynasty with distaste, when they saw the judgement of wrath falling upon

---

[1] J. Maurice, *Numismatique constantinienne*, i (1908), 126 ff. and pl. xi. 10, 11; cf. also the representation of Fausta on the multipla from Trier in M. R. Alföldi, 'Die constantinische Goldprägung in Trier', *Jahrbuch für Numismatik und Geldgeschichte*, ix (1958), 112 ff. and pls. viii. 8, ix. 10, 11.

[2] Th. K. Kempf, 'Die Ausgrabungen am Trierer Dom', *Spätantike und Byzanz*, Neue Beiträge zur Kunstgeschichte des ersten Jahrtausends, i (1952), 103 ff.; id., 'Trierer Domgrabungen 1943–1954', *Neue Ausgrabungen in Deutschland* (Berlin, 1958), pp. 368 ff.; A. Alföldi, 'Zur Erklärung der konstantinischen Deckengemälde in Trier', *Historia*, iv (1955), 131 ff.; new interpretation by M. R. Alföldi, 'Helena nobilissima femina', *Jahrb. f. Numismatik und Geldgesch.* x (1959–60), 79 ff.

[3] H. Dörries, *Das Selbstzeugnis Kaiser Konstantins*, pp. 189 ff.; A. Piganiol, *L'Empereur Constantin*, pp. 169 f.; *L'Empire chrétien*, pp. 34 f. On the subject of Christian influences upon this legislation recently H. Wolff, 'Doctrinal Trends in Postclassical Roman Marriage Laws', *Zeitschr. d. Savignystift.*, Rom. Abt. lxvii (1950), 261 ff.

near relatives, must have remembered the stern words of the Constantinian code in which the parricide was denied honest punishment and burial with pagan severity:

If any person should hasten the fate of a parent or a son or any person at all of such degree of kinship that killing him is included under the title of parricide, whether he has accomplished this secretly or openly, he shall not be subjected to the sword or to fire or to any other customary penalty, but he shall be sewed in a leather sack and, confined within its deadly closeness, he shall share the companionship of serpents. As the nature of the region shall determine, he shall be thrown into the neighbouring sea or into a river, so that while still alive he may begin to lose the enjoyment of all the elements, that the heavens may be taken away from him while he is living and the earth, when he is dead (*Cod. Theod.* ix. xv. 1,[1] translated by C. Pharr).

The blow which had hit Constantine in his own house did not harden him. He continued to tolerate the pagan religion,[2] even though Christian forms prevailed among the representatives of court and government. The official works of art and the coins of the period celebrate the union of the dynasty with the new faith. There is a lead medallion in Nantes in which the portraits of the principal members of the family appear in a curious combination. It shows the busts of Constantine and Helena turned towards each other; in the centre, below them, is the young Constantine, accompanied on the right by his brother Constantius and on the left by the emperor's sister Constantia. In other words, it represents Augustus and Augusta with the two Caesars and the *nobilissima femina* who belonged to the reigning members of the family. In the upper field there appears the Constantinian monogram, here a symbol of the religious foundation of the dynasty.[3]

Helena held the leading position which she occupies here for only a few more years. After her death Constantine restored the members of the lateral branch of the Flavian house to the position withheld from them for so long, and they were included in the plans for the imperial future. His half-brother Julius Constantius was called to the court, where he married Basilina, the future mother of the emperor Julian. She was a Christian, and when she

---

[1] A. A. T. Ehrhardt, 'Some aspects of Constantinian Legislation', *Studia Patristica*, ii (Texte und Untersuchungen zur Geschichte der altchristlichen Literatur, lxiv, 1957), 119 f., traces this law back to a pagan opposition among Constantine's officials.

[2] Cf. the excellent account by H. Dörries, *Constantine and Religious Liberty* (The Terry Lectures, New Haven, Conn., 1960).

[3] J. Lafaurie, loc. cit., pp. 227 ff. and pl. ix f.

died she bequeathed her large estates to the Church.[1] Julius Constantius' daughter by his first marriage became the wife of the emperor's son Constantius, proclaimed Caesar in 324. The emperor's second surviving half-brother, Dalmatius, was made consul in 333 and received the title of censor before he was put in charge of the important investigation of the case against Athanasius.[2] His son Dalmatius was proclaimed Caesar in 335 and was given the greater part of the Balkan peninsula; his second son Hannibalianus was made King of Armenia and married the emperor's daughter Constantina. Thus the two branches of the family of Constantius Chlorus were to be re-united by their descendants. Finally, the emperor affianced his youngest son Constans, Caesar from 333, with Olympias, the daughter of a man, Ablabius, who enjoyed the emperor's highest favour and as *Praefectus praetorio* directed the imperial policy, now openly Christian. The Christian dynasty seemed to rest on such firm grounds that Eusebius' speech on the occasion of the thirtieth anniversary of Constantine's reign could celebrate him as the ruler who guided the quadriga of Caesars over the whole earth (*Triak.* iii. 4).

Was it, then, really true that the preservation of the clan had been visible proof of God's grace? When Constantine had gone to rest in the tomb which he had prepared for himself amid the stelae of the Twelve in the Church of the Apostles in his new capital,[3] there was only a short moment of time in which this belief could be held. A few months after his funeral the soldiers in Constantinople revolted in protest against the co-regency of the emperor's nephews. They killed his brothers and six nephews, and many personages of the former court, without being held back by Constantius. But this was only the opening of the epilogue. Constantine, the eldest of the sons who now shared the reign, perished soon afterwards in a raid on the territory of his brother Constans. Ten years later Constans himself fell a victim to the messengers of the pagan usurper Magnentius. The only one left was Constantius, who had no children; and it was he who experienced the full force of pagan protest against the Christian dynasty and the religious ground on which it had been

---

[1] H. von Schoenebeck, loc. cit., pp. 76 f.
[2] W. Ensslin, 'Dalmatius Censor', *Rhein. Mus.* lxxviii (1929), 205 ff.
[3] J. Vogt, 'Der Erbauer der Apostelkirche in Constantinopel', *Hermes*, lxxxi (1953), 111 ff. For religious questions involved here cf. *Reallexikon für Antike und Christentum*, iii (1956), 370 f.

built. His cousin Julian, spared from the blood-bath of Constantinople and shaken by the horrors through which he had lived, turned from Christianity back to the old gods. He tells us that he saw the root of all the ills in the connexion of emperor and empire with the revolutionary new religion.[1] He still made some allowance for the founder of the dynasty in his speeches on the emperor Constantius; but after having been proclaimed Augustus he accused his cousin, the younger Constantius, of being the murderer of his family, and the great Constantine of having wrought the destruction of law and custom by his revolutionary actions. He was the last survivor and became sole ruler of the empire after Constantius' death. In the autobiographical myth which he inserted in his pamphlet against the cynic philosopher Heraclius, he drew a picture of Constantine as a greedy, blinkered despot who had done nothing for the education of his sons, deeming 'their number to be sufficient'. In this way, he says, Constantine had been responsible for the disorders which had broken out after his death and which had led to the razing of venerable sanctuaries. In all this distress he, Julian, had received an order from Helios to punish the godless and purify the ancestral house. His satire *Caesares* is even more violent in its indictment of Constantine. He works up the tyrant's baseness and degeneration to their climax in the crime of parricide, and makes the culprit take refuge with Jesus, the demon of murderers, seducers, and accursed men. Godlessness is denounced as the origin of all vices, and the annihilation of the race is made to appear the inevitable result of the desertion of the gods. This is the complete reversal of all the ideas which, as I have tried to show, governed the family policy of the dynasty's founder.

We are at the end of our discussion of some important aspects of the history of Constantine's house. We have had no Tacitus to guide us; but from the fragmentary evidence at our disposal there arises the picture of a powerful family head who seems to hark back to the first Augustus in his fateful grandeur. Constantine sought to impart the message of his own faith to the citizens of his realm[2] and, as his letter to King Sapor of Persia shows, even beyond its frontiers. He began with his own family, inspired by

---

[1] For the following cf. my article 'Kaiser Julian über seinen Oheim Constantin den Grossen', *Historia*, iv (1955), 339 ff.

[2] For the inner reasons for Constantine's striving to christianize the pagans, see A. A. T. Ehrhardt, *Politische Metaphysik von Solon bis Augustin*, ii (Tübingen, 1959), 271 ff.

the hope of ensuring the dominion of his house and the stability of his empire with the help of his God. This union of dynastic aspirations with religious convictions left its imprint on the population and produced at all levels that sense of pious expectation which is expressed in Optatianus' poem:

> summe, fave! te tota rogat plebs gaudia rite,
> et meritam credit, cum servat iussa timore
> Augusto et fidei, Christi sub lege probata (viii 3–5).

As the creator of this dynastic faith Constantine has become the prototype of numerous Christian rulers. We choose from a long line only one who resembles him in power and drama: when Charles V wrote his last political testament in 1548 he urged his son to attract the help of God by defending His holy faith and advised him that 'it is always best to secure realms by means of one's own children'.[1]

The establishment of the *domus divina* on religious foundations had proved powerless to control the passions. We have heard of the tension between Helena and the lateral branch of the family; of the catastrophe of Fausta and Crispus; of the excessive zeal of the army; and of the sons' fratricide. The story ends with the outcry of Julian, who hurled the reproach of *theomachos* in the teeth of his dynasty's founder: the death of the race was the penalty for deserting the gods. These were the last words of dying paganism, spoken with the voice of a pious heathen. Certainly, his arguments are as faulty as those of his adversaries, and his judgement of his uncle is unjust. It is a natural impulse, νόμος φύσεως, to found power on heritage, as even Eusebius admits in one of his clearer moments (*Vit. Const.* I. xxi. 2), but it has nothing to do with the law of the Christian. The attempt to obtain divine help by force and receive it as a tangible counter was a remnant of pagan beliefs, a symptom of religious restlessness in a Christian era.

However, we must not forget that not all Christians thought so; and to give Constantine his due we must remember that we have passed in review no more than a small section of his political and religious achievements. Those scholars who have recently studied his theology have arrived at the conclusion that he had gained a certain understanding of suffering and endurance which are of the nature of martyrdom. They point to the letter which

---

[1] K. Brandi, *Kaiser Karl V*, i (3rd ed., 1941), 500 ff.

Constantine addressed to the African bishops and communities after the collapse of his intervention with the Donatists,[1] in which he writes: nihil ex reciproco reponatur iniuriae; vindictam enim, quam deo servare debemus, insipientis est manibus usurpare, maxime cum debet fides nostra confidere, quicquid ab huiusmodi hominum furore patietur, martyrii gratia apud deum esse valiturum. quid est enim aliud in hoc saeculo in nomine dei vincere quam inconditos hominum impetus quietae legis populum lacessentes constanti pectore sustinere? It is not our intention to raise fresh questions here. We shall never discover if Constantine learned from his experiences of family policy what it means to conquer in the name of God. But we have reason to believe that he may have had a presentiment of the tragedy which is the peculiar fate of all rulers who attempt to make the world a Christian place.

[1] Optatus, *App.* Nr. 9 (= H. von Soden, loc. cit., No. 31); cf. H. Dörries, loc. cit., pp. 38 f.; H. Kraft, loc. cit., pp. 60, 196 f.

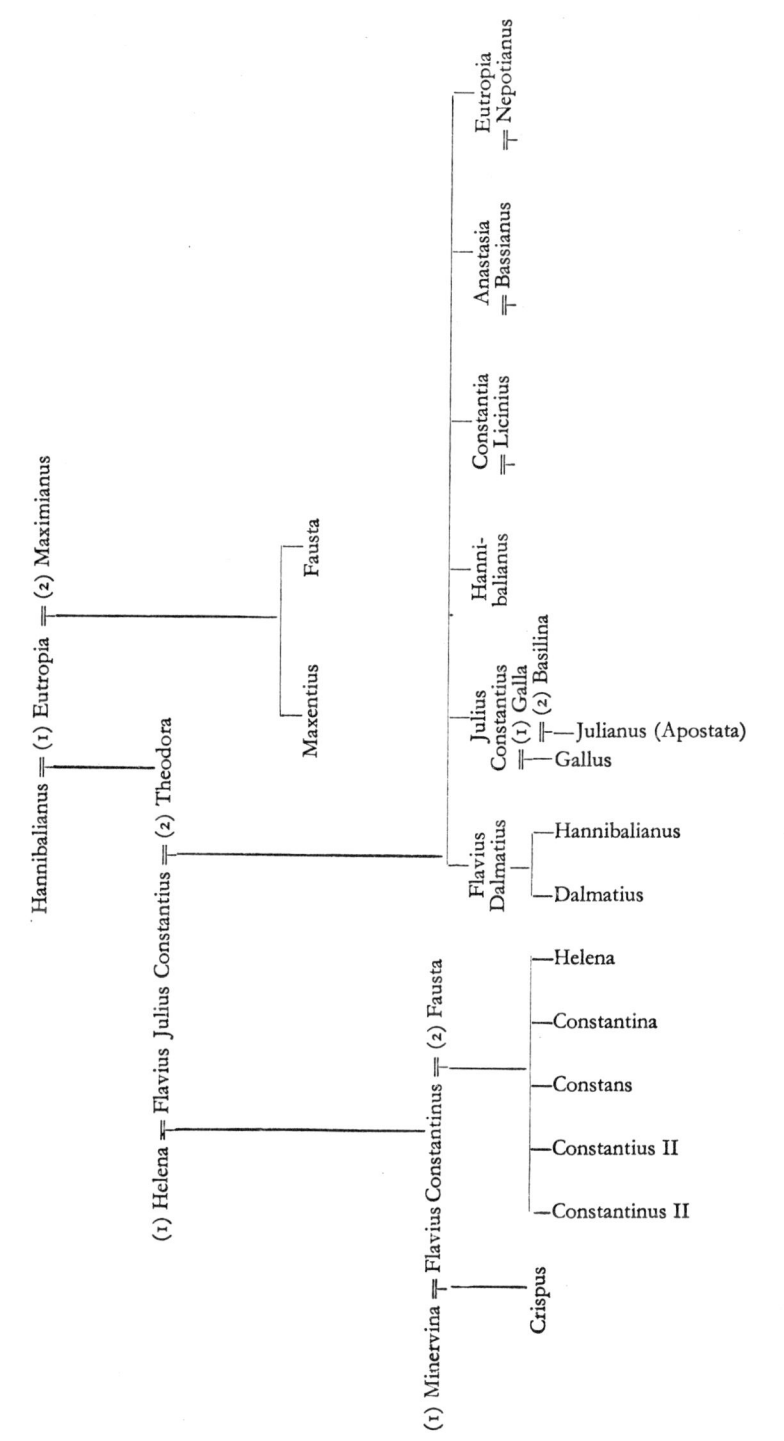

CONSTANTINE'S FAMILY TREE

Hannibalianus = (1) Eutropia = (2) Maximianus

(1) Helena = Flavius Julius Constantius = (2) Theodora

├─ Flavius Dalmatius
│ ├─ Hannibalianus
│ └─ Dalmatius
├─ Julius Constantius = (1) Galla / = (2) Basilina
│ ├─ Julianus (Apostata)
│ └─ Gallus
├─ Hannibalianus
├─ Constantia = Licinius
├─ Anastasia = Bassianus
└─ Eutropia = Nepotianus

Maxentius — Fausta

(1) Minervina = Flavius Constantinus = (2) Fausta

Crispus

- Helena
- Constantina
- Constans
- Constantius II
- Constantinus II

III

Christianity and the Northern Barbarians*

E. A. THOMPSON

AT the second ecumenical Council, held at Constantinople in 381, the assembled Fathers discussed certain aspects of the administration of the Church. Among the decisions taken by them was one to the effect that the churches of God among the barbarian peoples must be governed according to the established custom.[1] What churches existed among the northern barbarians at that date? How and to what extent was Christianity diffused among the Germanic peoples in the fourth and fifth centuries? And when those peoples crossed the imperial frontiers what steps were taken by the Church to convert them to Christianity in cases where they were still pagan?[2]

I

Barbarian warriors who had enlisted in the imperial armies might come to know and accept the religion to which many of their Roman fellow soldiers subscribed. We have the explicit testimony of a fifth-century author that this sometimes happened, and his word cannot be doubted.[3] But it is not easy to believe, and

---

* This essay was originally published in *Nottingham Medieval Studies*, I, 1957.

[1] Hefele, *Hist. des conciles*, II. i (Paris, 1908), 22.

[2] We are not concerned here with the steppe nomads, for whom see G. László, 'Die Reiternomaden der Völkerwanderungszeit und das Christentum in Ungarn', *Zeitschr. f. Kirchengeschichte*, lix (1940), 125–46; E. A. Thompson, *Attila and the Huns*, Oxford, 1948, pp. 37–39, and note some interesting pages of pseudo-Zachariah of Mytilene, transl. F. J. Hamilton and E. W. Brooks, London, 1899, 329–31. Nor shall we dwell on the archaeological evidence for Christianity beyond the northern frontier. Most of it comes from Romania and seems to be derived from the Romano-Dacians who continued to live there under the Visigoths: see references in *Journal of Ecclesiastical History*, vii (1956), 1 f. Note also W. Kubitschek, *Römerfunde von Eisenstadt* (Vienna, 1926), p. 56.

[3] Pseudo-Prosper, quoted below, p. 57, n. 3. It would be interesting to know to what extent, if any, returning German mercenaries brought back Mithraism with them to their homes. No evidence has been found: C. Clemen, 'Mithrasmysterien und germanische Religion', *Archiv f. Religionswissenschaft*, xxxiv (1937), 217–26. But, of course, when so many Germans served in the Roman army, the *argumentum ex silentio* is dangerous. No safe conclusions can be drawn from the fact that the ashes of a Visigoth were buried *c*. 300 at Lechinta de Mureș in Transylvania in a snake-handled urn of a type which is alleged to have been often associated with Mithraic ritual: see E. Beninger, 'Ein westgotisches Brandgrab von Maros-Lekencze (Siebenbürgen)', *Mannus*, xxx (1938), 122–41, esp. 129–35. The urn may have been

Christianity and the Northern Barbarians

our authority does not claim, that many such warriors on their return to their people were able to induce any considerable section of their tribe to abandon their traditional cult and to begin to worship the God of the Romans. Much would depend, of course, on the character and status of the returned warrior himself. If he had been a respected tribesman or even a chief before his departure, his influence might be far from small after his return. Even a lesser figure might enjoy a temporary prestige when he came back with his Roman ways and his knowledge of the world and his pocket full of Roman money. On the other hand, it is easy to see that he might well run the risk of becoming something like an outcast if when he returned home he refused to take part any longer in the clan feasts and the ceremonies of his kindred. The Visigoth St. Sabas was expelled outright from his village and was eventually abandoned to his fate because of his persistent refusal to worship with his fellow villagers.[1] And even if the punishment were not so severe, even if there were no formal punishment at all, the mockery and abuse of his neighbours might well daunt the new convert, compel him to hold his opinions in silence, and outwardly to conform to the old ways.[2] In such circumstances the converts whom he might win to his faith would probably be few, and it has never been claimed that any of the great Germanic peoples was converted by returned mercenaries: their activities will only account for the presence of individual Christians beyond the frontier.

Secondly, that same fifth-century author who mentions the conversion of barbarian soldiers serving in the Roman armies says also that sons of the Church, when carried off captive by the barbarians, would sometimes enslave their masters to the gospel of Christ and win them to the faith.[3] Here again his word cannot

---

taken as booty from the provinces by the Visigoth whose remains it finally contained. But C. Daicoviciu, *La Transylvanie dans l'antiquité* (Bucharest, 1945), p. 224, n. 2, argues that the urn is in a traditional Geto-Dacian style. For a Mithraeum at Kreta, 12 miles south of the Danube on the right bank of the Utus (Vid), which seems to have been destroyed by the Goths towards the end of the third century, see I. Welkov, *Bulletin de l'Institut archéologique bulgare*, viii (1934), 90 f.

[1] *Passio S. Sabae*, ed. H. Delehaye, *Analecta Bollandiana*, xxxi (1912), 216–21.

[2] The Christian Roman prisoners in Gothia also had to put up with some mockery at what were considered the oddities of their religion: Sozomen, II. vi. 3. Cf. St. Patrick, *Conf.* xlii. Here is what an Irishman is reported to have said to Patrick: 'tu filio meo babtismum da, quia tener est. ego autem et fratres mei non possimus tibi credere usque dum ad nostram plebem pervenerimus, ne inrideant nobis', Tírachán, *Brev.* xiv = p. 309. 13, Rolls ed. The response of a German tribesman would perhaps not have been very different.

[3] Pseudo-Prosper, *de Invoc. omnium Gentium* ii. 33 (Migne, *P.L.* li. 717 f.): 'quidam ecclesiae filii ab hostibus capti dominos suos Christi Euangelio manciparunt, et quibus

be doubted; and the importance of these prisoners in converting their captors was far greater than that of returned soldiers. There is a famous story that the Georgian people were converted in Constantine's reign by the efforts of a single captive woman; and the story is usually regarded as being substantially true.[1] But even if it is not true, its mere existence illustrates the part which Christian prisoners were thought to play in spreading their religion beyond the frontiers. And there can be no denying that the very basis of the Christian communities in Gothia before the days of Ulfila and throughout much, if not all, of his lifetime was formed by the Christians, both clergy and lay, who had been taken in the great third-century Gothic raids on the Roman provinces, and by their descendants, of whom Ulfila himself was one. They earned the respect of the Visigoths, we are told, by using their medical skill (which would be far higher than anything known beyond the Danube), by curing the possessed, by the steadfastness of their faith, and by the blamelessness of their lives.[2] Their influence on Visigothic history was not negligible. They undoubtedly made a number of converts, at any rate in the poorer strata of Visigothic society; and although the Visigoths were still an essentially pagan people when they entered the Roman empire in 376, the course of the conversion might well have been altered had it not been for these men and women. It does not follow, of course, that an appreciable number of converts was won in every place where Christian prisoners were to be found. Thus, Arnobius tells us that there were Christians—and he may well include Christian prisoners from Gaul—among the Alamanni at the beginning of the fourth century. Yet few would believe that Christianity made any significant impression on the Alamanni for many a generation after that date.[3]

condicione bellica serviebant, eisdem fidei magisterio praefuerunt. at alii barbari dum Romanis auxiliantur, quod in suis locis nosse non poterant, in nostris didicere regionibus, et ad sedes suas cum Christianae religionis institutione remearunt.' See also Sozomen, II. vi. 2, who seems to have considered the conversion of barbarians by their Christian prisoners, and especially by the clergy among the prisoners, to have been a common occurrence.

[1] Rufinus, H.E. i. 10. The general truth of the story is accepted by P. Peeters, 'Les débuts du Christianisme en Géorgie d'après les sources hagiographiques', *Analecta Bollandiana*, l (1932), 5–58; C. Toumanoff, 'Christian Caucasia between Byzantium and Iran', *Traditio*, x (1954), 109–89, at p. 126, &c. Cf. the legendary Phemion among the Arabs of the Nejd: T. Nöldeke, *Tabari* (Leyden, 1879), pp. 178–82, and the Christian prisoners of the Bulgars, Theophanis Contin. v. 4 (pp. 216 f., ed. Bonn), Theophylact, *Hist. Mart.* xxix ff. (Migne, *P.G.* cxxvi. 192 ff.). For a Moorish parallel see Victor Vitensis, *Hist. Persec.* i. 35 f.

[2] Sozomen, loc. cit. On the value of a medical training to a prisoner of the barbarians see *Anthol. Lat.* ii, No. 1414; and for the value of a high Christian morality see Jerome, *Vita Malchi* vi (Migne, *P.L.* xxiii. 58). [3] Arnobius, *Adv. Gent.* i. 16, cf. Sozomen, II. vi. 1.

A third means by which Christianity is sometimes thought to have crossed the Roman frontier into the northern barbarian world is less explicitly discussed by our ancient authorities. It is sometimes contended that Christianity travelled with commerce. Now the strong influence of commerce on some of the post-Roman, medieval missions, especially those of the Church of Hamburg, can be seen very clearly. Then a missionary would travel along the trade routes in the company of merchants; and he might base his work on the trading settlements of the north, like Birca (Björkö) or Sliaswich (Hedeby, near Schleswig), for here he could find, especially at the great pagan religious festivals, not only a considerable number of Christian prisoners held as slaves but also throngs of Christian merchants who had come to these distant waters to trade the rich goods of the south for the fish, furs, honey, wax, and slaves of the north. He could also find a number of native merchants who had imbibed Christianity on their long voyages abroad. The missionary's first step would be to win the favour of the local chieftain and his leading men by means of lavish bribery,[1] obtain permission to preach openly, and secure a guarantee that there would be no penalization of any convert whom he might win. Finally, he would take all possible steps to establish a church building with a preacher permanently on the spot so that the pagans might be exposed to continuous Christian influence. The whole process might well be backed by the interest, authority, and money not only of the Church in the German empire but also of the emperor himself, who might regard the mission as a sound political investment. In the Scandinavian world, for example, the missions had to be based on the merchants and the trading posts, or they could not be undertaken at all.[2]

But is it possible to project these or similar conditions back into Roman times, and to suppose that commerce and trading communities played some considerable part in extending Christianity beyond the northern frontier? It is said that shortly before

---

[1] I cannot refrain from quoting Herbord, *Dial.* II. vii. 12 (*M.G.H. Scriptores*, xx), where he describes how Otto of Bamberg gave an ivory staff to the local Pomeranian chief: 'donariis ducem honorans, baculum quoque dedit eburneum, quo ille statim usus ipsoque incumbens gratulabundus huc illucque deambulabat, conversusque ad milites, "qualem", ait, "patrem nobis dedit Deus et qualia patris dona, et haec nunc quidem magis quam alio tempore gratiora".'

[2] All these points will be found abundantly illustrated in St. Rimbertus, *Vita S. Anskarii*, and in the anonymous *Vita* of Rimbert himself (both edited by G. Waitz, *S.S. rer. Germ.*, 1884).

St. Ambrose's death in 397 a Christian who had travelled from Italy into the country of the Marcomanni north of the middle Danube spoke about Ambrose to the local queen Fritigil. He spoke to such effect that the queen believed in Christ and sent to Ambrose for written instruction in the Christian faith. Ambrose, who had done nothing, so far as we know, to introduce the Marcomanni to Christianity, seized this opportunity and wrote 'an excellent letter in the manner of a catechism' to the queen. Now the anonymous traveller who won the queen's confidence is thought to have been a merchant; and this may well have been the case.[1] A more instructive figure in this connexion (though he was not concerned with the northern frontier) is Frumentius, whose life fell in the first half of the fourth century and whose story is so familiar that there is no need to summarize it here.[2] After he was established in power at Axum in Ethiopia he began to seek out any Roman merchants in the town who happened to be Christian. He gave them exceptional privileges, and urged them to provide themselves with meeting houses at which they could gather together for prayer in the Roman fashion. Eventually he went to Alexandria where he was consecrated as Bishop of Axum by St. Athanasius. Up to this point in his career his efforts had been directed solely towards the Roman merchants in Axum,[3] and hence his activity hitherto is no parallel to that of Ansgar (801–65) and Rimbert in Scandinavia. But having been appointed bishop he then proceeded to work for the conversion of the native inhabitants of the town. He did not become a missionary among the barbarians until he had consolidated his position among the Roman traders of the port and until he had won official recognition for his work. The Christian Roman traders themselves do not appear to have been doing anything to win over the barbarians, or their pagan fellow Romans, to Christianity before Frumentius' rise to power. Indeed, if Frumentius had not obtained his high office and if the Christian merchants had been left in their former state of indifference towards the natives of the place and their own pagan Roman companions, it is not easy to see how Christianity could have registered any appreciable success in Axum in the mid-fourth

---

[1] Paulinus, *Vita S. Ambrosii*, xxxvi, cf. J. Zeiller, *Les Origines chrétiennes dans les provinces danubiennes* (Paris, 1918), p. 544. But there is no Roman parallel to Adam of Bremen, IV. 16 'una ibi [sc. in Curland] nunc facta est ecclesia, cuiusdam studio negotiatoris', &c.

[2] Rufinus, *H.E.* i. 9.

[3] Socrates, I. xix. 10, and Sozomen, II. xxiv. 8, go astray on this point.

century. Moreover, throughout Rufinus' account of Frumentius' career there is no indication that the Bishop of Alexandria was carefully watching events in Axum or that he took any initiative in fostering the work of Frumentius. He acted when Christian communities were already flourishing in the city, and then only when Frumentius drew his attention to the position. His attitude towards the Axumites was very different from that of Gregory the Great towards the English or of St. Ansgar towards the Danes and the Swedes. Finally, there is still less any indication that the emperor far away in Constantinople took any heed of the work of Frumentius until Athanasius had consecrated him. And even then the emperor only interfered, so it would seem, in order to counteract his sectarian opponents: he did not wish to allow heretics (as the Catholics were, in his eyes) to gain the upper hand among the Roman traders or the native inhabitants at the mouth of the Red Sea.[1] His attitude was very different from that of Louis the Pious and other medieval rulers towards the evangelistic activities of the Church of Hamburg and other centres. In fact, it could scarcely be claimed that Axum is in any significant way a parallel to Birca and Sliaswich. The energy and capacity of one prisoner acting on his own initiative used the presence in the city of Christian Roman merchants so as to establish a church *among* but not in the first instance *for* the barbarians. There is no true parallel here to the great systematic, organized missionary enterprises of the Church of Hamburg.

Now Axum was a thriving port of great importance on the trade routes to Africa and India. Can it be thought that anything like such conditions as existed even at Axum (to say nothing of Birca) could be found among the Germanic barbarians beyond the Rhine and the Danube? Only one community of Roman merchants permanently resident among the northern barbarians is reported by ancient writers. That is the community of which Tacitus speaks as existing in the capital of Maroboduus' kingdom in the early days of the Roman empire;[2] and that this was in many ways unique throughout the whole history of the Germans' relations with the empire is strongly suggested by the archaeological evidence. We know of no great pagan festivals among the Germans of the Roman period at which throngs of Christian

---

[1] Cf. Philostorgius, iii. 4 (pp. 32 f., ed. Bidez), 6 (p. 35), and Constantius' letter quoted by Athanasius, *Apol. ad Const.* xxxi (Migne, *P.G.* xxv. 636 f.).
[2] Tacitus, *Ann.* II. lxii. 4.

Roman merchants would be present. Nor is there any reason to suppose that substantial numbers of Germanic merchants had been to the empire and had been converted there. And, finally, it is highly unlikely that any Roman Christian ever managed to secure a position among a Germanic people comparable to that which Frumentius won at Axum. In a word, all the prerequisites for the achievements of Axum and Birca (such as they were) were lacking beyond the northern frontier. If we wish to speculate we may suppose no more than that small communities of Roman traders, with some Christians among them, living in less favourable conditions than those of Maroboduus' kingdom, may have existed somewhere in Gothia in the days of Athanaric, or somewhere in the Ukraine in the time of Ermanaric, or among the fourth-century Vandals or Gepids. But for such a supposition there is no evidence; and even if such communities existed, it would scarcely be claimed that they resulted in the conversion of whole peoples, or even substantial sections of peoples, to the Christian faith.

Christianity, then, filtered across the northern imperial frontier by way of some of the prisoners taken in the barbarian raids on the Roman provinces and by way of Germanic soldiers who returned home after completing their service with the Roman armies; and to a slight extent it may have reached the barbarians of the north in the wake of the Roman traders who hawked their wares beyond the Rhine and the Danube. But the efforts of prisoners, mercenaries, and traders were haphazard and unorganized, and in themselves they won no major victories for the Church. It is salutary to remember that all three of these influences were brought to bear upon the early ninth-century Swedes. Christian war-prisoners, Christian merchants from Frisia, and Christian Swedes who had been converted abroad when serving as traders or as mercenaries could all alike be found in substantial numbers in southern Sweden; and yet their combined influence, together with the strenuous and sustained efforts of Ansgar and Rimbert, made little impression on the paganism of the country.

Evidence has been found in the Gothic language for the existence of Latin- as well as Greek-speaking 'missionaries' in Gothia before the days of Ulfila.[1] But there is no reason to

---

[1] W. Schulze, *Kleine Schriften* (Göttingen, 1934), p. 513; M. H. Jellinek, *Gesch. d. gotischen Sprache* (Berlin and Leipzig, 1926), pp. 188 ff.

suppose that these missionaries were sent out by the Church with the explicit aim of converting the Visigoths: they may well have been war-prisoners—Christians, both clergy and lay, are known to have been carried off by the Goths in the third century.[1] In fact, the Catholic Church is not reported to have sent any bishops or lesser clergy to minister to the Catholic prisoners in Gothia during the later third century or the first decades of the fourth; and the Arians consecrated Ulfila as bishop only in 341. That is to say, for two generations after the prisoners had been carried off from their homes in Asia Minor and elsewhere they were neglected, so far as we know, by the Churches. Moreover, although Ulfila is known to us as 'the Apostle of the Goths', he was originally appointed by Eusebius of Nicomedia not to act as bishop of the Goths in general but to serve as bishop of those Christians who were already living in Gothia in 341 and who were, we may suppose, for the most part not Visigoths at all but Roman prisoners or their descendants.[2] In other words, Ulfila was not appointed in the first place in order to evangelize the Visigoths and to win a pagan people to Christianity but simply to minister to those Romans and others in Gothia who were already converted:[3] Eusebius did not necessarily envisage a Gothic Bible when he consecrated Ulfila. The Gothic bishop's position was similar to that of Palladius when Pope Celestine sent him in 431 as bishop to the Scots in Ireland who believed in Christ.[4] Those whom our authority calls 'Scots' undoubtedly included many Roman Christians who had been carried off in Irish raids on Britain—towards the end of the fourth century, for example, 'thousands' of persons, including the young Patrick, were carried off from Britain in a single raid;[5] and no doubt many of these were Christian. It would, of course, be an error to think that the majority of the Christians in Ireland at that time were Romans;[6] and in this there is a difference from the position in Gothia ninety years earlier. But two points of similarity should be noted. First, such of the Christians in Ireland as were in fact

---

[1] Philostorgius, ii. 5 (p. 17. 11, ed. Bidez).
[2] *Journal of Ecclesiastical History*, vii (1956), 1–11.
[3] Philostorgius, ii. 5 (p. 18. 1 f.). His words are not contradicted by Auxentius, p. 75, 6 f. (ed. Kauffmann); 'propter multorum salutem in gente Gothorum ... episcopus est ordinatus', who in that passage is summarizing the results of Ulfila's mission rather than giving us Eusebius' motives for appointing him in the first instance.
[4] Prosper, *Chron. Min.* i. 473: 'ad Scottos in Christum credentes ordinatus a papa Caelestino Palladius primus episcopus mittitur.'
[5] Patrick, *Conf.* i.   [6] Prosper, loc. cit.

Roman provincials languished in captivity for many a year (as the experience of Patrick shows) before Palladius was sent to comfort them; and the fate of the Christian Roman prisoners in Gothia was similar. Secondly, just as there is no indication that Celestine intended Palladius to set about converting the pagan Scots, so there is no indication that Eusebius intended Ulfila to convert the pagan Visigoths. True, Ulfila and Palladius' successor, Patrick, when once they had been consecrated, worked to convert the barbarians. But this was not the purpose for which they had been consecrated in the first place, and neither of them is known to have received any help or encouragement in his evangelistic work from the clergy or the secular rulers of the empire.[1]

In a word, the Churches of the fourth and fifth centuries delayed for a curiously long time to send bishops to their captive sons and daughters beyond the frontier; and they made little or no organized or planned effort to save the barbarians from the fire everlasting. With the minor exception of the exiled Audius (who was neither a Catholic nor an Arian, but the founder of a sect of his own), we do not know of a single bishop of a Roman frontier town who went into German territory with a view to converting the natives. If a Christian community were found to exist beyond the frontier, as, for example, in Ireland, Gothia, and Ethiopia, the Church would consecrate a bishop to minister to it (though presumably it would do so only if requested by the community in question);[2] but it made no effort to bring such communities into existence. The reasons for this attitude on the part of the Church need not detain us, and the sharp contrast with the practice of Carolingian times has more than once been pointed out.[3]

II

What then of the barbarians who had crossed the frontier and were moving through the Roman provinces? The evangelistic work of Niceta, the eminent bishop of Remesiana in the province

---

[1] Contrast the policy of the Church of Hamburg in the early ninth century, which sent out presbyters *both* to preach to the gentiles *and* to console the Christian prisoners: *Vita S. Rimberti* xvi (p. 94, ed. Waitz).

[2] Pope Celestine, *Ep.* iv. 5 (Migne, *P.L.* l. 434).

[3] K. Holl, *Gesammelte Aufsätze zur Kirchengeschichte*, iii (Tübingen, 1928), 117–29, cf. R. E. Sullivan, 'The Carolingian Missionary and the Pagan', *Speculum*, xxviii (1953), 705–40, at 709–11.

of Dacia Mediterranea, some 24 miles south-east of Naissus (Nish), a man who is sometimes thought to have been the author of the *Te Deum*, was applauded by his friend Paulinus of Nola at the turn of the fourth and fifth centuries. Two points are noteworthy in Paulinus' words. First, as one of the most important results of Niceta's success among the barbarians he sees the fact that the Goths will now live at peace with the Romans of the neighbourhood in which they had settled.[1] For him the conversion of certain Goths has a political side: it will mitigate some of the horror of the invasions. This was a point which the fourth- and fifth-century emperors seem to have missed: none of them is known to have conceived the idea that to convert a barbarian people to Christianity might well be to win an ally or at any rate to modify the hostility of an enemy. Secondly, Paulinus expresses no less satisfaction at the work of Niceta among the Bessian brigands of the neighbourhood. We do not always realize the extent to which the poorer classes among the Roman provincials co-operated with the barbarian invaders, or at any rate used the occasion of a barbarian invasion to revolt against the established order. And yet this co-operation and this tendency to rebel are not the least remarkable facts in late Roman history. Hence, Niceta seems to have devoted no less time and energy to the Bessi than he gave to the Goths: they were no less a threat to law and order than were the barbarians themselves, and the upshot of Niceta's mission, according to Paulinus, was that the Bessian brigands became monks![2] There may be some exaggeration here, but it would seem that the missionary had restored law and order among the native population as well as, and perhaps better than, any contemporary general could have done. What Niceta in fact achieved was to turn Gothic invader and Bessian brigand alike to Christianity and incidentally to some sort of acquiescence in the harsh and oppressive rule of the emperors.[3]

---

[1] Paulinus, *carm.* xvii. 245 ff., 261 ff. Cf. Jerome, *Ep.* lx. 4.

[2] Paulinus, *carm.* xvii. 213 ff.

[3] By coincidence a papyrus shows us two Bessians named Boraides and Zemarchus working side by side in 561 with two Germans (as it seems) named Illerich and Tangilas (Ilderic and Tancila); they are all four of them *buccellarii* in Egypt, P.Oxy. xvi. 1903 (cf. 2046), with the edd. ad loc. Cf. F. Zucker, 'Germanen im römischen und byzantinischen Ägypten', *Geistige Arbeit*, vi, No. 13 (1939), 3–6, at 4; H. Kortenbeutel, 'Germanen in Ägypten', *Mitteilungen d. Deutschen Instituts f. ägyptische Altertumskunde in Kairo*, viii (1939), 177–84, at 183. (To their references to Germans in the papyri add H. Zilliacus, *Vierzehn Berliner griechische Papyri* (Helsinki, 1941), pp. 85 f., No. 13 Οὐλιάριχ.)

Paulinus also tells us in a letter which he wrote either in 398 or in 400 of the missionary work carried out in Belgica Secunda by the last continental Roman author known to have visited Britain, Victricius of Rouen. The poet recalls how once the woods and shores of Belgica II were empty and unsafe because of the visits of 'foreign barbarians and native brigands'. But since Victricius began his missionary effort islands and woods are at peace and are thronged with churches and monasteries and the angelic choirs of the saints. It is not clear that he converted any of the Saxon sea-raiders; but it is clear that his aims did not differ from those of Niceta. It was part of his purpose to win over to a peaceful way of life both the barbarians from outside the frontier and the oppressed classes within it. But in the end, his Christian communities appear to have been wiped out in the great invasion of the Vandals, Alans, and Sueves in 406.[1]

We have already mentioned Queen Fritigil of the Marcomanni (p. 60). In his letter to her St. Ambrose not only discussed the faith but also urged her, according to his biographer, 'to persuade her husband to keep peace with the Romans. When the woman received the letter she persuaded her husband to entrust himself and his people to the Romans', i.e. they entered the provinces by agreement with the Roman authorities and settled there as Federates.[2] In fact, so able a statesman as Ambrose did not fail to regard peace with the Roman authorities as not the least of the benefits which would result from the acceptance of the Christian faith by a Germanic people.

Also contemporary with Niceta was a certain Amantius of Aquileia, whom we know only from the inscription on his sarcophagus, which was found in 1771 at Beligna near Aquileia. Amantius left his native city and travelled far off to a people who were led by two chieftains. He laboured among them and among the native Roman population for twenty years (either 378–98 or 393–413) as Bishop of Jovia on the road from Poetovio to Mursa. That it was he who converted the two chieftains from paganism to orthodox Christianity is not explicitly stated but may well be the case.[3] At any rate, the barbarian people thought Amantius

---

[1] Paulinus, *Ep.* xviii. 4, discussed by E. de Moreau, 'St. Victrice de Rouen', *Revue Belge de Philologie et d'Histoire*, v (1926), 71–79, cf. E. Vacandard, *Saint Victrice, évêque de Rouen* (2nd ed., Paris, 1903), pp. 122 ff.; P. Grosjean, 'Notes d'hagiographie celtique', *Analecta Bollandiana*, lxiii (1945), 94–99.

[2] Paulinus, *Vita S. Ambrosii*, xxxvi.

[3] *C.I.L.* v. 1623 = O. Fiebiger, *Inschriftensammlung zur Gesch. d. Ostgermanen: Neue Folge* (Vienna, 1939,) p. 25, No. 34. That the people in question were the Ostrogoths of

worthy to partake of the Holy Sacrament in company with their two chiefs and also 'to guide them with his counsel'.[1] Now if we do not know all the ways in which Amantius used his general ascendancy over the chiefs, we can be fairly sure of one: it is hardly credible that he would have failed to 'guide them' away from any move that might have damaged Roman peace and property. The high influence of Amantius with the two leaders was some guarantee, however frail, that local life and property would be spared the full fury of the invaders.

If we failed to find much evidence for Roman missionary activity beyond the frontier, we can at any rate be sure that, once the barbarians had crossed the frontier, there were not wanting churchmen who were prepared to go among them (apparently on their own initiative) and win them for the Gospel. But these seem to have been purely local efforts, and they do not represent any general policy on the part of the Church. Moreover, it is curious that all our evidence relates to a short period before and after A.D. 400. Whether this is coincidence we do not know: there may have been other local priests who won successes among the barbarians without finding any Paulinus to celebrate their work. But even when we make all allowance for gaps in our information, it can hardly be thought that evangelistic work was general in every region where pagan barbarians settled down. Again, Orosius says that a barbarian people who had become Christian lived in obedience to the Roman clergy whom they admitted to their society, and accordingly they treated the Roman population, in whose midst they had settled, not as subjects but as brother Christians, and refrained from oppressing and plundering them.[2] Orosius undoubtedly felt that the conversion of a barbarian people to Christianity was something of an insurance against damage to person and property. We have seen that some

---

Alatheus and Saphrax is suggested by R. Egger, 'Historisch-epigraphische Studien in Venezien', *Jahreshefte d. Österreichischen Archäologischen Instituts in Wien*, xxi-xxii (1922-4), Beiblatt 309-44, at 332 f., and his opinion is shared by Fiebiger, loc. cit., but seems improbable: see L. Schmidt, *Gesch. d. deutschen Stämme: die Ostgermanen* (Munich, 1934), p. 261. In addition to two chiefs (*geminis ducibus*) two peoples (*binis populis*) are also mentioned; and Egger, art. cit. p. 339, is puzzled as to the identity of the second people. But since they are living deep in the empire we require some reference to the native inhabitants, and I suggest that the Romans of the locality are themselves meant. If that is right, the *plebs aliena* (a phrase which does not suggest two barbarian peoples) had the dual command which is so widespread in the early Germanic communities. On Amantius see also J.-R. Palanque, *St. Ambroise et l'empire romain* (Paris, 1933), p. 82, n. 16.

[1] Lines 3-4 of the inscription: 'dignus ita geminis ducibus consortia sacra participare fidei, consilio regere.'

[2] Orosius vii. 32. 13. Cf. Origen, *C. Cels.* viii. 68.

at least of those who went out among the barbarians, in addition to their spiritual reasons for working for the conversion, were not unaware of the political implications of their undertaking. But the threat to society came not only from the invaders but also from the masses of uprooted and propertyless people who could be found in every province at the end of the fourth century. Now it is not said that the Romans among whom Amantius worked were brigands; but certainly Niceta and Victricius directed their efforts at the local outlaws as well as at the foreign invaders. What is curious is that the Roman government drew no conclusions from the success of the missionaries.

III

Although the results at which we have so far arrived are largely negative, the fact remains that several of the great Germanic peoples were converted to Arianism before the western empire disappeared in 476. What is known about the conversion of each of them?[1]

We have already mentioned the Marcomanni. The incident of Fritigil leaves little room for doubt that the Marcomanni, apart from Fritigil's tribe, were pagan at the end of the fourth century; and the people later known as the Bavarians, of whom the Marcomanni became a part, were pagan long after the close of our period. The Heruls only became Christian when they entered the Roman Empire and Justinian gave them land around Singidunum (Belgrade) somewhat after 535.[2] The Lombards, too, were not converted in our period. According to a tradition preserved by themselves—and although we know it only from a late source, its truth cannot reasonably be doubted—they were won over to Christianity by Rugian missionaries during the years 488–505, when they had occupied the lands of the Rugi in Lower Austria.[3] The conversion of the Franks, Alamanni, Frisians, and Saxons also does not concern us. These peoples did not enter the

---

[1] For similar reviews see Zeiller, op. cit., pp. 534–42; K. D. Schmidt, *Die Bekehrung der Germanen zum Christentum* (Göttingen, 1939), *passim*.

[2] Procopius, *B.G.* vi. 14. 33 ff.

[3] *Historia Langobardorum Codicis Gothani*, ii (*M.G.H. S.S. rer. Langob.* viii), with Schmidt, op. cit., pp. 392–5. Whether they were Catholic before they became Arian is a question which does not concern us. The protagonist of the priority of Catholicism among them is C. Blasel, 'Der Übertritt der Langobarden zum Christentum', *Archiv f. katholisches Kirchenrecht*, lxxxiii (1903), 577–619, cf. Zeiller, op. cit., pp. 571 ff., who believes that they were introduced to Christianity by the remnants of Fritigil's Marcomanni.

provinces *en masse* while the Western empire was in being (though the first two encroached upon it), and they were not converted until after 476. In fact, we may conclude that with one exception (the Rugi: *v. infra*) the peoples who did not enter the Roman Empire before 476 did not become Christian before that date.

The question now arises, did any of the peoples who entered the provinces before 476 become Christian before crossing the frontier? It has been argued elsewhere that the conversion of the Visigoths must be dated to the period 382–95, when they were settled as Federates in Moesia.[1] Although we know something about certain Catholic missionaries who tried in vain to convert them, there is unfortunately no hint in our sources at the identity of the Arian missionaries who successfully won them over in 382–95; but it is natural to suppose that they were not Romans but Gothic disciples of Ulfila who went among them with the Gothic Bible in their hands. At any rate, after they had settled on Roman soil, the considered and characteristic attitude of Roman Arians towards them is probably suggested by a passage in the Arian commentary on Matthew's Gospel known as the *Opus Imperfectum*. In this work, which may have been composed in the first half of the fifth century, the author has a word to say about his barbarian fellow-heretics. 'The barbarian nations', he writes, 'are in the habit of giving their sons names which recall the havoc caused by wild beasts or scavenging birds: they think it glorious to have such names, suitable for war and raging for blood.' These words would scarcely have rung with a very welcome sound in the ears of men who had been brought up to reverence Ulfila, the Little Wolf. Although the author of the *Opus* admits that God is prepared to call barbarians as well as civilized men, he castigates priests who propagate the word of God among 'unlearned, undisciplined, and barbarian peoples, who neither seek nor hear it with judgement and who have the name of Christians but the manners of pagans'.[2] If this was the general attitude of Roman Arians towards the barbarians it can hardly be doubted that the conversion was the work of Gothic missionaries.

The date of the conversion of the Vandals is disputed. Recent inquirers have tended to believe that they were converted by Visigothic missionaries towards the end of the fourth century

[1] *Journal of Ecclesiastical History*, vii (1956), 1–11.
[2] *Opus Imperfectum*, Homily i (Migne, *P.G.* lvi. 626), xxxv (ibid. 824, cf. 864).

when they were living in the Körös-Mures region north of the lower Danube.[1] But the theory may be doubted. Jordanes tells us that the Visigoths sent out missionaries to the Ostrogoths and the Gepids.[2] He does not mention the Vandals. But why should he specify the two Visigothic missions which were not successful in the fourth century, while omitting to mention the only one which (on this theory) was a success? It was certainly not Jordanes' purpose to minimize the achievements of the Goths. Moreover, if we accept the date of the conversion of the Visigoths themselves as 382–95 it should be noted that Courtois has shown reason for thinking that $c.$ 392 the Vandals had begun their long journey towards the west. The Visigoths had been living south of the Danube since 376 and so were no longer in direct contact with the Vandals. Are we to suppose, then, that at the very moment when they were beginning to win a decisive success among their own people and when all their efforts were needed at home, the Visigothic Christians sent preachers away to the north, beyond the Roman frontier, through the dominions of the Huns, where travel was at precisely this date exceedingly difficult?[3] And are we to suppose further that these missionaries converted the Vandals almost overnight—when they were, so to speak, in the very act of packing their bags? It seems a hazardous supposition. It is supported by no evidence, and some may find it safer to accept the alternative theory and to believe that when the Vandals crossed the Rhine on 31 December 405 they were still a pagan people. This would account for the fact that some Romans who joined them in Gaul lapsed from Christianity and reverted to paganism.[4] But what seems decisive is that Orosius appears to have regarded the conversion of the Vandals as a very recent event when he was writing in 417.[5] The conversion, he seems to imply, had taken place in Spain, i.e. in the years 409–17.

[1] So K. D. Schmidt, op. cit., pp. 351 f., followed by L. Schmidt, *Gesch. d. Wandalen* (2nd ed., Munich, 1942), p. 184. So, too, K. Helm, *Altgermanische Religionsgeschichte*, ii, 1 (Heidelberg, 1937), p. 75; H. Giesecke, *Die Ostgermanen und der Arianismus* (Leipzig and Berlin, 1939), pp. 167 f.; M. Jahn *apud* H. Reinerth, *Vorgeschichte d. deutschen Stämme*, iii (Leipzig and Berlin, 1940), 1022; C. Courtois, *Les Vandales et l'Afrique* (Paris, 1955), pp. 35 f. *Contra*, Zeiller, op. cit., p. 538.
[2] Jordanes, *Get.* xxv. 133.
[3] Sozomen, vii. xxvi. 6 ff.
[4] Orientius, *Common.* ii. 313 ff. For a later stage of the Vandal invasion see Quodvultdeus, *de Tempore Barbarico*, iii–iv (ed. G. Morin, *S. Aur. Augustini Tractatus sive Sermones Inediti*, Campoduni et Monaci, 1917, 202 f.). Similar lapses had taken place when the pagan Goths and Boradi invaded Pontus in the third century.
[5] Orosius, vii. xli. 7 f. It is not clear to me why Courtois, op. cit., p. 35, n. 7, takes this passage to refer to the Silings alone.

The safest conclusion then would be to reject the theory of a conversion in the wilds of Hungary at a time when the Visigoths themselves were barely Christian.

The Sueves who travelled to Spain in company with the Vandals and founded a kingdom in the north-west of the peninsula were still ruled by a pagan named Rechila who died in 448; but Rechila's son Rechiarius (448–56), who succeeded him in spite of secret opposition, was a Catholic.[1] There is some reason to suppose, however, that he was a convert and had not been born a Catholic.[2] It has not been doubted, I think, that the conversion of the Sueves took place when they were already settled in Spain.

The Burgundians were still pagan in 370, and Ammianus gives no indication that the pagan priesthood and the pagan practice which he describes had disappeared *c.* 395 when he was writing his History.[3] The common belief is that they were still pagan when they entered Gaul in 406: it is difficult to see how or why missionaries would have made their way through the lands of the Alamanni and other pagan peoples in southern Germany in order to single out the Burgundians for special attention.[4] At the end of the fifth century they were so warmly attached to their Arianism that they must have been Arian for at least a generation by then;[5] and it is noteworthy that the family traditions of King Gundobad (*c.* 480–516) were Arian.[6] In fact, the author of the *Gallic Chronicle* suggests that the major Germanic peoples settled in Gaul were all of them Arian by 451, and in this he is supported by Gregory of Tours.[7] (The notorious statement of Orosius that by 417 the Burgundians had been converted not to Arianism but to Catholicism is generally discounted and may be dismissed.[8]) There can

---

[1] Hydatius, *Chron. Min.* ii. 25.
[2] Ibid. ii. 301: 'Recciarius . . . catholicus factus.'
[3] Amm. Marc. xxviii. v. 14.
[4] Cf. A. Coville, *Recherches sur l'histoire de Lyon du Vme siècle au IXme siècle* (Paris, 1928), pp. 150 f.; A. Hauck, *Kirchengeschichte Deutschlands*, i (Leipzig, 1922), 93. An exception is K. D. Schmidt, op. cit. i. 410, who believes that towards the end of the fourth century (presumably after 370) Visigothic missionaries came up the Danube (from Moesia?) to the upper Main valley and converted them before they entered Gaul. To me this seems very improbable. That the Burgundians were converted during the period of the kingdom of Worms is also the view of Ihm, P.-W. iii. 1064; D. Bohnsack *apud* Reinerth, op. cit. iii. 1140.
[5] Greg. Tur. *Hist. Franc.* ii. 34.
[6] Alcimus Avitus, *Ep.* vi (p. 34. 33 f., ed. Peiper): there is every reason to believe him cf. K. D. Schmidt, op. cit., p. 412.
[7] *Chronica Minora*, i. 662, Greg. Tur. *Hist. Franc.* ii. 9 (p. 58. 5).
[8] Orosius, vii. xxxii. 13, whose story was long ago doubted by C. Binding, *Das burgundisch-romanische Königreich*, i (Leipzig, 1868), 40 f. See esp. H. von Schubert, 'Die Anfänge des Christentums bei den Burgunden', *Sitzungsberichte d. Heidelberger Akad. d. Wiss., phil.-hist.*

be little doubt, then, that the conversion must be dated between the years 406 and 451, and the analogous case of the Visigoths suggests a narrowing of these limits. We might suppose that just as the Visigoths were converted to Arianism when settled as Federates in Moesia between 382 and 395, so the Burgundians were converted when settled as Federates in Germania Prima between 412 and 436. This dating would help to explain why a story arrived at Constantinople which, highly coloured though it had become on its journey, was designed to explain why the eastern Burgundians had seen fit to become Christian about the year 430.[1] These Burgundians had remained east of the Rhine when the bulk of the people had crossed into Gaul in 406; and although we do not know what were the relations between the two groups of Burgundians there is at least a presumption that if the eastern Burgundians were converted c. 430 their companions in Gaul were converted at about the same time.

Now if this were all, we could conclude with some assurance that before the year 476 none of the great Germanic peoples living outside the frontier was Christian. There were individuals and groups of persons who had been converted, but the peoples as a whole were all of them pagan. Unfortunately, little information has survived about three great peoples who had been absorbed into Attila's empire towards the close of the fourth century and so were largely withdrawn from the sight of Roman authors. These peoples are the Ostrogoths, the Gepids, and the Rugi.

There were Catholic communities among the Ostrogoths in the Crimea c. 400.[2] But the bulk of the Ostrogoths were still pagan in 406 when human sacrifices were performed in the army

---

Klasse, iii (1911), to whose arguments little of value is added by G. Köhler, 'Die Bekehrung der Burgunden zum Christentum', *Zeitschrift f. Kirchengeschichte*, lvii (1938), 227–43, or by K. D. Schmidt, op. cit., pp. 404–11. A long but wholly unconvincing attempt to uphold Orosius is made by Coville, op. cit., pp. 139–52, cf. Zeiller, op. cit., p. 580. An intermediate position seems to be taken up by M. Burckhardt, *Die Briefsammlung des Bischof Avitus von Vienne* (Berlin 1938), p. 25, n. 1.

[1] Socrates, VII. xxx. 3, cf. *Chronica Minora*, ii. 491. The story does not specify whether these Burgundians became Catholic or Arian. There is no reason to reject the general truth of the tale: E. A. Thompson, *Attila and the Huns* (Oxford, 1948), pp. 66 f.

[2] John Chrysostom, *Ep.* xiv, ccvi, who himself tried to counteract the Arianism of the Goths in Constantinople by setting aside for them a church to be used for Catholic services by the Catholic Goths there. He appointed presbyters and deacons who knew the Gothic language. One or two sermons still exist which John himself preached to them in 399: Theodoret, H.E. v. 30, John, *Homilia habita postquam Gothus*, &c. (Migne, P.G. lxiii. 499–510), with P. Batiffol, 'De quelques homélies de S. Jean Chrysostome et de la version gothique des écritures', *Revue Biblique*, viii (1899), 566–72. But there is no evidence that he sent missionaries to win over the pagan Germans as he did to win over the Huns: Theodoret, H.E. v. 31.

Christianity and the Northern Barbarians

of Radagaisus which invaded Italy in that year.[1] Now Jordanes says, apparently referring to the fourth century, that Visigothic Arian missionaries went out among the Ostrogoths.[2] There is no reason to doubt him; but he does not claim that they won any significant successes. It is also true that many Christian Goths lived in Constantinople in the first half of the fifth century under the leadership of Gainas, Plinthas, Ardaburius, and others; but it is difficult to envisage circumstances in which Gothic missionaries from Constantinople or from Ulfila's old settlement at Nicopolis could have worked among those Ostrogoths who had been overrun by the Huns *c.* 370 and who lived in great hardship under the oppressive rule of the nomads until 455. Unauthorized travellers, even bishops, were distinctly unwelcome in the Hun empire and if discovered would have been put to death out of hand.[3] It would be absurd, of course, to suppose that these conditions would have made a conversion impossible. But is it not more likely that the Ostrogoths were converted when they were living in the Roman province of Pannonia in 456–72, where access to them would have been unimpeded?[4] As for the identity of those who converted them, one or two pieces of evidence suggest that these were Goths from Constantinople (or Nicopolis). The extant fragment of the Gothic Calendar, in the form in which we have it, is an Ostrogothic document and was written in the Ostrogothic kingdom of Italy in the period 493–553. But originally it had been a Visigothic document: it was drawn up in its earliest form towards the end of the fourth century when the Visigoths lived south of the lower Danube.[5] The Calendar, however, was not handed on directly by the Visigoths to those Ostrogoths who later settled in Italy. There is one entry in the Calendar, as we have it and as the Ostrogoths in Italy had it, which was only added to the original text some years after the Visigoths had marched away from the Balkans to the West. The Goths in Constantinople, as is well known, had been warmly engaged in the Psathyrian dispute at the turn of the fourth and fifth centuries; and they were not reconciled to their adversaries until 419.[6]

---

[1] Orosius, VII. xxxvii. 4 ff.
[2] Loc. cit. in n. 2, p. 70 above.
[3] Sozomen, VII. xxvi. 6 ff., Priscus of Panium, frag. 8, p. 320.
[4] Cf. Zeiller, op. cit., pp. 536 f., a judicious summary of the probabilities.
[5] This has been established by H. Achelis, 'Der älteste deutsche Kalender', *Zeitschrift f. d. Neutestamentliche Wissenschaft*, i (1900), 308–35, at 314 ff., 322 f.; R. Loewe, 'Der gotische Kalender', *Zeitschrift f. Deutsches Altertum*, lix (1922), 245–90, at 274 ff., 278 ff., 283.
[6] Socrates, V. 23; Sozomen, VII. xvii. 9 ff.; Suidas, s.v. Ἀρειανοί.

After the reconciliation these Goths as a gesture to their opponents allotted a festival in their Calendar to the opposing leader, Dorotheus of Antioch, although he had died a natural and not a martyr's death in 407 at the unusual age of 119.[1] But in 419 the Visigoths were already settled in their kingdom of Toulouse and perhaps had not even heard of these events—at any rate, it can hardly be supposed that they would have included so far-distant a figure as Dorotheus in their Calendar, especially as they themselves are not known to have been involved in the Psathyrian controversy. The Calendar, therefore, in its present form derives from Constantinople or Nicopolis and was handed on to the bulk of the Ostrogoths, when they became Christian, not by the Visigoths in Gaul but by the Goths living in or near the eastern capital. Secondly, it has been shown that the Gothic text of the Gospels of Luke and Mark as preserved in the *Codex Argenteus* is a much revised and Latinized version in which the original renderings of Ulfila have been in many places altered by Visigothic scholars in Gaul.[2] On the other hand, the text of Matthew and John is in a purer and more Ulfilian style and had evidently escaped the attentions of the Visigothic scholars.[3] Now when the Ostrogoths entered Italy in 489 and came again into close contact with the Visigoths for the first time since 376, the revision of Ulfila's text by Visigothic scholars must already have reached an advanced stage (for they are referred to by Salvian in 440). How then did the Ostrogoths come to possess so pure a text of Matthew's Gospel as the *Codex Argenteus* shows them to have had? They cannot have received it from the Visigoths of Toulouse, for they can hardly be thought to have waited until 489 before receiving a text of Ulfila at all; and if they had received it from the Visigoths in or after 489 it would not have been so pure and Ulfilian as the Argenteus shows it to have been. The only possibility would seem to be that the pure text was that which had been in the hands of the Goths at Constantinople throughout the fifth century since the departure of Alaric for the west in 401. The Goths of the eastern capital, it seems, had not tampered with Ulfila's work on anything like the scale of the Visigoths at Toulouse.[4] But if it is agreed that the Ostrogoths on

---

[1] See the Calendar at 6 Nov., and cf. H. Delehaye, art. cit., p. 277; Loewe, art cit., pp. 271 f.
[2] Their activities are referred to by Salvian, v. 5 ff.
[3] G. W. S. Friedrichsen, *The Gothic Version of the Gospels* (Oxford, 1926), pp. 160 f., 243.
[4] See id., *The Gothic Version of the Epistles* (Oxford, 1939), pp. 261–4, from whom I differ

their conversion received both their New Testament and their Church Calendar from the Goths at Constantinople, it can hardly be denied that the latter had played a decisive part in their conversion. There is some reason, in fact, to think that Gothic missionaries won the Ostrogoths to the new faith, whereas there is no reason to think that Roman missionaries concerned themselves with them at all.

In the fourth century the Gepids lived in the Carpathian mountains north of the Visigoths in Transylvania. Visigothic missionaries had gone among them, as among the Ostrogoths, in the fourth century; but although they may have made a few converts, no claim is made that they were any more successful than they were among the Ostrogoths.[1] And in fact the Gepids were still pagan when Salvian mentioned them in 440–1: indeed, a phrase which Salvian uses of them may perhaps suggest that human sacrifice was still known among them in his day.[2] After the collapse of the Hun empire in 455 they were still living east of the Tisza and received annual subsidies from the East Roman government.[3] Later still, in 472, they occupied land on both sides of the Danube around Singidunum and Sirmium. It is only in the sixth century that they are reported as being Arians.[4] Now if they were converted when still under the rule of the Huns their conversion must be dated to the period 441–55. But of all times when the conversion of a people subject to the Huns may have been possible, this surely is the most improbable. In 441–3 and again in 447 Attila carried out his two great attacks on the eastern empire. After 447 there was mounting tension on the lower Danube frontier. In 451 Attila turned abruptly against the west and invaded Gaul. In 452 he was in Italy. In 453 he died, and wars broke out between his sons, and in 455 the great Hun empire was overthrown by the rebellion of their subjects, led by the Gepids. In all their campaigns the Huns brought with them the warriors of their subject peoples, partly so as to strengthen their own manpower and partly because it would have been dangerous to leave them behind when the Hun warriors themselves were far away. Can we reasonably suppose that in these conditions

on some points. How has it come about that a Visigothic text of Luke and Mark was included in the *Codex Argenteus*?

[1] Jordanes, *Get.*, loc. cit.
[2] Salvian, iv. 67, cf. 82: 'Gipidarum inhumanissimi ritus.'
[3] Jordanes, *Get.* l. 264.
[4] Procopius, *B.V.* iii. 2. 5 f.; *B.G.* vii. 34. 24; Cyril of Scythopolis, *Vita S. Sabae*, p. 176. 5, ed. E. Schwartz.

Christian missionaries were able to convert the Gepids under Attila's very eyes? Is it not easier to believe that missionaries came peacefully up the Danube to Sirmium and Singidunum and converted the Gepids in and after 472?

Finally, the Rugi in Lower Austria north of the Danube were Arian before the death of St. Severinus in 482; and here we have a clear case of a Christian Germanic people living outside the Roman frontier. It is true that, although their headquarters were north of the Danube, the Rugi controlled a considerable area of Roman territory south of the river, had stationed garrisons in it, and exacted a tribute from it. But that hardly alters the case: they were a Germanic people who had been converted to Christianity while living outside the frontier in our period. It does not necessarily follow, however, that the Rugi were converted as a result of Roman or Gothic missionary activity outside the frontier. Some Rugi had not been absorbed into Attila's empire but had settled in the Roman provinces. We catch a glimpse of them in the period 434-41, when they rebelled and seized Noviodunum on the lower Danube—evidently their settlement lay in that region.[1] Here it would have been easy for the Goths at Nicopolis or Constantinople to make contact with them and instruct them in the Arian faith. The rest of the Rugi, when they freed themselves from the rule of the Huns, will have followed the example of this section of the people.[2] This, of course, is no more than a hypothesis: there is no evidence of any kind for the conversion of the Rugi. But perhaps it accounts for the conversion more simply than can otherwise be done, and it suggests that there is no compelling reason to posit the existence of a Gothic mission in Attila's empire.

IV

However we may account for the conversion of the various Germanic peoples, we have no evidence for supposing that Roman missionaries played any substantial part in the process. True, we know the names of several Catholic bishops who worked among the invaders once they had crossed the frontier. But the Germans were not won to Catholicism in this period,

---

[1] Priscus of Panium, frag. 1 a, with Thompson, op. cit. 217f.
[2] Rappaport, in Pauly-Wissowa, *Realencyclopädie*, 1 A. 1222, assumes that the Rugi became Christian after the fall of the Huns' empire in 455.

and the work of these bishops was a failure. It has sometimes been thought that the Burgundians were converted by Roman Arians of the Rhineland; but until some evidence is produced for the existence of a community of Roman Arians on the Rhine in the first half of the fifth century—and evidently a flourishing and vigorous community—we may consider it safer to suppose that Visigothic missionaries came up from Toulouse after the foundation of the kingdom there in 418. On the other hand, the claims which have sometimes been made for a vast and successful Gothic mission outside the Roman frontier and within the territories of Attila may well be exaggerated:[1] the phenomena which this alleged mission is assumed to explain can in fact be accounted for otherwise. That our evidence is defective is only too apparent; but the conversion of the Ostrogoths and the Gepids may most easily be explained if we date it to a time when these peoples were settled inside or on the Roman frontiers and when Gothic missionaries could work among them in comparative peace. The achievement of the Gothic mission was on any showing a very considerable one,[2] but there is no convincing evidence that it was conducted under the eyes of the Huns. The final conclusion which we may draw is that until the year 476, when the western empire ceased to exist as a political entity, none of the great Germanic peoples with the single exception of the Rugi was converted to Christianity while still living outside the Roman frontier. The central issue concerns the subjects of the Huns. There can be no mathematical proof of any opinion; and we can only say that, given what we know of the fierce rule of the nomads, our conclusion is not improbable and that it conflicts with nothing in the scanty evidence. Moreover, even if we move our lower limit from 476 to, say, the death of Justinian in 565, we shall find only one more exceptional case of a people who, like the Rugi, were converted to Christianity while living in territory which had not once been Roman. This exception is the Lombards (p. 68 above), who curiously enough were converted in Lower Austria, where the Rugi had lived before them, and were won over by Rugian missionaries. Again, it is certain that none of the great Germanic peoples who entered the Roman provinces in the fourth and fifth centuries remained pagan for

---

[1] See, for example, K. D. Schmidt, op. cit., pp. 419 ff.
[2] It is confirmed by the existence of a Greek element in ecclesiastical German: see Schulze, op. cit., pp. 526 f.

more than a generation after they crossed the frontier. No people, in fact, is known to have delayed its conversion longer than the Sueves who entered Gaul in 406 and were first ruled by a Christian forty-two years later—and even the Sueves in some cases were turning to Christianity as early as 417.[1] It would seem to follow that the act of crossing the imperial frontiers and settling down as landlords or the like on Roman soil necessarily and inevitably entailed the abandonment of paganism and conversion to the Roman religion. Neither phenomenon is found except in company with the other; and if our arguments are valid the cases are numerous enough to justify us in ruling out coincidence as the explanation. That is to say, the religious history of the Germans in the Roman period cannot be divorced from their political history. Their transference from the wilds of *barbaria* into the social relationships of *Romania* brought about a marked and comparatively sudden transformation in their religion. The move into a new economic and social world was necessarily followed by a move into a new spiritual world.

[1] Orosius, VII. xli. 8.

IV

Pagan and Christian Historiography in the Fourth Century A.D.[1]

ARNALDO MOMIGLIANO

I

ON 28 October 312 the Christians suddenly and unexpectedly found themselves victorious.[2] The victory was a miracle—though opinions differed as to the nature of the sign vouchsafed to Constantine. The winners became conscious of their victory in a mood of resentment and vengeance. A voice shrill with implacable hatred announced to the world the victory of the Milvian Bridge: Lactantius' *De mortibus persecutorum*.[3] In this horrible pamphlet by the author of *De ira dei* there is something of the violence of the prophets without the redeeming sense of tragedy that inspires Nahum's song for the fall of Nineveh. 'His fury is poured out like fire and the rocks are broken asunder by him. The Lord is good, a strong hold in the day of trouble': this at least has an elementary simplicity which is very remote from the complacent and sophisticated prose of the fourth-century rhetorician. Lactantius was not alone. More soberly, but no less ruthlessly, Eusebius recounted the divine vengeance against those who had persecuted the Church. To us it naturally appears that there is something in common between the Jews who died in defending the old Jerusalem and the Christians who died in building up the new Jerusalem against the same Roman empire. Modern scholars have found it easy to prove that in form and substance the Jewish martyr is the prototype of the Christian martyr. Such scholarly discoveries have little relevance to the realities of the

---

[1] The notes to this lecture are meant to provide no more than an introduction to the recent literature.

[2] Cf., however, P. Bruun, 'The Battle of the Milvian Bridge: The Date Reconsidered', *Hermes*, lxxxviii (1960), 361–70, which puts the battle in 311.

[3] The standard commentary is by J. Moreau, *Sources Chrétiennes* (Paris, 1954). Cf. W. Nestle, 'Die Legende vom Tode der Gottesverächter', *Arch. f. Religionsw.* xxxiii (1936), 246–69, reprinted in *Griechische Studien* (1948), p. 567. In general J. Stevenson, *Studia Patristica*, i (Berlin, 1957), 661–77. Not convincing S. Rossi, *Giorn. Ital. Filol.* xiv (1961), 193–213.

fourth century. The pupils hated their masters, and were hated in their turn. With a cry of joy Eusebius, possibly a man of Jewish descent, retells from Josephus the story of the siege and capture of Jerusalem: thus may perish the enemies of Christ. Perhaps it is no chance that personally neither Lactantius nor Eusebius had suffered much from Diocletian's persecution. Like Tacitus in relation to Domitian, they voiced the resentment of the majority who had survived in fear rather than in physical pain. Eusebius had been near his master Pamphilus who had carried on his work on the Bible in prison while awaiting death.[1]

If there were men who recommended tolerance and peaceful coexistence of Christians and pagans, they were rapidly crowded out. The Christians were ready to take over the Roman empire, as Eusebius made clear in the introduction of the *Praeparatio evangelica* where he emphasizes the correlation between *pax romana* and the Christian message: the thought indeed was not even new. The Christians were also determined to make impossible a return to conditions of inferiority and persecution for the Church. The problems and the conflicts inside the Church which all this implied may be left aside for the moment. The revolution of the fourth century, carrying with it a new historiography, will not be understood if we underrate the determination, almost the fierceness, with which the Christians appreciated and exploited the miracle that had transformed Constantine into a supporter, a protector, and later a legislator of the Christian Church.

One fact is eloquent enough. All the pioneer works in the field of Christian historiography are earlier than what we may call their opposite numbers in pagan historiography. *De mortibus persecutorum* was written by Lactantius about 316. Eusebius' *Ecclesiastical History* probably appeared in a first edition about 312.[2] His life of Constantine—the authenticity of which can hardly be

---

[1] The facts are gathered by H. J. Lawlor and J. E. L. Oulton, *Eusebius, The Ecclesiastical History and the Martyrs of Palestine*, translated with introduction and notes (London, 1928; reprint, 1954), ii, 332. Cf. S. Liebermann, *Ann. Inst. Phil. Hist. Orient.* vii (1939-44), 395-446.

[2] On the controversial question of the various editions of the *Ecclesiastical History* with which I do not intend to deal here, see especially E. Schwartz, introduction to his *ed. maior* (Berlin, 1909), vol. iii, and article in Pauly-Wissowa, *Realencyclopädie*, s.v. Eusebius (now reprinted in *Griechische Geschichtschreiber*, 1957, pp. 540 ff.); R. Laqueur, *Eusebius als Historiker seiner Zeit* (Berlin and Leipzig, 1929); H. J. Lawlor and J. E. L. Oulton, introduction to their translation (1928); H. Edmonds, *Zweite Auflagen im Altertum* (Leipzig, 1941), pp. 25-45 (with bibliography).

doubted—was written not long after 337.[1] Athanasius' life of St. Anthony belongs to the years around 360. Among the pagan works none can be dated with absolute certainty before the death of Constantine. The *Historia Augusta* purports to have been written under Diocletian and Constantine, but the majority of modern scholars prefer—rightly or wrongly—a date later than 360.[2] The characteristic trilogy, to which the *Caesares* by Aurelius Victor belong, was put together later than 360.[3] The lives of the sophists by Eunapius—which are pagan hagiography—were published about 395.[4] Ammianus Marcellinus, too, finished his work about 395.[5] On the whole, the Christians come before the pagans in their creative writing. The Christians attack. The pagans are on the defensive.

Towards the end of the century the situation changed. Theodosius' death precipitated a political crisis, and the barbarians were soon taking advantage of it with invasions on an unprecedented scale. The intervention of the state in theological matters appeared less attractive to people who had witnessed the trials of the Priscillianists and the cruel executions that concluded them. Many Christians became less certain of themselves and went back to paganism. Many pagans became more aggressive and dared to say openly that the new religion was responsible for the collapse of the empire. In the pagan field resignation yielded to fury, and in the Christian field aggressiveness had to be turned into self-defence. This incidentally brought about a revival of pagan historical writing in Greek: pagan Greek historiography had been conspicuously absent from the ideological struggles of the fourth century. It thus becomes clear that the years between 395 and 410 saw new developments in historiography which are beyond the scope of this lecture. Though we shall not disregard them altogether, we shall confine our analysis to the years 312–95.

[1] Bibliography until 1956 in B. Altaner, *Patrologie* (5th edn. Freiburg im Br., 1958), p. 209. Add J. Straub, *Studia Patristica*, i (Berlin, 1957), 679–95.

[2] My essay reprinted in *Secondo Contributo alla storia degli studi classici* (Rome, 1960), pp. 105–43 gives the bibliography to which I wish to add W. Ensslin, *Studi Calderini-Paribeni*, i (1956), 313–23; J. Straub, *Bonner Jahrbücher*, clv-clvi (1955–6), 136–55, and more particularly E. M. Staerman, *Vestnik Drevnej Istorii*, 1957, 1, 233–45 translated in *Bibl. Class. Orient.* v (1960), 93–110, and A. I. Dovatur, *V.D.I.* quoted, pp. 245–56. I am not moved by the arguments of J. Schwartz, *Bull. Fac. Lettres Strasbourg*, xl (1961), 169–76.

[3] The problem is discussed in my *Secondo Contributo alla storia degli studi classici*, pp. 145–89. A later date is suggested by G. Puccioni, *Studi Ital. Fil. Class.* xxx (1958), 207–54 and *Ann. Scuola Normale Pisa*, xxvii (1958), 211–23.

[4] Cf. also W. R. Chalmers, *Class. Quart.*, N.S., iii (1953), 165–70.

[5] Cf., however, O. J. Maenchen-Helfen, *A. J. Ph.* lxxvi (1955), 384–400.

II

The clear-sighted determination of the Christians, which became suddenly apparent about 312, was the result of centuries of discipline and thought. In times of persecution and of uneasy tolerance the Church had developed its idea of orthodoxy and its conception of the providential economy of history. It emerged victorious to reassert with enhanced authority the unmistakable pattern of divine intervention in history, the ruthless elimination of deviations. The foundations of Christian historiography had been laid long before the time of the battle of the Milvian Bridge.

We all know the story of the man who went into a London bookshop and asked for a New Testament in Greek. The assistant retired to a back room and after ten minutes came back with a grave look: 'Strange, Sir, but Greek seems to be the only language into which the New Testament has not yet been translated'. The story may remind us of two facts. The first is that there was a time in which the New Testament was only available in Greek. The second and more important is that at that time it was as difficult as it is now to find a bookshop with a New, or for that matter an Old, Testament in Greek. About A.D. 180 a man like Galen could walk into a bookshop only to discover that they were selling an unauthorized edition of his own lectures. But though he was interested in the Christians, Galen would hardly have found a Bible. The Bible was no literature for the pagan. Its Greek was not elegant enough. Lactantius noted: 'apud sapientes et doctos et principes huius saeculi scriptura sancta fide care(a)t' (*Inst.* v. i. 15). If we find a pagan who had a slight acquaintance with the Bible, such as the anonymous author of *On the Sublime*, we suspect direct Jewish influence: justifiedly so, because the author of the *Sublime* was a student of Caecilius of Calacte, who, to all appearances, was a Jew.[1] Normally the educated pagans of the Roman empire knew nothing about either Jewish or Christian history. If they wanted some information about the Jews, they picked up second-hand distortions such as we read in Tacitus. The consequence was that a direct acquaintance with Jewish or Christian history normally came together with conversion to Judaism or to Christianity.

[1] Cf. A. Rostagni, *Anonimo–Del Sublime* (Milan, 1947); E. Norden, 'Das Genesiszitat in der Schrift vom Erhabenen', *Abh. Berlin. Akad.* (1954), p. 1.

Pagan and Christian Historiography in the Fourth Century A.D. 83

People learnt a new history because they acquired a new religion. Conversion meant literally the discovery of a new history from Adam and Eve to contemporary events.[1]

The new history could not suppress the old. Adam and Eve and what follows had in some way to be presented in a world populated by Deucalion, Cadmus, Romulus, and Alexander the Great. This created all sorts of new problems. First, the pagans had to be introduced to the Jewish version of history. Secondly, the Christian historians were expected to silence the objection that Christianity was new, and therefore not respectable. Thirdly, the pagan facts of life had to get into the Jewish-Christian scheme of redemption. It soon became imperative for the Christians to produce a chronology which would satisfy both the needs of elementary teaching and the purposes of higher historical interpretation. The Christian chronographers had to summarize the history which the converts were now supposed to consider their own; they had also to show the antiquity of the Jewish-Christian doctrine, and they had to present a model of providential history. The result was that, unlike pagan chronology, Christian chronology was also a philosophy of history. Unlike pagan elementary teaching, Christian elementary teaching of history could not avoid touching upon the essentials of the destiny of man. The convert, in abandoning paganism, was compelled to enlarge his historical horizon: he was likely to think for the first time in terms of universal history.

The spade-work in Christian chronology was done long before the fourth century.[2] The greatest names involved in this work, Clemens Alexandrinus, Julius Africanus, and Hippolytus of Rome, belong to the second and third centuries. They created the frame for the divine administration of the world; they transformed Hellenistic chronography into a Christian science and

---

[1] On the implications of the Christian vision of history see, for instance, L. Tondelli, *Il disegno divino nella storia* (Turin, 1947); O. Cullmann, *Christus und die Zeit* (2nd edn., Zürich, 1948); W. Kamlah, *Christentum und Geschichtlichkeit* (2nd edn., Stuttgart, 1951); R. L. P. Milburn, *Early Christian Interpretations of History* (London, 1954); K. Löwith, *Weltgeschichte und Heilsgeschehen*, (Stuttgart, 1953); C. Schneider, *Geistesgeschichte des antiken Christentums* (Munich, 1956). See also H. Rahner, *Griechische Mythen in christlicher Deutung* (Zürich, 1945), and the studies by S. G. F. Brandon and K. Löwith in *Numen*, ii (1955).

[2] Besides the fundamental H. Gelzer, *Sextus Julius Africanus und die byzant. Chronographie* (Leipzig, 1880–98), I shall only mention A. Hamel, *Kirche bei Hippolyt von Rom* (Gütersloh, 1951); M. Richard, *Mél. Sciences Religieuses* vii (1950), 237, and viii (1951), 19 (on Hippolytus); B. Kötting, 'Endzeitprognosen zwischen Lactantius und Augustinus', *Hist. Jahrb.* lxxvii (1957), 125–39; P. Courcelle, 'Les Exégèses chrétiennes de la quatrième églogue', *Rev. Étud. Anc.* lix (1957), 294–319; A.-D. Van Den Brincken, *Studien zur Lateinischen Weltchronistik bis in das Zeitalter Ottos von Freising* (Düsseldorf, 1957; with bibliography).

added the lists of the bishops of the most important sees to the lists of kings and magistrates of the pagan world. They presented history in such a way that the scheme of redemption was easy to perceive. They showed with particular care the priority of the Jews over the pagans—in which point their debt to Jewish apologetic is obvious. They established criteria of orthodoxy by the simple device of introducing lists of bishops who represented the apostolic succession. Calculations about the return of Christ and the ultimate end had never been extraneous to the Church. Since the Apocalypse attributed to St. John had established itself as authoritative in the Church, millennial reckonings had multiplied. Universal chronology in the Christian sense was bound to take into account not only the beginning, but also the end; it had either to accept or else to fight the belief in the millennium. Chronology and eschatology were conflated. Both Julius Africanus and Hippolytus were firm believers in the millennium, without, however, believing in its imminence. But the higher purpose of philosophy of history was never separated from the immediate task of informing and edifying the faithful. Hippolytus' introduction to his *Chronicon* is explicit. To quote a sentence from one of its Latin translations (another was incorporated in the Chronographer of 354), it was his purpose to show 'quae divisio et quae perditio facta sit, quo autem modo generatio seminis Israel de patribus in Christo completa sit'.

At the beginning of the fourth century Christian chronology had already passed its creative stage. What Eusebius did was to correct and to improve the work of his predecessors, among whom he relied especially on Julius Africanus.[1] He corrected details which seemed to him wrong even to the extent of reducing the priority of the Biblical heroes over the pagan ones. Moses, a contemporary of Ogyges according to Julius Africanus, was made a contemporary of Kekrops with a loss of 300 years. Eusebius was not afraid of attacking St. Paul's guesses about the chronology of the Book of Judges. He freely used Jewish and anti-Christian sources such as Porphyrios. He introduced a reckoning from Abraham which allowed him to avoid the pitfalls of a chronology according to the first chapters of Genesis.

[1] The essential work after E. Schwartz is R. Helm, 'Eusebios' Chronik und ihre Tabellenform', *Abh. Berl. Akad.* (1923), p. 4. Cf. also R. Helm, *Eranos*, xxii (1924), 1–40, and A. Schöne, *Die Weltchronik des Eusebius in ihrer Bearbeitung durch Hieronymus* (Berlin, 1900). D. S. Wallace-Hadrill, 'The Eusebian Chronicle: the extent and date of composition of its early editions', *J.T.S.*, N.S. vi (1955), 248–53.

Pagan and Christian Historiography in the Fourth Century A.D. 85

He seems to have been the first to use the convenient method of presenting the chronology of the various nations in parallel columns. None of the earlier chronographers seems to have used this scheme, though it has often been attributed to Castor or to Julius Africanus. He made many mistakes, but they do not surprise us any longer. Fifty years ago Eduard Schwartz, to save Eusebius' reputation as a competent chronographer, conjectured that the two extant representatives of the lost original of Eusebius' *Chronicon*—the Latin adaptation by St. Jerome and the anonymous Armenian translation—were based on an interpolated text which passed for pure Eusebius. This conjecture is perhaps unnecessary; nor are we certain that the Armenian version is closer to the original than St. Jerome's Latin translation. Both versions reflect the inevitable vagaries of Eusebius' mind to whom chronology was something between an exact science and an instrument of propaganda.

But we recognize the shrewd and worldly adviser of the Emperor Constantine in the absence of millenarian dreams. Eusebius, and St. Jerome who followed him, had an essential part in discrediting them. Of course, they did not stamp them out. Millenarian reckonings reappear in the *De cursu temporum* which Bishop Hilarian wrote at the end of the fourth century.[1] They also played a part in the thought of Sulpicius Severus about that time.[2] As we have already said, the disasters of the end of the century made a difference to dreams, as they made a difference to the other realities.

Thanks to Eusebius, chronography remained the typical form of Christian instruction in the fourth century. It showed concern with the pattern of history rather than with the detail.

The Christians indeed were not alone in having a problem of historical education. The pagans had their own problem. But we can state immediately the difference between pagans and Christians in the teaching of history. The pagans were not concerned with ultimate values in their elementary teaching. Their main concern was to keep alive a knowledge of the Roman past. After the social and political earthquakes of the third century a new leading class had emerged which clearly had some difficulty in remembering the simple facts of Roman history.[3] This explains

---
[1] The text is edited in C. Frick, *Chronica Minora*, i (1892).
[2] S. Prete, *I chronica di Sulpicio Severo* (Città del Vaticano, 1955).
[3] E. Malcovati, *I Breviari del IV secolo*, in Annali Università Cagliari, xii, 1942.

why Eutropius and (Rufius?) Festus were both commissioned by the Emperor Valens to prepare a brief summary of Roman history. Eutropius was the first to obey the royal command. But the seventy-seven pages of his Teubner text must have proved too many for Valens. Festus, who followed, restricted himself to about twenty pages. He was not modest, but literal, when he commended his work to the 'gloriosissimus princeps' as being even shorter than a summary—a mere enumeration of facts. The new men who, coming from the provincial armies or from Germany, acquired power and wealth, wanted some knowledge of the Roman past. They had to mix with the surviving members of the senatorial aristocracy in which knowledge of Roman history and antiquities was *de rigueur*. The establishment of a new senate in Constantinople, by adding another privileged class, complicated this educational problem. The senators of Constantinople, picked as they were from the municipal upper class of the East, were not likely to be uneducated, but they were not particularly strong either in the Latin language or in Roman history. These people too needed *breviaria*. Eutropius was soon translated into Greek by a friend of Libanius and began his momentous career in the Byzantine world. There can be few other Latin authors able to boast of at least three successive translations into Greek.

In their characteristic neutrality, the pagan *breviaria* presented no danger to the Christians. They were so devoid of religious content that they could not give offence. On the contrary, the Christians could easily exploit them for their own purposes. Eutropius was very successful in Constantinople where the aristocracy soon became predominantly Christian. The Christian compiler known as the Chronographer of 354 incorporated in his own work a pagan recapitulation of the history of Rome—the so-called *Chronica urbis Romae*.[1] When St. Jerome decided to continue Eusebius' *Chronicon* to 378 he used pagan writers such as Aurelius Victor and Eutropius, not to mention the *Chronica urbis Romae* which he probably knew as a part of the Christian chronography of 354. All this, however, only emphasized the fact that the Christians had no compilation comparable to Eutropius and Festus. If *breviaria* were not needed during the fourth century when the Christians felt very sure of themselves, they

[1] Mommsen, *Über den Chronographen vom J. 354* (1850), partially reprinted in *Ges. Schriften*, vii, is still the standard work. Text in Mommsen, *Chronica Minora*, i (1892).

appeared less superfluous towards the end of the century when the pagan version of Roman history gained in authority. Sulpicius Severus, who had absorbed pagan culture in Gaul, was the first to realize the deficiency and to fill the gap just about A.D. 400. He combined Christian chronographers and the Bible with *historici mundiales*, the pagan historians. His purpose was still the dual one of the earlier Christian chronography: 'ut et imperitos docerem et litteratos convincerem.' Later, about 417, Orosius followed his example when he was requested by St. Augustine to produce a summary of the history of Rome in support of his *Civitas dei*. Orosius gave what from a medieval point of view can be called the final Christian twist to the pagan epitome of Roman history.[1]

III

Epitomes are only on the threshold of history. So far we have considered books which were meant to remind the reader of the events rather than to tell them afresh. But an important fact has already emerged. Whether in the form of chronographies or, later, in the form of *breviaria*, the Christian compilations were explicit in conveying a message: one can doubt whether the majority of the pagan compilations conveyed any message at all. Sulpicius Severus and Orosius fought for a cause, and it is to be remembered that Sulpicius Severus expressed the indignation felt by Ambrosius and Martin of Tours against the appeal to the secular arm in the Priscillianist controversy. Consequently, it was very easy to transform a pagan handbook into a Christian one, but almost impossible to make pagan what had been Christian. Later on we shall consider one possible exception to the rule that the Christians assimilate pagan ideas, while the pagans do not appropriate Christian ones. The rule, however, stands: it is enough to indicate the trend of the century—and, incidentally, to explain why the Christians were so easily victorious. Just because the trend is so clear, we can perhaps conjecturally add yet another case of the easy transformation of pagan historical *breviaria* into Christian ones. All is in doubt about the first part of the *Anonymus Valesianus*—which is a brief life of

---

[1] Among the recent literature see K. A. Schöndorf, *Die Geschichtstheologie des Orosius* (Munich, 1952). Cf. also J. Straub, 'Christliche Geschichtsapologetik in der Krisis des römischen Reiches,' *Historia*, i (1950), 52–81.

Constantine under the name of *Origo Constantini imperatoris*. But a fourth-century date seems highly probable; and it also seems clear that the few Christian passages are later interpolations from Orosius. If so, the *Origo Constantini imperatoris* is a beautiful example of a short pagan work which was made Christian by the simple addition of a few passages.[1] The Christians could easily take it over because of the relatively neutral character of the original text. The pagans for their part kept away from Christian explosives.

Christian initiative was such that it did not hesitate to appropriate Jewish goods also. Pseudo-Philo's *Liber antiquitatum Biblicarum* was originally a Jewish handbook of Biblical history. It seems to have been written in Hebrew for Jews in the first century A.D., it was later done into Greek, and, to all appearances, in the fourth century it was changed into a Christian handbook and translated into Latin.[2]

The question then arises whether the Christians became the masters of the field also on the higher level of original historical writing and whether here, too, they confirmed their capacity for assimilating without being assimilated.

If the question were simply to be answered by a yes, it would not be worth asking. The traditional forms of higher historiography did not attract the Christians. They invented new ones. These inventions are the most important contributions made to historiography after the fifth century B.C. and before the sixteenth century A.D. Yet the pagans are allowed by the Christians to remain the masters of traditional historiographical forms. To put it briefly, the Christians invented ecclesiastical history and the biography of the saints, but did not try to christianize ordinary political history; and they influenced ordinary biography less than we would expect. In the fourth century A.D. there was no serious attempt to provide a Christian version of, say, Thucydides or Tacitus—to mention two writers who were still being seriously studied. A reinterpretation of ordinary military, political, or diplomatic history in Christian terms was neither achieved nor even attempted. Lactantius in the *De Mortibus persecutorum* is perhaps the only Christian writer to touch upon social and political

---

[1] Text and discussion by R. Cessi in his ed. of the *Anonymus Valesianus* (Rer. Ital. Script., 1913), but his conclusions are not accepted here. The Groningen dissertation by D. J. A. Westerhuis, 1906, is still very valuable. New edition by J. Moreau (Leipzig, 1961).

[2] See the edition by G. Kisch, *Pseudo-Philo's Liber Antiquitatum Biblicarum* (Notre Dame, Indiana, 1949).

events. He does so in a conservative and senatorial spirit which must be embarrassing to those who identify the Christians with the lower middle class, but he never seriously develops his political interpretation: he is not to be compared as an analyst with Ammianus Marcellinus or even with the *Scriptores historiae Augustae*.

The consequence is plain. No real Christian historiography founded upon the political experience of Herodotus, Thucydides, Livy, and Tacitus was transmitted to the Middle Ages. This is already apparent in the sixth century when a military and political historian like Procopius was basically pagan in outlook and technique. When in the fifteenth and sixteenth centuries the humanists rediscovered their Herodotus, Thucydides, Livy, and Tacitus, they rediscovered something for which there was no plain Christian alternative. It is not for me to say whether an alternative was possible: whether an earlier 'Tacitus christianus' would have been less foolish than the post-Reformation one. What I must point out is that the conditions which made Machiavelli and Guicciardini possible originated in the fourth century A.D. The models for political and military history remained irretrievably pagan. In the higher historiography there was nothing comparable with the easy christianizing of the pagan *breviaria*.

Here again Eusebius was the decisive influence. How much he owed to predecessors, and especially to the shadowy Hegesippus, we shall never know, unless new evidence is discovered.[1] But it is fairly clear that Hegesippus wrote apologetic, not history. Apart from him, there is no other name that can seriously compete with Eusebius' for the invention of ecclesiastical history. He was not vainly boasting when he asserted that he was the 'first to enter on the undertaking, as travellers do on some desolate and untrodden way'.[2]

Eusebius, like any other educated man, knew what proper history was. He knew that it was a rhetorical work with a maximum of invented speeches and a minimum of authentic documents. Since he chose to give plenty of documents and refrained

[1] Among the recent literature see K. Mras, *Anz. Oesterr. Akad.* (1958), pp. 143–45; W. Telfer, *Harv. Theol. Rev.* liii (1960), 143–54.

[2] Cf., among many, H. Berkhof, *Die Theologie Eusebius' von Caesarea* (Amsterdam, 1939); Id. *Kirche und Kaiser* (Zürich, 1947); F. E. Cranz, *Harv. Theol. Rev.* xlv (1952), 47–66; K. Heussi, *Wissenschaftl. Zeitschr. Univ. Jena* vii (1957–8), 89–92; F. Scheidweiler, *Zeitschr. f. d. Neut. Wissenschaft* xlix (1958), 123–9; D. S. Wallace-Hadrill, *Eusebius of Caesarea* (London, 1960).

from inventing speeches, he must have intended to produce something different from ordinary history. Did he then intend to produce a preparatory work to history, an ὑπόμνημα? This is hardly credible. First of all, historical ὑπομνήματα were normally confined to contemporary events. Secondly, Eusebius speaks as if he were writing history, and not collecting materials for a future history.

It was Eduard Schwartz who in one of his most whimsical moments suggested that German professors of *Kirchengeschichte* had been the victims of their poor Greek. They had not understood that Ἐκκλησιαστικὴ ἱστορία did not mean *Kirchengeschichte*, but *Materialien zur Kirchengeschichte*. Eduard Schwartz, of course, was fighting his great battle against the isolation of ecclesiastical history in German universities, and we who share his beliefs can hardly blame him for this paradox. But a paradox it was.[1]

Eusebius knew only too well that he was writing a new kind of history. The Christians were a nation in his view. Thus he was writing national history. But his nation had a transcendental origin. Though it had appeared on earth in Augustus' time, it was born in Heaven 'with the first dispensation concerning the Christ himself' (1. i. 8). Such a nation was not fighting ordinary wars. Its struggles were persecutions and heresies. Behind the Christian nation there was Christ, just as the devil was behind its enemies. The ecclesiastical history was bound to be different from ordinary history because it was a history of the struggle against the devil, who tried to pollute the purity of the Christian Church as guaranteed by the apostolic succession.

Having started to collect his materials during Diocletian's persecutions, Eusebius never forgot his original purpose which was to produce factual evidence about the past and about the character of the persecuted Church. He piled up his evidence of quotations from reputable authorities and records in the form that was natural to any ancient controversialist. As he was dealing with a Church that represented a school of thought, there was much he could learn in the matter of presentation from the histories of philosophic schools which he knew well. These dealt with doctrinal controversies, questions of authenticity, successions of *scholarchs*. But he did away with all that was anecdotal and worldly in the pagan biographies of philosophers. This is why we shall never know whether Clemens Alexandrinus was fond of

[1] 'Über Kirchengeschichte' (1908) in *Gesammelte Schriften*, i (1938), 110-30.

eating green figs and of basking in the sun; which are established points in the biography of Zeno the Stoic. At the same time Eusebius certainly had in mind Jewish-Hellenistic historiography, as exemplified for him and for us by Flavius Josephus. In Josephus he found the emphasis on the past, the apologetic tone, the doctrinal digression, the display (though not so lavish) of documents: above all there was the idea of a nation which is different from ordinary pagan nations. Jewish historiography emphatically underlined the importance of the remote past in comparison with recent times and the importance of cult in comparison with politics.

The suggestion that Eusebius combined the methods of philosophic historiography with the approach of Jewish-Hellenistic historiography has at least the merit of being a guide to the sources of his thought. Yet it is far from accounting for all the main features of his work. There were obvious differences between the history of the Church and that of any other institution. Persecution had been an all-pervading factor of Christianity. Heresy was a new conception which (whatever its origins) had hardly the same importance in any other school of thought, even in Judaism. An account of the Christian Church based on the notion of orthodoxy and on its relations with a persecuting power was bound to be something different from any other historical account. The new type of exposition chosen by Eusebius proved to be adequate to the new type of institution represented by the Christian Church. It was founded upon authority and not upon the free judgement of which the pagan historians were proud. His contemporaries felt that he had made a new start. Continuators, imitators, and translators multiplied. Some of them (most particularly Sozomen) tried to be more conventional in their historiographical style, more obedient to rhetorical traditions. None departed from the main structure of Eusebius' creation with its emphasis on the struggle against persecutors and heretics and therefore on the purity and continuity of the doctrinal tradition.

Eusebius introduced a new type of historical exposition which was characterized by the importance attributed to the more remote past, by the central position of doctrinal controversies and by the lavish use of documents.

I am not yet able to answer two questions which are very much on my mind: whether in the Middle Ages there was a school of pure ecclesiastical history from Cassiodorus to Bede, to Adam of Bremen and to John of Salisbury; and whether this school, if any, was characterized by a special interest in documents. What is certain is that from the sixteenth to the eighteenth century ecclesiastical history (especially of the early Church) was treated with a much greater display of erudition, with much more care for minute analysis of the evidence than any other type of history. There is no work in profane history comparable with the Magdeburg Centuriators and with Baronius. Naturally this is the expression of the fiercely controversial character which ecclesiastical history assumed with the Reformation. But we may well wonder whether the ecclesiastical historians of the Renaissance would have entered upon the path of erudition and documentation—and incidentally of illegibility—without the powerful precedent of Eusebius and his immediate pupils. Conversely, we may well wonder whether modern political historiography would ever have changed from rhetoric and pragmatism to footnotes and appendixes without the example of ecclesiastical history. The first man who applied careful scrutiny of the evidence to the history of the Roman empire was Le Nain de Tillemont, who came from ecclesiastical history and worked in both fields. Among the Maurists of St. Germain-des-Prés erudition spread from ecclesiastical to profane, even to literary history. Perhaps we have all underestimated the impact of ecclesiastical history on the development of historical method. A new chapter of historiography begins with Eusebius not only because he invented ecclesiastical history, but because he wrote it with a documentation which is utterly different from that of the pagan historians.[1]

Thus we are brought back to our main point. Eusebius made history positively and negatively by creating ecclesiastical history and by leaving political history alone. In a comparable manner another Christian invented the biography of the saints and left the biography of generals and politicians to the pagans. The inventor was Athanasius, whose life of St. Anthony was promptly made available in Latin by Evagrius. The complicated pattern of suggestions which lies behind the rise of hagiography—*exitus illustrium virorum*, Jewish legends, lives of philosophers, 'aretalogies', &c.—cannot detain us here. The studies by K. Hoil and R. Reitzenstein seem to have established that Athanasius was more

[1] W. Nigg, *Die Kirchengeschichtsschreibung* (Munich, 1934). Cf. H. Zimmermann, 'Ecclesia als Objekt der Historiographie', *Sitzungsb. Akad. Wien*, ccxxxv (1960).

directly inspired by the Pythagorean type of the θεῖος ἀνήρ, such as we find in the life of Apollonius of Tyana by Philostratus and in the life of Pythagoras himself by Iamblichus.[1] Athanasius intended to oppose the Christian saint who works his way to God with the help of God to the pagan philosopher who is practically a god himself. By imparting a mortal blow to the ideal of the pagan philosopher, he managed to produce an ideal type which became extremely popular among ordinary Christians. Only small groups of pagans believed that Pythagoras or Diogenes was the best possible man. The great majority of pagans was more interested in Hercules, Achilles, and Alexander the Great. But in Christian society the saint was soon recognized as the only perfect type of man. This gives hagiography, as begun by Athanasius, its unique place. It outclassed all other types of biography because all the other types of men became inferior to that of the saint. In comparison, the ordinary biography of kings and politicians became insignificant. One of the most important features of the lives of saints is to give a new dimension to historiography by registering the activity of devils in the plural. It is no exaggeration to say that a mass invasion of devils into historiography preceded and accompanied the mass invasion of barbarians into the Roman empire. A full treatment of 'Devils in historiography' must be reserved for a future course at the Warburg Institute on 'Devils and the Classical Tradition'. But so much can be said here: the devils seem to have respected the classical distinction of literary genres. They established themselves in biography, but made only occasional irruptions into the field of *annales*.

The difficulty of writing a Christian biography of a king as distinct from the life of a saint is already apparent in the life of Constantine by Eusebius, though it was produced perhaps twenty years before the composition of the life of St. Anthony by Athanasius. Eusebius had no other choice but to present the life of Constantine as a model of a pious life—παράδειγμα θεοσεβοῦς βίου, as he himself says. The task was certainly not beyond Eusebius' ingenuity, but it flouted anybody's respect for truth. Moreover, it implied neglect of all that counts in a life of a general and a politician: military glory, political success, concern for ordinary

[1] Cf. R Reitzenstein, *Sitzungsb. Heidelberg. Akad.* 1, 1914, n. 8; K. Holl, *Ges. Aufsätze* ii (1928), 249–69; K. Heussi, *Ursprung des Mönchtums* (Tübingen, 1936); A.-J. Festugière, *Rev. Et. Grecques*, 1 (1937), 470–94; H. Dörries, *Nachr. Ges. Wiss. Göttingen*, xiv (1949), 359–410. Cf. also the English translation of the life of St. Anthony by R. T. Meyer (Ancient Christian Writers, x, 1950).

human affairs, and the rest of the passions power carries with it. No wonder that this life of Constantine was never a success, had hardly any influence on later biographies, and found some modern scholars ready to deny the Eusebian authorship even at the risk of being contradicted by papyrological evidence. It continued to be easier for a Christian to work on the life of a saint than to write the life of an emperor. We may sympathize with Eginhard when he decided to go back to Suetonius for his life of Charlemagne.

IV

We can thus see that a direct conflict between Christians and pagans is not to be expected on the higher level of the historiography of the fourth century. The Christians, with all their aggressiveness, kept to their own new types of history and biography. Eusebius' life of Constantine was an experiment not to be repeated—historiographically a blind alley. The pagans were left to cultivate their own fields. This perhaps reinforced their tendency to avoid any direct discussion with their formidable neighbours in the field of historiography. The opposition to Christianity can be guessed rather than demonstrated in the majority of the pagan students of history. It shows itself in the care with which pagan historians of the past—such as Sallust, Livy, and Tacitus—were read and imitated. It is also apparent in the implicit rejection of the most characteristic Christian values, such as humility and poverty. But it seldom takes the form of direct critical remarks. There are two or three sentences in the *Historia Augusta* which sound like a criticism of the Christians. One is the good-humoured remark that in Egypt 'those who worship Serapis are, in fact, Christians and those who call themselves bishops of Christ are in fact devotees of Serapis' (Firmus, viii. 2). In the last sentence of Aurelius Victor's *De Caesaribus* there is perhaps a criticism of Constantius II's Christian ministers: 'ut imperatore ipso praeclarius, ita apparitorum plerisque magis atrox nihil'. But notice with what care the emperor is declared blameless. Finally, there are the well-known criticisms of Ammianus Marcellinus against the Roman clergy and other bishops, such as Bishop George of Alexandria. But here again notice that the same Ammianus praises Christian martyrdom, and respects the blameless life of provincial bishops. The pagans were bound to be prudent—and their mood was altogether that of a generous

Pagan and Christian Historiography in the Fourth Century A.D.

and fair-minded liberalism. The *Historia Augusta* is by no means the big anti-Christian pamphlet which some scholars have seen in it. On the contrary, the ideal emperor Severus Alexander worships Jesus with Abraham in his private chapel. Ammianus Marcellinus makes an effort to disentangle what is *absoluta* and *simplex religio* and what is *anilis superstitio* in Christianity (XXI. xvi. 18). According to him what matters is *virtus*, not paganism or Christianity. As we all know, this attitude is also to be found in Symmachus, in some of the pagan correspondents of St. Augustine and in the Panegyricus by Nazarius (IV. vii. 3). Rufius Festus, who was an unbeliever, but whose pagan sympathies are shown by the disproportionate amount of space he devotes to Julian, is full of deference towards the Christian god of his master Valens: 'Maneat modo concessa dei nutu et ab amico cui credis et creditus es numine indulta felicitas.' 'May long last the happiness that was granted to you by the friendly god whom you trust and to whom you are entrusted.' This is a very decent way of saving one's conscience without offending one's master.

The only exception is Eunapius, whose history of the fourth century was so anti-Christian that, according to Photius, it had to be re-edited in a less offensive form. The greater part of this history is lost, but Eunapius' attitude is clear enough from the extant fragments and even more so from his lives of the Sophists, where Julian is the hero and the apology for Neoplatonic paganism is unbridled. If Julian won victories it was because the right gods helped him. We can still read in the margins of the *Codex Laurentianus* of Eunapius' lives of the Sophists the indignant remarks of one of his Byzantine readers. Eunapius clearly meant his lives of the Sophists to compete with the lives of the Christian saints whose cult he despised (*Vit. soph.* 472). But Eunapius reflects the changed mood of the end of the century when even the most optimistic pagan could no longer nurture illusions about Christian tolerance.[1] Furthermore, his particular type of reaction is that of a professor who wrote for Greek *literati* rather than for the pagan aristocracy of the West. As we observed, the Greek pagans of the East seem to have become vocal only at the end of the century. During the century itself Latin was the main language of pagan historiography.

In the West, among the Latin historians, the resistance to

[1] The *Vitae sophistarum* are now to be read in the ed. by G. Giangrande (Rome, 1956).

Christianity showed itself in a mixture of silence and condescension; Christianity is rarely mentioned. If it is mentioned, kindness and good humour prevail. What counts is the vast zone of silence, the ambiguity which gives Latin pagan historiography of the fourth century its strange imprint of reticence and mystery. Seldom are historians of historiography faced by works so difficult to date, to analyse in their composite nature and to attribute to a definite background. For the first time we come across historical work done in collaboration—which adds to its elusiveness.

The *Historia Augusta* is the classic example of historiographic mystery. The work purports to have been written by six authors at various moments of the reigns of Diocletian and Constantine. Some at least of the alleged authors claim to have written in collaboration. This very claim of team-work is baffling: co-operative 'Cambridge histories' were not common in antiquity. The writing is sensational and unscrupulous, and the forged documents included in this work serve no obvious purpose. One or two passages may point to a post-Constantinian date either for the whole collection or at least for the passages themselves. But the date and the purpose of the *Scriptores historiae Augustae* remain an unsolved problem.

A less famous, but no less remarkable, mystery is the tripartite corpus under the title *Origo gentis Romanae*—a title which incidentally must be translated as 'History of the Roman people'. It includes a history of Roman origins from Saturnus to the murder of Remus, a collection of short biographies from Romulus to Augustus (the so-called *De viris illustribus*), and, finally, short and accomplished biographies of Roman emperors to A.D. 360. The imperial biographies were written by Aurelius Victor whom we know to have been a friend of Julian and a *praefectus urbi* under Theodosius. The other two sections of the trilogy are anonymous: they were written by two different authors, neither of whom can be identical with Aurelius Victor. A fourth man acted as editor and put together the three pamphlets to form the present trilogy. All these people were pagan. I have elsewhere suggested that the editor of the trilogy may have tried to produce a complete pagan history of Rome at the time of the emperor Julian. But this is a pure guess, though not an unreasonable one I trust. The compiler himself does not say anything about the precise meaning and date of his compilation. He may have known the Christian

Chronographer of 354: he has certainly adopted a compositional scheme which reminds us of the *Chronica urbis Romae* included in the Chronographer of 354. What is extraordinary and, to my mind, important in this trilogy is the absence of any direct allusion to Christianity. The author is pagan: there is no reference to the Christians.

Ammianus Marcellinus is not a mystery in the sense in which the *Historia Augusta* and the tripartite *Origo gentis Romanae* are mysteries.[1] He speaks about himself more than the majority of the ancient historians ever did. His keen eye is constantly on the look-out for individual features. He is a man full of delightful curiosity. Yet what do we ultimately know about Ammianus? He does not even tell us why he, a Greek from Antioch, chose Latin as his literary language. He says very little about the theological controversies of his time and almost nothing about the religious feelings of the people he must have known best. Magic seems to interest him more than theology. Yet theology counted most. He was a soldier. Yet he is apparently not interested in military organization. He has an uncanny ability to describe a character without defining a situation. He never gives himself away. His histories might have for motto his own words: 'quisquis igitur dicta considerat, perpendat etiam cetera quae tacentur' (XXIX. iii. 1). It is symbolic that the greatest feat of his military career was to escape unnoticed from besieged Amida while the Persians were breaking into the city. He may have become more reticent about religion in the books XXVI–XXXI which he wrote after 392 when Theodosius hardened against the pagans. But even the earlier books, written as they were in more tolerant years, are not much more explicit. He dislikes the Germans, yet his unwillingness to analyse the causes of the barbarian successes is notorious. He deplores the greed and avarice of some Roman aristocrats, especially of the Anicii who were just then turning to Christianity. But he cannot have had any general objection against the senatorial class among which he had his pagan friends, Praetextatus, Eupraxius, and Symmachus. An acute and passionate judge of individuals, he avoids our direct questions

[1] It will be enough to refer to the two well-known monographs on Ammianus by W. Ensslin (*Klio*, Beiheft xvi, 1923) and E. A. Thompson (Cambridge, 1947). Full bibliography will be found in Ch. P. Th. Naudé, *Am. M. in die lig van die antieke Geskiedskrywing* (diss. Leiden, 1956). V. S. Sokolov, *Vestnik Drevnej Istorii*, 1959, 4, 43–62. Cf. also S. Mazzarino, 'La propaganda senatoriale nel tardo impero', *Doxa*, iv (1951), 121–48. Id. 'La democratizzazione della cultura nel Basso Impero', *Rapports XI Congrès Intern. Sciences Historiques*, ii (Stockholm, 1960), 35–54. L. Dillemann, *Syria*, xxxviii (1961), 87–158.

and leaves us wondering. His master Tacitus is a paragon of directness by comparison.

If reticence, love of the pagan past, moderation, and erudition were the prominent features of these Latin historians, the Christians did not have much to fear from their work. Historians of this kind could please other historians. Ammianus Marcellinus, the *Historia Augusta*, and the now lost histories by Nicomachus Flavianus, were read in the sixth century in the circle of Symmachus and Cassiodorus, when there was a revival of interest in Roman history.[1] But Ammianus, the *Historia Augusta*, and Aurelius Victor were never popular for all we know. The fact that at least one of these historical works, the *Historia Augusta*, is guilty of professional dishonesty is not a sign of strength for historiography of this kind. It would be unfair to generalize when so much of the fourth-century historical production is lost. Within the limits of our knowledge we are constantly reminded of the fact that the true pagans of the fourth century found their most profound satisfaction not in writing new history, but in copying existing histories, trying to solve problems of antiquarianism, commenting on Virgil and other classics, reading and writing poetry in a pagan spirit. The real passion was in those who tried to revive the past by direct religious worship, by discussion of ancient customs, by the study of ancient writers. Our instinct is right, I think, when we consider Macrobius, Symmachus, Servius, and Donatus more typically pagan than Ammianus Marcellinus. Festus who wrote the historical *breviarium* has sometimes been identified with Festus Avienus, the translator of Aratus. The identification is not to be maintained. The historian Festus was even accused of atheism by Eunapius (p. 481). The poet Festus Avienus, a friend of the Nicomachi Flaviani, was warmly devoted to Jupiter and to the Etruscan goddess Nortia of his native country.[2] When he died, his son wrote on his tomb that Jupiter was opening the skies to him—the son echoing in his lines his father's lines:

> nam Iuppiter aethram
> pandit, Feste, tibi candidus ut venias
> Iamque venis (*I.L.S.* 2944)

This seems to have been the driving spirit of dying paganism in the West. Therefore, St. Augustine, who knew where to look

---

[1] See my *Secondo Contributo alla storia degli studi classici* (1960), p. 198.
[2] Cf. A. Garroni, *Bull. Comm. Arch. Com.* (1915), pp. 123-35.

for the real enemy, was not worried by contemporary pagan historians in the Latin tongue, such as Ammianus Marcellinus. Greek historians, such as Eunapius, worried him even less because he probably did not know them: his command of Greek was modest. But he was disturbed by the idealization of the Roman past which he found in fourth-century Latin antiquarians, poets, and commentators of poets. He saw in them the roots of the new resistance against Christianity which became evident towards the end of the century. He went back to the sources of their antiquarianism, and primarily to Varro, in order to undermine the foundations of their work. He fought the antiquarians, the sentimental and emotional pagans, of his time—not the contemporary historians. The latter might be left to die from natural causes. But the former had to be fought. The result is to be seen in the *De civitate dei*. It is also to be seen in the work of St. Augustine's pupil Orosius who was induced by him to write against the readers of Livy, not against the readers of the *Historia Augusta* or of Ammianus. All went according to plan, except that the pagan historians of the fourth century were not really going to die. They were only going to sleep for some centuries. They belonged to that classical tradition in historiography for which ecclesiastical history, whatever its merits, was no substitute. Though we may have learnt to check our references from Eusebius—and this was no small gain—we are still the disciples of Herodotus and Thucydides: we still learn our history of the late empire from Ammianus Marcellinus.[1]

[1] Cf. also J. Sirinelli, *Les Vues historiques d'Eusèbe de Césarée durant la période prénicéenne*, thèse (Paris, 1961), and W. Lammers (ed.), *Geschichtsdenken und Geschichtsbild im Mittelalter* (Darmstadt, 1961) with bibl.

V

The Survival of Magic Arts

A. A. BARB

THE comfortable belief in evolution which used to make scholars regard magic as a crude stage in human development preceding, and only under certain unfavourable social conditions retarding, the development of science and religion proper—this belief has been badly shattered by what we have lived to see in the present century.[1] Nowadays, when hardly anybody with open eyes still believes in optimistic evolutionism, it seems to be the general tendency to deny altogether that a fundamental difference exists between magic and religion and to stress that magical elements form part of even the most highly developed religious systems, at least in the form in which these are generally practised.[2] A paper on Magic and Religion published last year[3] maintains, for instance, 'that the scientific debate over the relation between "magic" and "religion" is a discussion of an artificial problem created by defining religion on the ideal pattern of Christianity. The elements of man's beliefs and ceremonies concerning the supernatural powers which did not coincide with this ideal type of religion was—and is—called "magic". . . . Magic became—and still becomes—a refuse-heap for the elements which are not sufficiently "valuable" to get a place within "religion".' And the author concludes: 'The study of comparative religion would win in clearness, honesty and stringency, the aspects of valuation would be avoided etc. if the term "magic" were given a decent burial.'

Well, if this is so I had better pack up and leave the room without delivering my lecture. But I beg to differ. I have not come to bury the term 'Magic'; but neither do I want to praise what it denominates (as certain neo-gnostic occultists are nowadays

[1] G. Widengren, 'Evolutionism and the Problem of the Origin of Religion', *Ethnos*, x (1945), 57 ff. Cf. also the literature quoted by M. Eliade, *Traité d'histoire des religions* (1949), pp. 45 f.

[2] R. Ehnmark, 'Religion and Magic', *Ethnos*, xxi (1956), 1 ff.; E. R. Goodenough, *Jewish Symbols in the Greco-Roman Period*, ii (1953), 155–61.

[3] O. Pettersson, 'Magic–Religion', *Ethnos*, xxii (1957), 109 ff.

inclined to do). The fundamental difference between magic and religion is still the same as it always was. On the one hand, we have the religious man, offering his adorations in humble submission to the Deity; always careful to add to any supplication the reservation 'if it be according to Thy will'. On the other hand, we have the magician, attempting to force the supernatural powers to accomplish what he desires and avert what he fears.

This difference stands in spite of those who—quite rightly—object that not one man in a thousand fully lives up to this theoretical idea of religion and that there are in ritual and liturgy elements which scarcely differ from magical acts and incantations. Let me try to clarify my meaning by taking food as a simile, which is not exactly inappropriate if you remember the Biblical saying that man 'does not live by bread alone'. As Man is no longer in his original paradisal state, his religion tends by nature to deteriorate, just as food deteriorates through various stages, becoming first stale, then tainted, decayed, and finally poisonous. Magic cannot develop without religion—without the belief in the supernatural—and to that extent it cannot be separated from religion. But I propose to reverse the evolutionist thesis.[1] Religion does not evolve from primitive magic; on the contrary magic derives from religion, which, as it becomes tainted by human frailty, deteriorates into so-called white magic (the Greeks called it *theurgia*—working things divine[2]), gradually losing its whiteness and turning from more or less dirty grey into black magic, called in Greek *goēteia*, from the evil-sounding recitation of spells. Both are the illicit arts 'nefariae curiositatis', to use the words of St. Augustine, 'quam vel magian vel detestabiliore nomine goetian vel honorabiliore theurgian vocant'.[3] To complain that the current use of the word magic is libellous would be —to take up our simile again—as if we were to complain that the authorities concerned condemn rotten food to the refuse-heap as unfit for human consumption. Admittedly, their decision will not always be beyond dispute. It may be that one might argue

---

[1] I now find similar views expressed by D. W. Gundry in *Man*, lix (1959), 17 ('Magic and religion tend to exist side by side . . ., the former being a degeneration of the latter').

[2] Cf. H. Lewy, *Chaldaean Oracles and Theurgy* (Cairo, 1956), pp. 461 ff. Th. Hopfner's explanation of the term as 'compelling or forcing the Gods' (Pauly-Wissowa, *Realencyclopädie*, s.v. 'Theurgie') appears less convincing. For other explanations see S. Eitrem in *Symbolae Osloenses*, xxii (1942), 49 f.

[3] Augustine, *De civ. dei*, x. 8. 'The magical arts of the Chaldaean *Theurgists* did not differ in essentials from their competitors (the "*Goēts*")', states H. Lewy, op. cit., p. 238; cf. also S. Eitrem, loc. cit., pp. 72 f.

that sometimes quite nourishing foodstuff has been wasted, or, on the other hand, that food is passed as fit which causes severe indigestion to delicate stomachs; or that certain substances are pleasanter and more easily digestible when slightly 'high'. But the line has to be drawn somewhere if the daily bread of the community is to be kept safe from deadly poison. Whoever does not obtain his wholesome food from the acknowledged and controlled sources and instead fetches it stealthily from the refuse-heap does so not only at his own peril but also endangers the health and life of the community and has to be restrained as far as possible. One more observation: food-poisoning is caused more frequently by imported food than by home-grown stuff; just so we find again and again that the closest connexion exists between magic and alien imported cults.

The task, which is not always easy, of drawing this line between fit and unfit supernatural fare, if I may say so, has (perhaps with the exception of Ancient Egypt)[1] consistently been the concern of the lawful authorities, in Rome as elsewhere.[2] It confronted the *decemviri* who compiled the law of the twelve tables, the senate in its decision *De Bacchanalibus*, the dictator Sulla in his *Lex Cornelia de veneficiis*.[3] (The word *venenum*, originally a magic love-potion, gradually came to be used for all magic potions—good or evil, like the Greek φάρμακον—and only later meant what we call poison: *veneficium* always refers to magic generally.) The problem again faced Augustus, when he was invested with the office of *pontifex maximus* and ordered over 2,000 volumes of spurious books of divination to be burned.[4] It arose under Tiberius when professional divination was made a criminal offence and foreign soothsayers were deported from Italy. It was occasionally exaggerated to the point of absurdity when, for instance (if we can trust the *Scriptores historiae Augustae*), Caracalla condemned as criminals even those who wore magical amulets as a protection against malaria.[5] However, in a more

---

[1] Appropriately, however, an eminent egyptologist calls magic a cancerous growth (*Krebsgeschwür*) in the Egyptian religion (H. Junker as quoted by G. Thausing, 'Ethik und Magie', in *Wiener Zeitschrift f. d. Kunde des Morgenlandes*, liv (1957), 205 ff.). [See Addenda, p. 125.]

[2] For classical Greece cf. S. Eitrem in *Symbolae Osloenses*, xxi (1941), 51 ff. (Plato), 56 ff. (Athens).

[3] Julius Paulus, *Sentent.* v, xxiii, esp. §§ 14 ff.

[4] Sueton, *Augustus*, xxxi. 1; for his guiding ideas cf. also *Dio Cassius*, LII. xxxvi. 3. This standpoint of sound religious conservatism we find already two centuries earlier in Cato, *De agricultura*, v. 4—cf. E. Maróti, 'Das Verbot der Weissager bei Cato', *Annales Univ. Scient. Budapest.*, Sect. philol., i (1957), 91 ff.   [5] *Vita Caracallae*, v. 7.

The Survival of Magic Arts

reliable source, the fourth-century Roman historian Ammianus Marcellinus, we find practically the same words: reporting from his own lifetime he tells us that under Constantius II capital punishment threatened both people who wore such amulets and those remotely suspected of some kind of necromancy:

> For if anyone wore on his neck an amulet against the quartan ague or any other complaint, or was accused by the testimony of the evil-disposed of passing by a grave in the evening, on the ground that he was a dealer in poisons [the Latin has *veneficus* which means, as I have said before, a sorcerer], or a gatherer of the horrors of tombs and the vain illusions of the ghosts that walk there [that means a necromancer], he was condemned to capital punishment and so perished.[1]

We see here the most innocent 'white magic'—quite obviously such amulets were worn in the Roman empire as generally as lucky charms are worn today, and even a scholar like Galen, physician in ordinary to the Emperor Commodus, recommends a certain engraved stone as an effective amulet against dyspepsia[2] —we see this white magic treated on the same level as the blackest communication with the evil spirits of the dead. True, as Ammianus Marcellinus suggests, what lies behind such measures is the malevolence of informers and the constant fears of a superstitious emperor for his own safety. We remember the story in Philostratus of how the Emperor Domitian, three centuries earlier, received in audience the great (and if we are to believe his biographer of course snow-white) magician Apollonius of Tyana, and insisted that the magician should first deposit any amulet he might wear, any kind of book, even any writing, before being admitted into the imperial presence.[3] And as regards the 'horrors of tombs', the *sepulcrum horrores* mentioned by Ammianus, who has not read in Tacitus what, after the mysterious death of his Imperial Highness Prince Germanicus, was discovered under the floor and hidden in the walls of the princely residence?[4] 'The remains of human bodies, spells, curses, leaden tablets engraved with the name Germanicus [I shall have more

---

[1] Ammianus Marcellinus, XIX. xii. 13; I am quoting from the translation in the Loeb Classical Library, i. 541. Cf. also *Cod. Theod.* IX. xvi. 7 for similar measures under Valentinian and Valens.

[2] Galenus, *De simpl.* x. 19; cf. C. Bonner, *Studies in Magical Amulets* (Michigan, Ohio, 1950), p. 54, and Alexander Trallianus (ed. Puschmann), ii. 375, 579.

[3] Philostratus, *Vita Apollonii*, viii. 3.

[4] Tacitus, *Annales*, ii. 69; I am quoting from the translation in the Loeb Classical Library, ii. 495.

to say about these leaden tablets later], charred and blood-smeared ashes (from the funeral pyre), and others of the implements of witchcraft by which it is believed the living soul can be devoted to the powers of the grave.'

But apart from the personal fears and other all-too-human shortcomings, the task of a Roman emperor as health officer in things supernatural became increasingly difficult when the syncretistic, rotting refuse-heap of the dead and dying religions of the whole ancient world grew to mountainous height while wholesome supernatural food became scarce. It was perhaps never more difficult than in the fourth century. A thin but powerful layer of die-hard aristocrats and intellectuals tried stubbornly to preserve the religion by which their forefathers had built and cemented the Roman empire. For them the new Christian belief must have appeared to be detestable oriental superstition, and where it was successful, it must have seemed even more detestable magic, the more so, as for centuries persecutions had compelled Christianity to work of necessity in secrecy and darkness, those generally accepted characteristics of the magic arts. We know from St. Augustine[1] that certain people, trusting to a spurious oracle, saw in St. Peter an arch-magician,[2] who by his evil arts had brought it about that belief in Christ should survive for 365 years: 'Petrum autem maleficia fecisse ... ut coleretur Christi nomen per trecentos sexaginta quinque annos ...'. (We find here that ominous number of the days of the year which played a role in Gnostic systems and is contained in the word ABRAXAS, the *vox magica* kat'exochen of late antique sorcery.)[3] At the end of this period Christianity would suddenly disappear. A piece of wishful thinking, which attempted to explain the success, obviously quite preternatural, of that absurd religion, and which held out the hope of its final defeat. Christianity, on the other hand, now victoriously coming into the open, and supported mainly by the less-educated masses, was tainted with all the superstitions of the man in the street. And even where the clear voices of the New Testament and the Fathers of the Church were heard, the existence of evil demons (their legions swelled by all the pagan deities) and of powerful angels was unequivocally proclaimed, testifying for the masses to the real

---

[1] Augustine, *De civ. dei*, xviii. 53.

[2] Jesus himself, according to Bab. Talmud, *Sanhedrin*, vi. 1 (fol. 43a), was alleged to have been executed as a sorcerer! Cf. also the Koran, v. 110.

[3] Cf. A. A. Barb, 'Abraxas-Studien', in *Hommage à W. Deonna* (Brussels, 1957), pp. 67 ff.

existence of those infernal and celestial powers invoked by the current magic arts.

Thus, where we might have expected that evangelical truth, set free by Constantine the Great, would dispel all the unsavoury shadows of magic-ridden centuries, we find in the fourth century conditions which in many respects closely resemble the worst witch-hunting centuries at the end of the Middle Ages. With one difference, however: the Church, which (I think not quite fairly) is usually held more or less responsible for the witch scares flaring up, for instance, in the fifteenth century, had no part in the sad business of the fourth. It was the temporal power alone, that is to say, the emperor, who had actively to deal with these problems, just like the magistrates and rulers before him throughout antiquity. It cannot be excluded (nor as far as I can see can it be proved) that the actions of the emperors—from Constantine the Great all of them more or less convinced Christians—were in some way influenced by Christian doctrine in this respect. But while the Church consistently and uncompromisingly refused to make any distinction between magic and paganism, the emperors half-heartedly tolerated the old religious institutions which had been part and parcel of Roman public administration, but turned savagely against the prevalence of sorcery. The *haruspices*, whose office it was to interpret the abnormalities found in the intestines of sacrificial animals, and other portents, like lightnings, &c., were an ancient institution taken over from the Etruscans, who themselves had taken it over from the still older religion of the Near East. But the decay which had made these functionaries of semi-official Roman religion into private dispensers of eagerly sought evil magic had become clear even when the emperor Tiberius had made it an offence to consult them in private without witnesses.[1] I do not think it is quite fair to see here only the personal fears of a tyrant. For three centuries later Constantine the Great also found it necessary to decree that no *haruspex* should enter a private house, not even that of his best personal friend, on penalty of being burned alive, while the householder faced proscription and deportation; and Constantine added that whoever brought such cases to the knowledge of the authorities should not be considered a common informer but deserving of reward. He remarks somewhat contemptuously that if anybody wanted to make use of these superstitious practices he might do

[1] Sueton. *Tiberius*, lxiii.

so by all means as long as it was done openly, at one of the public shrines and according to the official rites.[1] However, hardly a year later, possibly under the pressure of the Roman conservatives,[2] Constantine turns the full rigour of the law only on those who contrive to injure their fellow men by magical arts or corrupt the innocent by love charms. The 'remedia humanis quaesita corporibus' are no longer a criminal offence (no execution for the wearers of, say, malaria-amulets, as under Caracalla before or under Constantius II after him), nor is it a criminal offence in agricultural regions to take measures against thunderstorms and the like, which may threaten the harvest.[3] This is a concession to 'white' magic which the Church would not have tolerated: for the Fathers there is—I have quoted St. Augustine before—no fundamental difference between *theurgia* and *goetia*. Both are *magia* founded on *idolatria*. In the same fourth century St. John Chrysostom praises as a martyr the steadfast Christian mother who would rather see her sick child or her husband die than try on them one of those magic amulets which were generally used. 'Even if ten thousand who deal in them advance philosophical arguments, telling her "All we do is to invoke God, nothing else" or similar stuff, the faithful old woman knows that this is idolatry.' If the objection is made 'But this is not idolatry but merely a charm' (the Greek has ἐπῳδή, incantation), Chrysostom answers: 'That precisely is the satanic idea, the method of the Devil, to gloss over the going astray and to offer the noxious drug (δηλητήριον φάρμακον) in a coating of honey.' One incantation only (if I may call it so) is left to the faithful: to praise the will of God; and one effective action or πρᾶξις (to use the Greek word which in the professional language of magic meant the ceremonial rituals): to make the sign of the cross.[4] This is stern, uncompromising religious theory. Nevertheless, in practice probably a very substantial percentage of contemporary Christians wore amulets of some kind or other. If this were not so, this part of the homily would not make sense, any more than similar condemnations by other Christian authors,[5]

[1] *Cod. Theod.* ix. xvi. 1–2. Cf. with this last passage Plato, *Leges*, x. 909 D f. For the activities of these Haruspices cf. the similar prohibition in Canon XXIV of the Synod of Ancyra (C. J. Hefele, *Conciliengeschichte*, i, 2nd ed., 24).
[2] Cf. A. Alföldi, *The Conversion of Constantine and Pagan Rome* (1948), pp. 77 f.
[3] *Cod. Theod.* ix. xvi. 3; cf. also ibid. xvi. x. 1.
[4] Chrysostom, *In epist. ad Coloss.*, Cap. III, Homil. viii. 5 = Migne, *P.G.* lxii. 357/8.
[5] Cf., for example, the references in F. X. Kraus, *Realencyclopädie der christl. Altertümer*, i. (1882), 49 f.

The Survival of Magic Arts

for Chrysostom's preaching is addressed to Christians, not to pagans. But would it not be some kind of magic act even to make the sign of the cross, if it were done without at the same time believing in and making submission to the true God?[1] As for pastoral duty, alas, there arose the problem of how far the standard of stern theory might be lowered,[2] to save from religious starvation the many, whose systems would not tolerate 'over-spiritualized' food, without poisoning them with some Christian brand of magic. That some kind of specifically Christian magic had in fact developed is clear from rulings of the Synod of Laodicea in the middle of the century when it was found necessary to forbid Christian clerics in major or minor orders to be magicians, charmers, soothsayers, or astrologers, or to fabricate amulets; wearers of such amulets were to be banned from the Christian community.[3] Incidentally, this same Council of Laodicea had to forbid the exaggerated cult of angels, which had apparently assumed the forms of magic.[4] At any rate the Church had her clearly and uncompromisingly defined dogmatic theology ('Christianam religionem absolutam et simplicem' as even the pagan Ammianus Marcellinus remarked with admiration)[5] to fall back upon where things threatened to get out of hand, when religion became more than slightly putrid.

The civil authority on the other hand, the emperors of the fourth century, were less lucky. No easy classification for them of magic, white or black, as a subsection of idolatry, that is pagan religion generally, and therefore evil. Contrary to Gibbon's suggestion, repeated by many subsequent historians, there is not, it must be stressed, a single imperial decree before Theodosius at the end of the century which under Christian influence prohibits any institution of the established pagan religion of the Roman state, as far as—and this is important—genuine public institutions, defined and ordered by sacred law, are concerned.[6] Where imperial decrees seem to condemn and forbid pagan

---

[1] Thus Julian the Apostate was alleged to have used this sign when frightened by demons, cf. Gregor. Nanzianz., *Oratio IV in Julianum*, lv–lvi = Migne, *P.G.* xxxv. 577–9.

[2] Cf. also C. Schneider, *Geistesgeschichte des antiken Christentums*, i (1954), 541 ff.

[3] Hefele, *Conciliengeschichte*, loc. cit., p. 770 (Can. 36). But cf. the 'Prophecy' (not 'soothsaying') by the Egyptian Christian hermit Johannes for Theodosius, as contrasted with the 'Curiositates sacrilegae et illicitae' by Augustine (*De civ. dei*, v. 26).

[4] Ibid., pp. 768 f. (Can. 35).

[5] Amm. Marc. xxi. xvi. 18.

[6] Cf. J. Maurice, 'Le Terreur de la magie au IVᵉ siècle', *Revue Historique de Droit français et étranger*, ser. iv (1927), 108 ff.; F. Martroye, 'La Répression de la magie et le culte des gentils au IVᵉ siècle', ibid. ix (1930), 669 ff.

religious practices as superstitions[1] they are concerned with what we should today call 'private devotions' (though 'devotions' might not always be the right expression here), practices which had grown up around and within the old religious institutions which had gradually become an empty shell. The intellectuals and aristocrats filled this empty shell for themselves with Stoic and Neoplatonic pseudo-philosophy, fatalistic astrology, or spiritualistic demonology, with the white magic of *theurgia*. The masses filled it with all the refuse of superstitions, questionable white magic, and an apparently alarming amount of *goetia*, that is to say unequivocal black sorcery. The Church, as I have said, had the dogma of divinely revealed truth as her theoretical support. The emperors, looking for guidance, found themselves on the horns of a dilemma. They wavered between respect for the empty husk of Roman paganism in which they no longer believed, and uncertain belief in a diluted Christianity, the full requirements of which they neither attempted to fulfil themselves nor dared to enforce on the state. In any case neither pagan nor Christian religion questioned the reality of good and evil spirits, the demons apparently far outnumbering the angels. The result was a state of vacillation between condonation and—more often —merciless savagery against any kind of magic, in which the emperors saw, or were advised to see, an affront, if not a plain danger, to their personal *majestas*. It is one of the ironies of history that, while the fashionable pagan philosophers of the Neoplatonic school glorified 'white' magic as *theurgia*, the decrees of the Christian emperors of the same century were actually far more consistent with Plato's strict tenets of the criminal character of the magic arts, as he set them out in the *Nomoi* of his later years.[2] I have already quoted a passage from Ammianus about the draconic measures of Constantius II against magical practices. In another chapter he writes:

If anyone consulted a soothsayer about the squeaking of a fieldmouse, or about the meeting with a weasel on the way, or any like portent, or used some old wife's charm to relieve pain (a thing which even medical authority allows), he was indicted (from what source he could not guess), was haled into court, and suffered death as penalty.[3]

There was a shrine of the age-old popular and rather undefined and slightly comic god Besa at Abydos in Egypt, that Eldorado of

[1] *Cod. Theod.* XVI. x. 2 ff.   [2] Plato, *Leges*, x. 908–910; xi. 933.
[3] Amm. Marc. XVI. viii. 1.

The Survival of Magic Arts

the magic arts, the role of which in the Roman empire, as regards the renown of all things mystic and theosophical,[1] might be compared to that which India used to play for the modern West. For some reason the oracle established there became fashionable at the time of Constantius and was consulted even by the upper classes. Some written petitions, alleged to have sinister intentions, were found by informers and sent to the emperor. He immediately dispatched his witch-hunter or grand-inquisitor, with unrestricted powers, a certain Paulus whom grim popular wit nick-named Tartareus ('Hell-fire Paul'). As we read in Ammianus, Paul established a court in a secluded city of Palestine, halfway between the great cities of Alexandria and Antiochia, which supplied most of his victims, and a reign of terror ensued.[2] With all due respect for Ammianus' generally acknowledged impartiality in these passages we must make allowances for his tendency towards over-statement and sensationalism.[3] But the three original decrees of Constantius II, incorporated later in the *Corpus iuris civilis*, show plainly the emperor's savagery against the large number of people making use of witchcraft, the 'multi magicis artibus usi', among whom are specified spell-casters, *haruspices* and astrologers, Chaldaeans, soothsayers, interpreters of dreams, and common sorcerers—all of them to suffer death for their activities. Even the aristocrat, otherwise legally exempt from torture, 'cruciatus et tormenta non fugiat'. If, though convicted, they persist in protesting their innocence, they must be put on the rack and the 'iron claws of the executioner must dig into their sides'.[4] There are certain decrees of Constantius which seem to go beyond the condemnation of the magic arts and to attack and restrict pagan religion as such. But if we evaluate the facts soberly we see that the intention of distinguishing magic from the old Roman religion was not abandoned. Like his predecessors and successors on the throne, including Valentinian I, Constantius retained among his titles that of *pontifex maximus*. When, for instance, during a threat of famine in Rome, the grain-ships were delayed by gales and the Prefect of Rome went to the temple of Castor and Pollux at Ostia to sacrifice to these patrons of sailors—with immediate success, as we read in

---

[1] Cf. also *Amm. Marc.* XXII. xvi. 17-22.
[2] Id. XIX. xii. 1 ff.
[3] Cf. A. Alföldi, *A Conflict of Ideas in the Late Roman Empire. The Clash between the Senate and Valentinian I* (1952), p. 3.
[4] *Cod. Theod.* IX. xvi. 4-6 = *Cod. Justin.* IX. xviii. 5-7.

Ammianus[1]—there could be no question of his doing something prohibited. Such official acts were quite a different thing from what Constantius had in mind when he ordered: 'Cesset superstitio, sacrificiorum aboleatur insania' or 'placuit claudi protinus templa',[2] or made similar prohibitions, which were bound to offend, in their ill-tempered harshness, even blamelessly religious pagans.

This harshness may well have contributed to the momentum of the pagan reaction, which burst forth under Constantius' successor Julian the Apostate, just at the time (*nota bene!*) when, according to the pagan prophecy I have already mentioned, the spell of the Christian sorcerer Peter was expected to come to an end. But after the short pagan interlude, the Christian emperor Valentinian I, more balanced than Constantius and more in harmony with the tactics and aims of Constantine the Great, again proclaimed freedom for both pagan and Christian religion in unmistakable terms. He has nothing, so he announces in one of his edicts, against the *haruspices* (to return to our old whipping-boys), nor against any kind of religion authorized by his forefathers ('aliquam concessam a maioribus religionem'). 'Nec haruspicinam reprehendimus, sed nocenter exerceri vetamus.'[3] But capital punishment awaits anyone who resorts 'at night to evil imprecations, magic rituals or necromantic sacrifices'.[4] Nor is there now any concession for 'white' magic. Prohibited is the consultation of the 'Mathematici', the astrologers, whether by night or day, in public or in private. Both parties to such consultations must be executed; for—the emperor adds—'to learn these forbidden things is not less criminal than to teach them'.[5] The extant books of Ammianus Marcellinus—even if we allow for his sensationalism and his personal dislike of Valentinian I—abound in case histories which show the appalling way in which these laws were handled. A simple-minded old woman, called in to cure the malaria of the daughter of the imperial governor of Asia, with an innocent charm ('levi carmine', writes Ammianus), was condemned to be executed as a criminal by the same girl's father. A horoscope for somebody called Valens was found among the papers of a distinguished citizen; although he insisted that this horoscope referred to his long dead brother of this name and not to Valens, the brother and co-emperor of Valentinian, a

---

[1] Amm. Marc. xix. x. 4.
[2] Cf. *Cod. Theod.* xvi. x. 2–6.
[3] Ibid. ix. xvi. 9.
[4] Ibid. ix. xvi. 7.
[5] Ibid. ix. xvi. 8.

The Survival of Magic Arts

contention which he offered to prove, he was tortured and killed.[1] Torture and execution were also the fate of a nobleman and high official for killing an ass, allegedly as a magic sacrifice, in spite of his defence that it was meant as a cure for his falling hair.[2] In the public bath 'a young man was seen to touch alternately with the fingers of either hand first the marble tiles and then his breast and to count the seven vowels, thinking it a helpful remedy for a stomach trouble'. Now these seven vowels of the Greek alphabet, co-ordinated with the seven planets and repeated in endless permutations, were, as we know from magic papyri and engraved stones, the stock-in-trade of every kind of late antique magic, even the whitest. Under Christian emperors this kind of vowel-permutation, now co-ordinated with the names of the seven archangels, was used in Asia Minor in an inscription in the theatre of Miletus (which had been adapted for use as a fortress) placing the town and its inhabitants under the protection of the supernatural powers.[3] In the fifth century such things might have passed. In the fourth century the unfortunate young man with his magical kind of counting-out game was hauled into court, tortured and beheaded.[4]

If there were no time limit for my lecture I might, I am afraid, go on indefinitely culling similar stories from the work of Ammianus, although he tells us that he has no intention of relating all such cases that he knows of since he is mainly interested in those involving better-class people.[5] But a few words must be said about the famous trial of the year 371 in Antiochia, the *cause célèbre* of the reign of the emperors Valentinian and Valens.[6] High treason (*crimen majestatis*) and magic practices[7] are interwoven in this case by which hundreds of people of all classes were led to torture and execution, accused, justly or unjustly, of taking part in an attempt to replace the emperor Valens by a brilliant young man of distinguished family and position, named Theodorus. The wire-pullers behind this plot employed two experts in divination, called Hilarius and Patricius, to discover by magical means the name of Valens' successor to the throne. Ammianus, who apparently went out of his way to study carefully the minutes of the proceedings—if indeed he was not an eyewitness—gives us an excerpt from the verbal statement of

---

[1] Amm. Marc. xxix. ii. 26–27. [2] Ibid. xxx. v. 11.
[3] Cf. Th. Hopfner, *Griechisch-ägyptischer Offenbarungszauber* i (1921), § 151.
[4] Amm. Marc. xxix. ii. 28. [5] Ibid. xxviii. i. 15.
[6] Ibid., xxix. i. 5 ff. [7] Cf. Julius Paulus, *Sentent.* v. 21.

Hilarius and Patricius in court.[1] According to this they constructed from olive twigs—in imitation of the Delphic oracle of Apollo—a small three-legged table (which was actually produced in court), consecrating it with the usual secret incantations and lengthy ritual ceremonies. When this table had been placed in the middle of a house which had been purified thoroughly by incense, they laid on it an exactly circular dish made from an alloy of various metals. Round the rim of this dish, at carefully measured intervals, were engraved the twenty-four letters of the Greek alphabet. The celebrant—or should we say medium?—in ceremonial priestly attire, stood above the dish, holding a consecrated magic ring swinging from a thread. This ring jumped fitfully and finally halted above single letters which accumulated to form words, which in turn formed elegant Greek hexameters of the kind by which the famous oracles of old proclaimed their answers. When questioned about the *name* of the successor to the throne, the ring jumped to the letters Θ, E, O, and Δ (Theod ...), at which moment one of those present cried out that inexorable fate had proclaimed the name of Theodoros—whereupon the session broke up, probably just as any spiritualistic meeting today would have to be discontinued after such an undisciplined incident.

Allow me now to interrupt the report of this trial for a short digression. A lucky find during the excavations in Pergamum, half a century ago, brought to light what might be called the tool-chest of a professional magician, probably of the third century.[2] It contained among other things a triangular table of just this kind, a round dish and two magic rings, quite obviously destined for the same procedure of divination for which the two accused had used rather more primitive tools. The little table, carefully cast in bronze and engraved (not simply an affair of olive-twigs), displays magical inscriptions invoking Hecate, the principal goddess of Graeco-Roman magic, who is also represented full length in her threefold image. The round dish, divided into carefully measured sections, like the one mentioned in the trial, does not show merely the letters of the Greek alpha-

---

[1] Amm. Marc. xxix. i. 28–33. Similarly Zosimus, iv. 13; a different and preposterous tradition (Cock-oracle, Libanius, Jamblichus!) by Cedrenus (eleventh century), see Migne, P.G. cxxi. 598, and Zonaras (twelfth century), P.G. cxxxiv. 1168, appears worthless.

[2] R. Wünsch, *Antikes Zaubergerät aus Pergamon* (Berlin, 1905) (= Jahrb. d. Deutsch. Archäol. Inst., Ergänzungsheft vi); S. Agrell, *Die pergamenische Zauberscheibe und das Tarockspiel* (Lund, 1936). [See Addenda, p. 125.]

The Survival of Magic Arts

bet—that would do only for amateurish fourth-century dabblers, when magic, in common with all other arts, was so sadly declining—but shows complicated and mysterious signs, in part such as we find on the so-called 'Gnostic' gems, in part obviously derived from Egyptian hieroglyphs. This circular device for divination, clearly descended from ancient astrology and here seen used in the third and fourth centuries, was taken over by the Arabs[1] who transmitted so much of ancient magic to the Middle Ages. It spread to the East as far as Tibet[2] and Indo-china,[3] and lives on in manuscripts and books all over Europe, was variously attributed to Ancient Egyptian kings, Greek philosophers, even Christian saints.[4] It appears again as an astrological calendar in the Renaissance[5] and finally degenerates into a half-serious, half-silly parlour-game.[6] But I must return into the fourth century and to our court case.

Asked by the judges whether the magic oracle had not told them their own fate, the accused quoted some of the oracular hexameters which foretold their own execution but also promised revenge. The emperor, who was about to condemn them, was to die by 'evil fate while Ares rages on the plain of Mimas'. Practising spiritualists—should there be any in this audience—will, no doubt, be pleased to hear that the spirits *were* right after all. Not only were the two prisoners in court, after giving evidence, put to death with savage tortures there and then; that part it was easy to prophesy. But the emperor himself, haunted by the verse 'While Ares rages on the plain of Mimas', became increasingly afraid to venture into Asia Minor, where, as he heard, there was a mountain called Mimas. When, seven years later, he actually died in battle against the Goths (on the plain of Adrianople, *not* in Asia Minor), it was found that near the spot where he was believed to have fallen there was an old tomb with a Greek inscription proclaiming it the burial-place of a certain

---

[1] Cf., for example, A. Kircher, *Oedipus Aegyptiacus*, II. i (Rome, 1653), 377, or the 'Zâirajah' described by Ibn Khaldûn, *The Muqaddimah*, transl. by F. Rosenthal (= Bollingen Series xliii), iii. 182 ff.
[2] See H. Bleichsteiner, *Die gelbe Kirche* (Vienna, 1937), figs. 71–72.
[3] See O. R. T. Janse, *Archaeological Research in Indo-China*, i (1947), pl. 130. 1.
[4] A. Kircher, op. cit. II. ii. 491; Cornelius Agrippa, *De speciebus magiae* (= *Opera*, ii. 486); C. Singer, *From Magic to Science* (London, 1928), p. 145, fig. 54; p. 161, fig. 58; p. 167, fig. 65; M. Förster, 'Sphaera Apulei und Glücksrad', *Archiv f. d. Studium der neueren Sprachen und Lit.* cxxix (1912), 45 f. [See Addenda, p. 125.]
[5] F. Boll and C. Bezold, *Sternglaube und Sterndeutung* (4th ed., 1931), pl. vi/13.
[6] Lorenzo Spirito, *Libro delle sorti* (Mantua, 1551); cf. also M. Förster, loc. cit., and I. Negri-V. Vercelloni, *I giochi di dadi d'azzardo e di passatempo* (Milan, 1958), *passim*.

distinguished man of bygone times called Mimas.[1] Moreover, the name of Valens' successor *de facto* began with THEOD . . .; only it was not Theodoros, as the magicians had precipitately concluded, but Theodosius, the emperor who did away with Graeco-Roman paganism for good.

It is interesting to observe how now on the more consistent basis of a Christian state religion the emperors, without in the least condoning magical practices (the magicians remain among those excluded from the general Easter amnesties),[2] feel it safe to replace the savagery of their predecessors with a more balanced *iustitia cum caritate*. Thus, while Valentinian I, as we have heard, decreed capital punishment both for the *mathematici*, the astrologers, and for those who consulted them, Theodosius I's successors, a generation later, allowed the *mathematici* to purge themselves by burning their books in the presence of the bishops, adopting the Christian faith, and promising not to relapse into their old errors. Only if they failed to do so or resumed their forbidden activities, were they to be punished, and even then they faced nothing worse than deportation.[3] But now, hand in glove with the Church, the emperors issued decree after decree against all the numerous heresies which had become rife on the fringes of orthodox Christianity.[4] These heresies, Jewish and Christian Gnosticism, Manichaeism (the latter condemned as a kind of evil magic as early as the beginning of the century by Diocletian), Neopaganism, and the rest were now thrown on the refuse-heap, a heavy bulk far more virulent and dangerous to spiritual health than the bones, by now rather dry, of the defunct religions of remote antiquity.

But with these decrees I am already trespassing into the fifth century and I must return to the fourth century and its historian Ammianus Marcellinus. Distinguished historians of our times have expressed some dismay that an educated and sober man like Ammianus evidently believed in the 'truth of the hocus-pocus of magic and witchcraft', which 'we know to be silly and harmless nonsense'.[5] But they forget that this rather dogmatic view which regards magic at best as hallucination and in general as fraud, pure and simple, is the result of a mere

---

[1] Amm. Marc. XXXI. xiv. 8–9.
[2] *Cod. Theod.* IX. xxxviii. 3–8.
[3] Ibid. IX. xvi. 12.
[4] Ibid. XVI. v. 7 ff.
[5] Alföldi, *A Conflict*, &c., p. 76; W. Ensslin, *Zur Geschichtsschreibung und Weltanschauung des Ammianus Marcellinus* (1923), pp. 94 f.; cf. also Th. Hopfner in Pauly–Wissowa, *Realencyclopädie*, s.v. 'Mageia', cols. 387 ff.

couple of centuries or so of 'Enlightenment' and, I am afraid, is gradually wearing a bit threadbare.[1] I for one sometimes feel sorry for those paragons of up-to-date scholarship, the social anthropologists, when they are confronted with the unexplained facts of witchcraft in primitive societies. Why, indeed, should Ammianus *not* have believed in magic? Everybody did so in antiquity except a few sceptics and agnostics—and they did not believe in religion either. If the more critical minds saw in much, or even most, of it a more or less fraudulent deception or superstition, that did not amount to dogmatic disbelief. We do not contend, say, that gold does not exist because most things which look like gold or even pretend to be gold are not genuine. All the Christian theologians believed in the existence of the magic arts; not to do so would mean disbelieving the stories of the Old and New Testament, from that of the witch of Endor to that of Simon Magus. All the fashionable pagan philosophers of the century, headed by the divine Iamblichus, believed in the magical arts of *theurgia* as part and parcel of their theosophic systems. The Christians, however, anathemized the use of magic. The self-righteous pagan philosophers apparently did not. Ammianus' admired idol, Julian the Apostate, who had more than a slight proficiency in such arts, knew by them of the impending death of Constantius II.[2] Under Valentinian and Valens, Maximus, Julian's revered and beloved master in Neoplatonic philosophy, paid with his life for a similar dangerous prescience.[3] We are told that Julian chose Maximus for his teacher when he heard how this great philosopher, using incense and incantations in front of a statue of the goddess Hecate (the goddess of magic, whom you have met before on the bronze table of Pergamum), had in the presence of his followers brought it about that the face of the goddess came to life, even smiled, and the torches in her hands began to burn. Although this story is related by a contemporary writer,[4] you may believe it or not. But what should we make of it if the century's glory in

---

[1] 'No intelligent person doubts the existence of sorcery', writes the fourteenth-century Arabic polyhistor Ibn Khaldûn (op. cit. iii. 159); 'It is definite that sorcery is true, although it is forbidden' (ibid., p. 179). Similar views are expressed by a modern English Roman Catholic writer, Montague Summers, cf., for example, his *History of Witchcraft and Demonology* (1926) or his *Witchcraft and Black Magic* (1945).

[2] Amm. Marc. xxi. i. 6 ff.   [3] Ibid. xxix. i. 42.

[4] Eunapius, *Vitae sophistarum*, 475 (ed. Giangrande, 1956, p. 44). We may assume that the Hekate statue of this story represents not just the goddess of the common sorcerer but the symbol of the Cosmic Soul as conceived in Chaldaean and Neoplatonic theosophy; cf. H. Levy, op. cit., pp. 88 ff., 248, 361 ff.

erudition and letters, the orator Libanius, tells us of his own experiences?[1] Not only was he himself more than once wrongly denounced for evil magic and necromantic practices, but he clearly shows that he *did* believe in magic, detesting the black kind, it is true, but not quite disinclined to use the more innocent aids of white magic. Suffering from severe headaches and other ailments he found, warned by friends and by a dream, that the black arts were being employed against his health. A dead chameleon, maimed and contorted, was discovered in his lecture room, proving that his and his friends' suspicions were well founded.

That is the sort of sorcery we find (with a wealth of more intricate and dangerous witchcraft) in the magic papyri which the soil of Egypt has preserved in such an abundant—or shall I say frightening?—number.[2] They are to a large extent copies written in the fourth century, in spite of the severe laws I have mentioned and for which I should like to quote another instance from Ammianus.[3] A silly young boy of aristocratic family was denounced under Valentinian I for having copied a magic book of this kind. Threatened with deportation he appealed through his father to the emperor, only to jump from the frying-pan into the fire: the boy was mercilessly executed. Incidentally, St. John Chrysostom, whose severe condemnation of magic amulets I have already quoted, escaped a similar fate only by a hair's breadth. He tells us how in his boyhood his native city Antiochia was once cordoned off by soldiers ordered to search for magic books (βίβλια γοητικὰ καὶ μαγικά). Somebody, in anticipation of his arrest, had thrown a half-finished book into the river Orontes. Chrysostom and a friend of his, on the way to church, saw something floating in the river and his friend fished it out, only to notice on opening the book, what it was. Just at this moment one of the soldiers on duty passed by. Nobody would have believed the boys' story and they did not dare throw the book away while the soldier was in sight. But with God's help they managed in the end to rid themselves of the wretched thing which might have spelled death for both of them.[4] No wonder people became frightened of their own libraries, when after the sensational trial of 371 the

---

[1] Cf. for the following C. Bonner, 'Witchcraft in the Lecture Room of Libanius', *Trans. of the American Philolog. Assoc.* lxiii (1932), 34 ff.

[2] Cf. K. Preisendanz, *Papyri Graecae Magicae*, i–ii (1928–31); iii (1941) (containing additions and the indexes) was destroyed but for a few advance copies during the war. The Warburg Institute acquired through the kindness of Professor Preisendanz a photostat copy of this volume.   [3] Amm. Marc. xxviii. i. 26.

[4] Chrysostom, *In Acta Apost. Hom. XXXVIII* = Migne, P.G. ix. 273 f.

The Survival of Magic Arts

judges ordered the wholesale public burning of vast quantities of codices and volumes containing in large part, as Ammianus insists, inoffensive scholarly literature;[1] many book-owners at that time spontaneously burnt whole libraries of their own merely in order to feel secure.[2] After all, where was the unequivocal dividing line between Neoplatonic philosophy—say, like Iamblichus' *De mysteriis Aegyptorum*—and Egyptian sorcery, between criminal investigation into the future by the *mathematici* (who, as we heard before, were condemned to death by Valentinian I and graciously allowed by Theodosius I to burn their books in the presence of the bishops) and, say, the handbook of astrology written by Firmicus Maternus, the same uncompromising Christian who loyally addressed *De errore profanarum religionum* to the emperors Constantius and Constans?

It is this sense of dangerous insecurity which makes it understandable why the author of the Greek poem on the magic powers of stones, the so-called *Lithica*, thought it safer to keep his name secret. This poem goes (merely because of the blunder of a medieval scholar) under the name of Orpheus, but it was written somewhere in Asia Minor in the latter part of the fourth century: its introduction alludes to the persecution of the old religion and its divine mysteries as abominable magic and to the recent execution of some grand old man, obviously Maximus, whom I have mentioned before as Julian the Apostate's master in Neoplatonic philosophy.[3] It is a rather insipid attempt to revive, with the help of injections of Greek mythology and with some superficial Hermetic colouring, the stale, popularized refuse of what long, long ago, in the imposing system of Old Babylonian astral religion, had been the punctiliously arranged correlation between individual divine powers and the single objects of the material world, all bound together by the supernatural forces of sympathy. Science, medicine, and philosophy had borrowed from this religion of the dead past, but the decomposing garbage was carried along in the teaching of the Persian Magi, by Chaldaean and Samaritan sorcerers, by Jewish and Egyptian dealers in amulets.

---

[1] Amm. Marc. xxix. i. 41.
[2] Ibid. xxix. ii. 4; cf. also Zonaras, iv. 14. On the burning of magical books see also Julius Paulus, *Sentent.* v. 23. 18; K. Preisendanz, 'Dans le monde de la magie grecque', *Chronique d'Égypte*, x (1935), 336 f.; idem, 'Zur Überlieferungsgeschichte der spätantiken Magie', in *Aus der Welt des Buches. Festgabe f. G. Ley* (Leipzig, 1950), pp. 226 f.
[3] Orpheus, *Lithica*, ed. E. Abel (Berlin, 1881), p. 17, vv. 61–81.

So that the full magical benefit might be obtained from the minerals, these had, preferably combined with the vegetable and animal substances corresponding to them,[1] to be duly consecrated and engraved with the proper images, names, and formulas. Together with the magic papyri tens of thousands of these so-called 'gnostic' intaglios,[2] mainly dating from the second to the fourth centuries A.D., still allow the most fascinating glimpses into the magic arts of these times. Like the papyri the majority of these stones appear to have been fabricated in Egypt, that is in Alexandria, and it seems to me that Alexandrian Jews of rather dubious orthodoxy might have a good deal to do with their manufacture. Throughout this age the Jews share with Persians and Chaldaeans a reputation as expert sorcerers second only to the Egyptian past masters. The Alexandrian Jews, being, as one might say, naturalized Egyptians and having absorbed a considerable amount of the Persian and Babylonian heritage, could well have provided the outstanding specialists in the magic arts. As to magic stones, they had in the most sacred books of the Old Testament the tradition of those mysterious twelve gems on the breast-plate of the high priest, wrought for Moses' brother Aaron. The Fathers inherited the tradition of speculation on these jewels and christianized it. In the fourth century, for instance, St. Epiphanius, Bishop of Salamis, wrote an *opusculum* on them, enumerating their medical and even miraculous powers, but steering clear of practical magic. I am also inclined to see an Alexandrian Jew in Damigeron, who is named as author in a frequently copied lapidary originally written in Greek and translated into Latin in the fifth century.[3] The name Damigeron[4] sounds like a literal translation in the singular of the term 'Elders of the People', used so frequently in the Old Testament as a synonym of the expression 'Children of Israel'. In this

---

[1] Cf. also Proclus, *De sacrificiis*, as quoted by Th. Hopfner in Pauly–Wissowa, *Realencyclopädie*, s.v. Theurgie', cols. 259, 2 ff. This is also the theory underlying the so-called *Kyranides*, the main redaction of which was done in the fourth century, cf. A.-J. Festugière, *La Révélation d'Hermès Trismégiste*, i (2nd ed., 1950), 201 ff.

[2] The standard work on these amuletic gems is Bonner, *Studies*, op. cit.; for their 'gnostic' character cf. A. A. Barb in *Journal of the Warburg and Courtauld Institutes*, xvi (1953), 202 and 227, nn. 157–8.

[3] Ed. by E. Abel in his edition of the *Lithica* (Berlin, 1881). Earlier and better manuscripts were edited by Pitra, *Analecta sacra*, ii (1884), 642 ff., and by Joan Evans, *Magical Jewels of the Middle Ages* (Oxford, 1922), pp. 195–213.

[4] Cf. M. Wellmann in Pauly–Wissowa, *Realencyclopädie*, iv, cols. 2055 f., and 'Die Stein- und Gemmenbücher der Antike', *Studien z. Gesch. d. Naturwiss. u. d. Medizin*, iv. 4 (1935), 147 f.

The Survival of Magic Arts

conjecture I am confirmed by the fact that a large number of the medieval magic lapidaries—and it is surprising how many translations of these nonsensical lists into practically all European languages circulated and were copied again and again—introduce themselves as being written by 'one of the Children of Israel in the desert after their departure from Egypt'.[1] It is less surprising to note that the main source for medieval lapidary lore was not the Greek verses of the fourth-century *Lithica*, which was far too highbrow, but the dull and stupid compilation of Damigeron. In the twelfth century no less a person than Bishop Marbod of Rennes took the trouble to turn it into Latin hexameters. For this reason you find this magical rubbish reprinted in Migne's *Patrologia Latina*,[2] while you find, by the way, in the *Patrologia Graeca* another jewel of Jewish magic, only superficially christianized, the *Testamentum Salomonis*.[3] It is one of the many magical books, among them also a lapidary which, unfortunately, is lost,[4] which that Jewish king and arch-magician was alleged to have written.

The magic stone-books and amuletic gems were almost exclusively used for what is generally called 'white' magic, although some of the stones were also used as love-charms, for making oneself invisible and similar less innocent arts. Stark black sorcery, on the other hand, is found in the so-called *Defixiones*,[5] sheets of the sinister metal lead, preferably pierced with nails and buried, after being inscribed with the names of the persons whom it was intended to harm by the proper invocation of the infernal demons. Many hundreds of them have been found, inscribed in Greek and in Latin, dating from early classical times to the late Roman period. I have mentioned how such leaden tablets were employed in the murder by magic of Prince Germanicus. Many of the late tablets were used to handicap chariG and horses on the race-course, horse-racing being a mass entertainment which in the fourth century aroused more passion than racing, greyhounds, football, and cricket rolled into one do in our time.

---

[1] Cf., for example, J. Evans, op. cit., pp. 102, 104, 158, 224, 235. The names Ethel, Cethel, Thetel, Techel, Chael, &c., quoted as author, are according to M. Steinschneider, 'Lapidarien', in *Semitic Studies in Memory of A. Kohut* (Berlin, 1896), corruptions of the name Bezaleel (cf. Exod. xxxi. 2 ff.; xxxv. 30 ff.). [See Addenda, p. 125.]

[2] Migne, P.L. clxxi. 1737 ff.

[3] Migne, P.G. cxxii. 1315 ff. Cf. also K. Preisendanz in Pauly-Wissowa, *Realencyclopädie*, Suppl. viii, cols. 684 ff.

[4] *Realencyclopädie*, loc. cit., col. 702. 16 ff. [See Addenda, p. 125.]

[5] Cf. A. Audollent, *Defixionum tabellae* (Paris, 1904).

The magic leads[1] bear the names of charioteers and horses, accompanied by horrible incantations, and the fact alone that our knowledge of antique horse-names is due mainly, not to literary writings, but to these tablets, makes one wonder whether the engraving and burying of these charms may not have been almost as popular then as the filling in and posting of football-pools is today. ['Darling, have you engraved our lead-tablet?—Yes, dear, but I haven't buried it yet.—Hurry up while it is still dark outside! The races start tomorrow.'] The jockeys themselves, of course, made ample use of this magical dope to disqualify their opponents. Ammianus Marcellinus reports several cases from the reign of Valentinian I where well-known charioteers, though they enjoyed a popularity which might well be the envy of any modern film star, were beheaded and burned alive for such sorcery.[2] Charioteers are mentioned in particular in one of the decrees against the magic arts issued under Theodosius.[3] It is illuminating to hear how the orator Libanius, having sadly realized, as I told you earlier, how a dead chameleon had been used to bewitch him, complained bitterly to his students: 'Now when you think that a charioteer or a horse has been crippled this way, everything is in an uproar as if the city were destroyed; whereas I have been honoured by your indifference to such practices in my own case.'[4] On some of the *Defixionum tabellae* the sorcerers have tried their hands at portraiture, drawing crude images of the poor jockey, fettered and nailed, assailed by a fierce serpent, &c.

Any image, made of wax, metal, or any other material, representing the person to be harmed, could, of course, be used for such evil spells, and, while lead tablets went out of fashion,[5] the practice itself has never died out, as folk-lorists will tell you.[6] The famous English mathematician and astrologer John Dee, who in spite of his denials was himself more than a dabbler in magic arts, was credited with successfully preserving Queen Elizabeth I

[1] See also the literature quoted by Preisendanz, 'Zur Überlieferungsgeschichte, etc.', loc. cit., and R. Mouterde, *Le Glaive de Dardanos* (Beyrouth, 1930), pp. 56 ff. (No. 34, 'Envoutement d'une écurie de course de la Béryte romaine').

[2] Amm. Marc. xv. vii. 2; xxvi. iii. 1–3; xxviii. i. 27; xxviii. iv. 25; xxix. iii. 5.

[3] *Cod. Theod.* ix. xvi. 11 = *Cod. Just.* ix. xviii. 9.

[4] Bonner, op. cit., p. 40.

[5] However, 'the burial of metal [= lead] tablets engraved with spells against an enemy is a learned species of magic to which educated Englishmen resorted now and then in the 16th and 17th centuries', see G. L. Kittredge, *Witchcraft in Old and New England* (Cambridge, Mass., 1929), p. 132.

[6] Cf. the references by Mouterde, op. cit., p. 58, nn. 5 ff.

The Survival of Magic Arts

from harm, when a wax image of her with a pin stuck in its breast was discovered.[1] This kind of sorcery, which was already practised in ancient Babylonia and which was quite common in Plato's time, can look back on a very long tradition indeed.

Among the durable materials—hardly anything magical written on paper, parchment, wax, or wood has survived—lead, as we have seen, was usually chosen by the magician with evil intent. For beneficial charms gold and silver were generally used, besides those engraved precious stones I have mentioned. We know by now a fair number of these thin inscribed metal sheets which were as a rule rolled up and enclosed in a cylindrical case, to be worn on the person. I have myself had the good fortune of unrolling and publishing a scroll of this kind of amulet, found in Austria in a Roman tomb of the later third century.[2] There were four sheets, one of gold and three of silver. The golden sheet and the smaller silver ones contained magic signs, names, and formulas of the usual kind. More interesting was the large silver sheet with a Greek charm against headache, or more precisely megrim (migraine), as the heading πρὸς ἡμίκρανιν shows. The charm is in the form of a little story: Antaura—that is the (obviously Neoplatonic) name of a female demon—arose from the sea crying out and shouting. Artemis of Ephesus (the goddess of magic, often identified with Hecate) met her, asked her where she was going, and exorcised her. This same charm is found several times in medieval Greek collections of magical prayers, which carry on, slightly modernized but otherwise very faithfully, the art of the ancient magic papyri. The name Antaura, however, has disappeared in the medieval charms, only the cursed, diabolical demon of the disease megrim is invoked. And instead of the goddess Artemis it is now 'our Lord Jesus Christ' or—as for instance in a modern Yugoslav version—the archangel Gabriel, who now deals appropriately with the evil demon.

This type of magic incantation—German scholars have coined the name *Begegnungssegen*[3] for it—which relates how the demon of disease in his wanderings encounters Christ, His Mother, or

[1] See the *Dictionary of National Biography*, v. 724 (A.D. 1577).
[2] Cf. A. A. Barb in *Der römische Limes in Österreich*, XVI (1926), cols. 53–68; id. in *Jedermann-Hefte*, iii (Vienna, 1933), 26–33.
[3] Cf. Weinreich in *Archiv für Religionswissenschaft*, xxix (1931), 259 f. (c. 21); F. Ohrt in *Hessische Blätter für Volkskunde*, xxxv (1936), 49 ff.

some saint or angel and is prevented by the more powerful being from doing further harm, lives on in countless charms in all languages and countries of Europe and the Near East. Seemingly plain folk-lore and, especially in their late dilapidated and bowdlerized forms, often downright silly, these charms are still founded on an eminently religious proposition, namely the conviction that mythical events, although they had happened 'once upon a time'—*in illo tempore*—remain for ever a timeless source of supernatural power.[1] Just as the story of the creation was recited at the New Year Festival in ancient Babylonia to ensure the continuation of law and order, so the cosmogonical first chapter of the Gospel of St. John was used throughout the Middle Ages and far into our times as an amulet and charm against all dangers. To counteract the bite of poisonous animals the Egyptians engraved on certain monuments the story of how the god Horus was bitten by a scorpion but healed by his mother Isis.[2] In fact, if you take the liturgical prayers of the Christian Church of today, the so-called 'Collects', you will find again and again this figure of speech: 'O god, who, *in illo tempore* didst this or that, grant now this or that analogous favour.' There was, of course, no lack of stories in the Old and New Testaments which could be repeated or referred to. More than a dozen such references are, for instance, contained in a single exorcism which has come down to us under the name of St. Ambrose, the great fourth-century Bishop of Milan,[3] and similar prayers rightly or wrongly attributed to his Greek contemporary in the East, St. Basil,[4] have fared better still. Their pattern is followed by the many apocryphal and often clearly magical prayers attributed to various other Fathers of the Church[5] such as St. Gregory Thaumaturgus (the Wonder-worker), or St. Cyprian, of whom legend made an ex-magician,[6] &c., down to the unashamedly magical compendia

[1] M. Eliade, *Le Mythe de l'éternel retour. Archétypes et répétition* (Paris, 1949); id., 'Kosmogonische Mythen und magische Heilung', in *Paideuma*, vi (1956), 194–204; cf. also H. Schwabl in Pauly–Wissowa, *Realencyclopädie*, s.v. 'Weltschöpfung', § 71. 4.

[2] For this and similar Egyptian magic *historiolae*, cf. F. Lexa, *La Magie dans l'Égypte antique*, i. 55 f.; Th. Hopfner in Pauly–Wissowa, *Realencyclopädie*, s.v. 'Mageia', col. 343, 46–59; J. Leipoldt–S. Morenz, *Heilige Schriften* (Leipzig, 1953), p. 187.

[3] Migne, *P.L.* xvii. 1109 f.

[4] Migne, *P.G.* xxxi. 1677 ff.

[5] Th. Schermann, *Spätgriechische Zauber- und Volksgebete* (Diss. Munich, 1919), pp. 27 ff.; id., *Griechische Zauberpapyri und das Gemeinde- und Dankgebet im 1. Klemensbrief* (1909); cf. also A. Delatte, *Anecdota Atheniensia*, i (1927), 228 ff.; A. Almazov in *Istoriko-filologicheskoe Obshchestvo: Lyetopis*, ix (Kiev, 1901), 45 ff.

[6] Cf. A.-J. Festugière, op. cit., pp. 37 ff., 369 ff.

like the much-copied *Enchiridion Leonis Papae*[1] and similar medieval pseudepigrapha, which are the substitutes for and heirs of the magic books of the third and fourth centuries.

As regards the simpler Christian charms, consisting, like the ancient Antaura-charm against headache, of a single short tale plus its application to the trouble in hand, it is interesting to find that practically all these very popular charms distinctly prefer apocryphal Christian stories to canonical ones[2] (and this again would show how magic develops from the more seedy fringes of religion). The apocryphal Gospel of St. James tells how the blood of Zacharias, the father of the Baptist, slain in the temple, turned to stone. This story was used as a charm against bleeding,[3] extant in Greek, Coptic, and Latin formulations; it was used in Russia and as far afield as Iceland.[4] There is a widely diffused charm against toothache, written down in Latin during the Anglo-Saxon period,[5] which exists on the Continent in Old Slavonic,[6] and of which corrupt vernacular forms are still current today in this country. 'As Peter sat on a marble stone, | The Lord came to him all alone. | Peter what makes thee sit there? | My Lord, I am troubled with the toothache. | Peter arise and go home. | And you, and whosoever for my sake | Shall keep these words in memory | Shall never be troubled with toothache.'[7] This charm can be traced back to an apocryphal Gospel of St. Bartholomew.[8] A magical prayer against serpents and all other poisons is attributed to St. Paul when he survived the bite of a poisonous viper in Malta, as told in the canonical Acts.[9] A far greater popularity, however, was achieved by a similar prayer against poisons attributed to St. John; this was taken from a collection of apocryphal Acts of the Apostles which tells how the Apostle drank poison without coming to any harm.

---

[1] See *Catal. général des livres imprimés de la Bibliothèque Nationale*, xciv (1929), col. 1129; C. De Clercq, *Catal. des mss. du Grand Séminaire de Malines* (= *Cat. gén. des mss. des bibl. de Belgique*, iv, 1937), pp. 173 f. (codd. 179-81).

[2] Cf. *Handwörterbuch des deutschen Aberglaubens*, vii. 1601 f. (s.v. 'Segen', 10, *b*).

[3] A. A. Barb, 'St. Zacharias the Prophet and Martyr', *Journal of the Warburg and Courtauld Inst.* xi (1948), 35 ff.

[4] H. Larsen, *An Old Icelandic Medical Miscellany* (Oslo, 1931), pp. 52 (and 138) [overlooked in the paper quoted above].

[5] O. Cockayne, *Leechdoms, Wortcunning and Starcraft in Early England* (= Rolls Series, xxxv), iii (1866), 64; cf. also R. Köhler, *Kleinere Schriften* (ed. Bolte), iii (1900), 544-58.

[6] M. Gaster, *Ilchester Lectures on Greco-Slavonic literature* [&c.] (London, 1887), pp. 85 f.

[7] *Notes and Queries*, i (1849-50), 429; cf. ibid., pp. 293, 349, 397, and iii (1851), 259.

[8] As I hope to show in a paper I am preparing.

[9] A. A. Barb, 'Der Heilige und die Schlangen', *Mitteilungen der Anthropol. Ges. in Wien*, lxxxii (1952), 1-21, esp. 4 ff.

This charm turns up in German, Anglo-Saxon, and Irish medieval manuscripts, and was even for some time officially admitted as sacramental by the Church.[1] It has more and more been realized lately that many an old German incantation, long treasured as a relic of primitive Germanic mythology, is nothing but an adaptation or even translation of some late antique, Greek, Roman, or Coptic charm, pagan or Christian.[2] And just as in the classical magic papyri we notice again and again the unmistakable activity of some Graeco-Egyptian priest or temple scribe, so the bulk of the surviving medieval charms was quite obviously written down by Christian clerics,[3] whether misguided, inquisitive, or simply playful. At last we have begun to understand that—as an eminent historian of religion put it recently—'the majority of popular incantations are the product of highly educated people, becoming more and more childish by a long process of dilapidation'.[4] They are not the products of some nebulous primitive folk-lore dating from an age before religion was invented.

In trying to suggest that Magic derives from Religion, decayed and decomposing, I feel somehow guilty of having simplified the matter. Like all human activities magic is a rather more complicated business than it appears to be and contains a variety of ingredients. There is in it a large proportion of philosophy run wild—Neoplatonic philosophy, for instance; there is half-baked and misunderstood medicine stupidly popularized; there is the tendency to borrow clauses and stipulations from learned legal phraseology.[5] It is appropriate that Goethe makes Dr. Faustus, that magician kat'exochen of our European heritage, say: 'Habe nun, ach, Philosophie, Juristerei und Medizin, und leider auch Theologie, durchaus studiert mit heissem Bemüh'n. . . .' Alas, also Theology, the most sublime of the four, last but by no means least: it is here that the really destructive decay sets in. As the

---

[1] A. A. Barb, 'Der Heilige und die Schlangen', pp. 9 ff.

[2] Cf. P. Merker-W. Stammler, *Reallexikon der deutschen Literaturgeschichte*, iii (1928/9), 514, § 7. Since then the tendency to reassert the Germanic origins has grown (cf. W. Kosch, *Deutsches Literatur-Lexikon*, 2. Aufl., iv (1958), 3494, who lists the literature). But see what I wrote in *Folklore*, lxi (1950), 26 ff., and the cautious, but enlightening recent treatment of the 'Merseburger Zaubersprüche' by A. Spamer (*Deutsches Jahrbuch für Volkskunde*, iii (1957), 347–65) and E. Riesel (ibid. iv (1958), 53–81).

[3] *Handwörterbuch des deutschen Aberglaubens*, vii. 1602 f.; cf. also A. Schirokauer, 'Form und Formel einiger altdeutscher Zaubersprüche', *Zeitschrift für deutsche Philologie*, lxxiii (1954), 353–64.

[4] M. Eliade, *Traité de l'histoire des religions* (1949), p. 258.

[5] Schirokauer, loc. cit.

proverb goes: 'A fish first begins to smell at the head.'[1] *Corruptio optimi pessima.*

And yet, however distasteful the products of a disintegrating religion may sometimes appear, however often we feel tempted to use expressions like 'rubbish', 'refuse', and 'garbage', the study of magic to which quite a large section of the library of the Warburg Institute is devoted is fascinating and important. Not mainly for the sake of the fragments which this study adds to our knowledge of ancient religions; nor mainly because the humanist must never close his eyes to the all-too-human. There are few human activities in the history of which an unbroken chain of tradition from the remotest antiquity to our days can be traced more clearly and conclusively than in the Magic Arts.

[1] M. P. Tilley, *A Dictionary of the Proverbs of England in the 16th and 17th Centuries* (1950), p. 217, F/304.

ADDENDA

p. 102, n. 1: For the carefully controlled compromise between Hittite religion and magic, cf. A. S. Kapelrud in *Numen*, vi (1959), 42 ff.

p. 112, n. 2: A tripod of olive or laurel wood with a table engraved with magic characters in a circle is also prescribed for divination in a magic papyrus—see Preisendanz, *P.G.M.*, pap. III, 284 ff.

p. 113, n. 4: Cf. also E. Wickersheimer, 'Figures médico-astrologiques des IXe, Xe et XIe siècles', *Janus*, xix (1914), 157 ff.

p. 119, n. 1: Cf. also L. de Laborde, *Notice des émaux, bijoux [etc.] du Louvre* (Paris, 1853), ii (Documents), pp. 442–4 ('Pierres d'Israel').

p. 119, n. 4: But cf. now L. Thorndike in *Ambix*, viii (1960), 14, n. 14.

VI

Synesius of Cyrene and Alexandrian Neoplatonism

HENRI IRÉNÉE MARROU

S1 la mémoire d'Hypatie demeure une des plus hautement honorées entre toutes les mémoires humaines, si elle a une situation presque unique dans un Panthéon des mémoires qui n'est pas au bout de la rue Soufflot, ce n'est point seulement parce que la fidélité dans le malheur, poussée, poursuivie jusqu'à demeurer fidèle dans une sorte de malheur suprême, et non plus seulement d'infortune et d'adversité (...), ce n'est point seulement parce que la fidélité dans le malheur (...) est peut-être le plus beau spectacle que la pure humanité ait jamais pu présenter. C'est peut-être, encore plus, et techniquement, ceci: Ce que nous admirons, et ce que nous aimons, ce que nous honorons, c'est ce miracle de fidélité (...) qu'une âme fut si parfaitement accordée à l'âme platonicienne, et à sa filiale l'âme plotinienne, et généralement à l'âme hellénique, à l'âme de sa race, à l'âme de son maître, à l'âme de son père, d'un accord si profond, si intérieur, atteignant si profondément aux sources mêmes et aux racines, que dans un anéantissement total, quand tout un monde, quand tout le monde se désaccordait, pour toute la vie temporelle du monde et peut-être pour l'éternité, seule elle soit demeurée accordée jusque dans la mort.

In these eloquent and profound words,[1] Charles Péguy celebrated the death of Hypatia in Alexandria in the month of March 415. Still a beautiful woman, virtuous and chaste, a philosopher and a pagan, she was set upon by a band of fanaticized Christians, and done to death.[2] There are many other passages I could have quoted from the literatures of Europe, for this episode has become in our general consciousness and in the Western literary tradition (if not in historical scholarship which, as we shall see, is likely to regard such matters in a more complex light), a

---

[1] It is the last page of the essay 'de la situation faite à l'histoire et à la sociologie et de la situation faite au parti intellectuel dans le monde moderne', published as an appendix to Jérôme and Jean Tharaud, 'Bar Cochebas', *Cahiers de la Quinzaine*, VIII. xi (3 Feb. 1907): reprinted in Péguy, *Œuvres en prose, 1898–1908* (Paris, 1959), pp. 1110–11.

[2] Socrates, *Ecclesiastica historia*, VII. xv. 5 (Hussey, ii. 76): Philostorgius, viii. 9 (Bidez, p. 111): Souda, Y 166, Adler, iv. 644–6.

symbol of the struggle at the beginning of the fifth century between dying paganism and the Church triumphant.

The same year that Péguy was writing his tribute, a professor of Freiburg im Breisgau, R. Asmus, published a study on 'Hypatia in Tradition und Dichtung'.[1] This, though very far from complete even in its own day (especially on French literature), nevertheless gives a clear indication of the importance that the theme had already assumed. It should at least have mentioned Leconte de Lisle's two poems—lyric and dramatic—on Hypatia in his *Poèmes Antiques* of 1852, which were probably Péguy's source; in English literature it is hardly necessary for me to recall that Hypatia and Synesius had become characters in a novel by Charles Kingsley, *Hypatia, or, New Foes with an Old Face*.[2] I am not sure whether Kingsley is still read, apart from his *Water Babies* and other fairy tales, and no doubt he is sometimes apt to make us smile. How artless the repressions lurking beneath the respectability of these Victorians! Hypatia's death was the occasion for a purple passage which, in its laboured eroticism, may remind French readers of Pierre Louÿs: 'She shook herself free from her tormentors and, springing back, rose for one moment to her full height, naked, snow-white against the dusky mass around . . .'.[3]

To pass from legend to history, however, we must remember that the conflict between paganism and Christianity did not always assume this bloody, brutal, and barbarous character. It was often, on the contrary, subtle and intricate—and therefore all the more interesting. It is paradoxical enough that a pupil of this pagan martyr, and the most true and devoted of her disciples, who venerated her throughout his life as 'mother, sister, teacher and withal benefactress, and whatsoever is honoured in name and deed',[4] should have been a gentleman from Cyrene who, though undoubtedly much against his will, ended by becoming a Christian bishop. (He had been one for two years when, shortly before his death,[5] he wrote the letter from which I have just quoted.) Moreover, whatever his misgivings and doctrinal difficulties, he

---

[1] *Studien zur vergleichenden Literaturgeschichte*, vii (1907), 11–44.
[2] First appeared in *Fraser's Magazine*, 1851–2: in book form in 1853.
[3] I have before me an *édition de luxe*, published by the Chesterfield Company in which this scene has been chosen for the frontispiece to vol. vi. 2 of *The Works of Charles Kingsley* (*Hypatia*) (London–New York, 1899): sepia drawing by Lee Woodward Zeigler.
[4] Synesius, *Ep.* xvi (Petavius, p. 173): I quote from Augustine Fitzgerald's English translation, *The Letters of Synesius of Cyrene* (London, 1926), p. 99.
[5] For these two dates, 411 and 413, see Charles Lacombrade, *Synésios de Cyrène, hellène et chrétien* (Paris, 1951), pp. 212, 273.

was a good, virtuous, and charitable bishop, even if not altogether a saintly one. A century after his death, at any rate, an edifying legend had grown up about his memory and was widely current among the monks of Palestine.[1]

The true problem here is not simply that a student from a pagan philosophical school in Alexandria should have become the Christian bishop of Ptolemais in Cyrenaica: the difficulty lies in the depths of the personality of Synesius himself, in the gradual development, always mysterious to our eyes, of an extremely complex way of thinking. His adherence to Christianity was not brought about by one of those conversions which suddenly 'annihilate' the past; it had been accompanied by reservations, misgivings, and resolves of a highly complicated nature. Here the conflict between paganism, as represented by the Neoplatonist philosophical tradition, and Christianity unfolds, and can be analysed, in the heart of one man: it is a typical case of what Arnold Toynbee has taught us to call 'schism in the soul'.

It is this that makes the delicate task of interpreting the often ambiguous evidence of Synesius' work so interesting, and so difficult. It also accounts for the profusion of works, frequently contradicting each other, which have been devoted to him. The latest of his commentators, Kurt Treu, points out, for example, that one and the same thesis, that of Professor Charles Lacombrade of Toulouse,[2] led to diametrically different conclusions in the minds of two critics, my colleague and friend P. Lemerle,[3] and myself.[4] Schism in the Sorbonne!

It would be interesting to recall here the entire bibliography devoted to Synesius: it represents one of those fine collective endeavours in which workers from all over the world, from western and from eastern Europe,[5] from the old and from the new world, come together in a common cause. Great Britain has not been the least active in honouring him: she has given us the

---

[1] John Moschus, *Pratum Spirituale*, 195, P.G. lxxxvii. 3077-80. I no longer dare to describe Synesius as a 'saint' without qualification, since the remarks addressed to me by the Bollandist F. H(alkin), *Analecta Bollandiana*, lxxi (1953), 257-8.

[2] K. Treu, 'Synesios von Kyrene, ein Kommentar zu seinem Dion', *Texte und Untersuchungen*, lxxi (Berlin, 1958), 26, n. 3.

[3] *Revue de Philologie*, lxxix (1953), 228-30.

[4] 'La "conversion" de Synésius', *Revue des Études Grecques*, lxv (1952), 474-84. The present account takes up and develops more fully suggestions put forward in that brief article.

[5] There is a Russian monograph on Synesius: A. Ostroumov, *Sinezij, episkop Ptolemaidskij* (Moscow, 1879).

Synesius of Cyrene and Alexandrian Neoplatonism

invaluable translation of Fitzgerald,[1] not to mention the slightly dated studies by Alice Gardner[2] and N. Crawford.[3]

But to return for the moment to Kingsley's novel: one good thing about the historical novel, as a literary genre, is that it constantly reminds the historian of the gap between historical scholarship, which recreates the past *wie es eigentlich gewesen*, and an imaginary history, which describes what could or might have happened. Kingsley introduces Synesius in chapter XXI, which has the apt title, 'The Squire-Bishop'. This term describes him very well. Before becoming a bishop, and indeed after, Synesius was very much of a gentleman-farmer, whose time was divided between his elegant hobbies, books and hunting, and the certainly heavy burdens imposed on a great landowner by the barbarian threat from the desert and the clumsy and corrupt administration of the Later Empire, with its crippling fiscal policy.

The Reverend Charles Kingsley, however, imagines him meeting none other than St. Augustine, his Holiness of Hippo. He was writing, of course, in the peaceful times of good Queen Victoria. If he had lived in our time of troubles, taking part perhaps in the campaign against Rommel's Afrika Korps, he might have contemplated the boundless desert sands which divided the Greek Cyrenaica of Synesius from the Latin Africa of St. Augustine. Though contemporaries,[4] it was impossible that the two men should have met. It was not simply the distance, but the lives they were destined to lead, and their different cultural environments, which kept them apart from each other.

Augustine never had the opportunities which were granted to Synesius. A humbly-born Latin, he was compelled by circumstances to cut short his education. He was self-taught in philosophy—it was the amateur Cicero, after all, who chiefly introduced him to it. He was never in a position to receive what Alexandria had to offer to our gentleman from Cyrene, a methodical and thorough higher education, which included a systematic initiation into the most authentic philosophical tradition. If historians were allowed to dream too, they might try to imagine

---

[1] The translation of the *Letters*, referred to above, was followed by *The Essays and Hymns of Synesius of Cyrene* (2 vols.; London, 1930).

[2] *Synesius of Cyrene, Philosopher and Bishop* (London, 1886).

[3] *Synesius the Hellene* (London, 1901).

[4] St. Augustine, as we know, lived from 354 to 430; the life of Synesius, as reconstructed by his most recent biographer, Charles Lacombrade (op. cit., pp. 12, 252, 273), was from 370 to 413.

what a powerful speculative genius like Augustine might have made of such an opportunity.

Are we to go so far as to say then that Synesius did not deserve his opportunity? The historian's first duty is to face the facts and we ought not to over-estimate our hero; he was not, by a long way, a figure of the first rank. He is more interesting for what he reveals, or rather the glimpses he allows us (his work, I repeat, is not easy to interpret) of the civilization to which he belonged, than for what he himself was able to achieve as an original thinker.

He was not so much a philosopher in the strict sense of the word as a rhetorician—and that he excelled in this capacity we know, alas, only too well: he was a true heir of the second Sophistic. He was also a letter-writer, and the Byzantines, who were so attached to the form, rightly regarded him as a master. And he was a poet; apart from the personal letters, it is probably the religious *Hymns* that move us most amongst all his works by the loftiness of their tone.[1]

The only treatise of his which might pass for a philosophical essay, the *De insomniis*,[2] is on analysis disappointing. One needs to be very charitable, as indeed Charles Lacombrade tried to be, to find any genuinely metaphysical questions in it. The problem is to discover 'dans quelle mesure la conscience individuelle, constituée par un conglomérat d'images, propre à une âme donnée, survit à l'anéantissement de l'être physique';[3] in other words, the relationship between consciousness and the individual person, psycho-physiology and anthropology. But, in fact, Synesius never comes to grips with the problem: the argument is cut short. Thus, when he comes to discuss the phenomenon of divination by dreams,[4] though he shows effectively how past and present experiences are reflected in the imagination,[5] he does not face the essential problem, namely how future events, which do not yet have an existence, can nevertheless send forth into our dreams images of themselves, 'advanced waves ($προκυλινδήματα$) of things not yet present, efflorescences of unfulfilled nature . . .'.[6] Instead of analysing this mysterious phenomenon, he abandons

---

[1] There is a French translation of the *Hymns* by Mario Meunier (Paris, 1947), who was Rodin's secretary after Rainer Maria Rilke.

[2] N. Terzaghi (ed.), *Synesii Cyrenensis . . . Opuscula* (Rome, 1944), pp. 143–89; Fitzgerald's translation, ii. 326–59. [3] Lacombrade, op. cit., p. 161.

[4] *De insomniis*, Terzaghi, 15, p. 177. 7 (Petavius, p. 149B); Fitzgerald, ii. 350.

[5] Ibid., Terzaghi, p. 177. 21 (Petavius, p. 149C).

[6] Ibid., Terzaghi, p. 178. 3–4 (Petavius, p. 149D).

abstract speculation and passes on to practical matters, insisting on the importance of a correct technique, which he at once begins to praise like a good rhetorician, ἐγκώμιον.[1]

Turning the leaves of his complete works is enough to confirm this. We do not find in them anything like the knowledge of earlier authors displayed by a Porphyry or a Proclus, no mention of learned commentaries on the classical mathematicians, Euclid and Ptolemy, nor on the great philosophers, Plato and Aristotle (though he claimed these latter as his 'leaders'—ἡγεμόνες).[2] No; at best Synesius remains one of those rhetoricians with some knowledge of philosophy who drew on it for nothing more than a background of general culture and a stock of equally general ideas (θέσεις), as material for their *inventio*. He belongs half way between the two characteristic forms of classical culture, rhetoric and philosophy. There were many such men in the Roman era who, following a distinction made by Philostratos and referred to by Synesius at the beginning of his *Dion*,[3] sought to distinguish themselves from the pure *litterati*,[4] who were simply rhetoricians, without ever managing to become as philosophical as they would have liked or as they claimed to be. One thinks of Philo of Larissa, one of Cicero's masters, of Dion of Prusa, long studied as a model and often imitated by Synesius, of Favorinus of Arles, or, nearer his own time, of Themistius and of the Emperor Julian.[5]

If, nevertheless, Synesius deserves to be studied today it is because he had after all followed a regular course in philosophy and can therefore tell us indirectly about the possibilities of philosophical teaching in his day in Alexandria, with Athens one of the two great centres of philosophical training and practice in the fifth century. He gives us a glimpse of another version of late Neoplatonism which, unlike that of Athens, had not hardened into a rigid hostility towards Christianity.

I have carefully avoided so far using the words school or university when referring to Alexandria: they have been used and abused often enough, without being clearly defined. In France it is a legacy from the old eclecticism of Victor Cousin:[6] a certain

---

[1] *De insomniis*, Terzaghi, 16, p. 178. 10 ff. (Petavius, x–xi. 150AB); Fitzgerald, ii. 351.
[2] *De regno*, Terzaghi, 8, p. 17. 9 (Petavius, iv. 8); Fitzgerald, i. 351.
[3] *Dion*, Terzaghi, 1, p. 233 (Petavius, p. 35A); Fitzgerald, i. 148.
[4] Like Synesius himself at times, as in his *Eulogy of Baldness*, Terzaghi, ibid., pp. 190–232 Petavius, pp. 63–87); Fitzgerald, ii. 243–74.
[5] Cf. my *History of Education in Antiquity* (London–New York, 1956), pp. 210–12.
[6] And also, until recently, even in England; e.g. Fitzgerald, *Essays*, i. 20 ff.; Introduction, 'The School of Alexandria . . .'.

grandiloquence has long been fashionable in describing a glorious and powerful 'School of Alexandria',[1] which included, at least as a forerunner, Philo the Jew, and which finally claimed as its own all the best minds of the closing years of Antiquity, from Ammonius Saccas to Plotinus, Porphyry, Iamblichus, and his successors.

But are we, as historians, entitled to speak of *a* school of Alexandria? We cannot, certainly, in an institutional sense, as an establishment of organized teaching, as had existed in Athens since the end of the fourth century B.C. There was nothing to compare with those religious brotherhoods or 'thiasoi' of the Muses,[2] the Academy, the Lyceum, and later the Garden and the Porch, where the position of the professional head of a school descended from master to disciple, in a direct line of succession (διαδοχή). We have a record of one such *diadoche* among the Neoplatonists of Athens, where from Plutarch 'the Great', who died 431/2, to Damascius and Simplicius who were expelled by Justinian in 529, we can follow the careers of nine successive heads of the school in seven generations (see table on p. 150). Here then we can speak of a Neoplatonist school in Athens: the only question is to what extent were these masters the direct and legitimate heirs of the *scholarchs* of the Academy, the descendants of Plato, through Speusippus, Xenocrates, Polemon, &c. There are too many gaps in our knowledge for us to be able to answer that question with any confidence.[3]

But in Alexandria there was nothing to compare with this, at least not until the end of the fifth century. Plotinus attended the classes of Ammonius Saccas there, but after 244–6 he left Alexandria for Rome and Italy, where the Syrian Porphyry became his pupil. Porphyry was succeeded by another Syrian, Iamblichus of Chalcis—at least he was succeeded in a doctrinal sense, for the biographical data is too meagre for us to know

---

[1] J. Barthelemy Saint-Hilaire (the translator of Aristotle), *De l'École d'Alexandrie* (Paris, 1845); E. Vacherot, *Histoire critique de l'École d'Alexandrie* (3 vols., Paris, 1846); J. Simon (the well-known statesman) 'Alexandrie (École d'—)' in A. Franck, *Dictionnaire des Sciences Philosophiques* (2nd ed., Paris, 1875). Édouard Herriot, before devoting himself to the more attractive subject of *Madame Recamier* (1904), and becoming the grand old man of French politics, had had time to write *Philon le Juif*, an essay on the Jewish school of Alexandria (Paris, 1898).

[2] This institution has been thoroughly studied by P. Boyancé, *Le Culte des Muses chez les phi osophes grecs* (Paris, 1936), pp. 249–327.

[3] One has only to look at the blanks and the question marks in the table *Sukzession der Scholarchen*, compiled by K. Praechter in F. Überweg, *Grundriss der Geschichte der Philosophie*, i (12th ed., Berlin, 1926), p. 666.

Synesius of Cyrene and Alexandrian Neoplatonism 133

with any certainty where Iamblichus was educated or where he taught.[1]

Unrelated to this line, however, there appeared suddenly, towards the end of the fourth century, Theon, the father of Hypatia. The brief reference to him in the *Souda*[2] places him in Alexandria during the reign of the emperor Theodosius (379–95), and associates him with the Museum (Θέων, ὁ ἐκ τοῦ Μουσείου). As an historian of education in antiquity I have been confronted, like many others, with the tantalizing problems surrounding the Museum of Alexandria. Our curiosity remains unsatisfied, but one thing at least is certain: we are not entitled to speak of it simply as a university.[3] We need to imagine rather an institution on the lines of an 'Institute for Advanced Study' or a 'Centre National de la Recherche Scientifique': a community of scholars paid by the state to devote themselves to their studies. And we imagine that they also taught and educated pupils, though this remains a conjecture based more upon the nature of the species (*bonum diffusivum sui* . . .) and on what we know of the Greek taste for education than on any precise documentation.[4]

There is one other line that I have tried to explore, however. Perhaps there were municipal chairs for philosophy in Alexandria, as there were in the principal towns of the empire for rhetoric.[5] Would not the proud and wealthy city of Alexandria have insisted on the equivalent of what, from the time of Marcus Aurelius, imperial munificence had assured to its rival Athens—four chairs of philosophy, one for each of the four great sects, Platonist, Aristotelian, Stoic, and Epicurian? I must confess that, put in this way, my hypothesis encounters a good deal of uncertainty, beginning with Eusebius of Caesarea's note to Anatolius, the future Bishop of Laodicea.[6] Nevertheless, that such chairs existed seems to me to be certain, though we do not know

---

[1] I do not think we have learned much more, on this point, since E. Zeller, *Die Philosophie der Griechen*, III. ii (4th and 5th eds., Leipzig, 1909–23), p. 236, nn. 1 and 3. When Eunapius, *Vitae sophist.* (Boissonade, p. 458), tells us that, abandoning his first master Anatolius, Iamblichus 'attached himself to Porphyry', we need not conclude that he attended the latter's teaching in person; it could mean simply a study of his books.

[2] Let us no longer write 'Suidas'—however obscure the name or sigla *Souda* that the manuscript tradition gave to this famous Byzantine encyclopaedia: on Theon, Θ 205, Adler, ii. 702.

[3] Even between prudent 'quotes'—like, e.g., Lacombrade, op. cit., p. 39.

[4] Cf. my *History of Education in Antiquity*, pp. 189–90.

[5] Ibid., p. 305.

[6] Ibid., pp. 190, 303, n. 10; and earlier in *Saint Augustin et la fin de la culture antique*, p. 217, n. 8, after Eusebius, *Historia ecclesiastica*, VII. xxxii. 6.

whether there were four, nor whether each had its own uninterrupted *diadoche*. One such chair was to be occupied by Hypatia. The formula used in the *Souda* to define her professorial activity: 'she was officially appointed to expound the doctrines of Plato, Aristotle, &c.', ἐξηγεῖτο δημοσίᾳ,[1] seems to me to be the exact equivalent of the one St. Augustine used of his own function at Carthage: 'cum ego rhetoricam ibi professus publica schola uterer'.[2]

We should be careful then in speaking of the museum or the university or school of Alexandria: all we can say, on our present knowledge, is that we find in Alexandria, from the fourth to the sixth centuries, philosophers and teachers of philosophy. I was most surprised to note that a papyrus, dating as far as we can tell from the first years of the reign of Anastasius (491–518), uses the words 'museums' and, apparently (it is badly damaged and almost illegible), 'academies', in the plural, in describing this pedagogical activity, as if there were many rival 'schools', run on similar lines.[3] Looking at the history of this activity as a whole, it is possible to list chronologically the most celebrated of the Alexandrian philosophers and place them side by side with the Neoplatonists of Athens (see table on p. 150). But such a list does not reveal a direct descent, a continuous *diadoche*, as it does on the Athenian side.

Hypatia was both the daughter and the pupil of Theon;[4] but immediately after her the succession was broken. In the following generation Hierocles, after having received his training in the school of Plutarch in Athens, established himself in Alexandria. Later, Hermias, a contemporary of Proclus in the school of Syrianus in Athens, did the same, and his son Ammonius also went to study at Athens before returning to settle in his native town. It is only from this Ammonius, son of Hermias, that we can trace an unbroken descent for two generations, as far as David and Elias, the commentators of Aristotle.

[1] *Souda*, Υ 166, Adler, iv, p. 644. 17.
[2] *Confessions*, vi. 7 (11).
[3] P. Cairo Maspero 67295, i. 15, μουσείους, 13, ἀκαδημίας (?), iii. 51, first published in 'Horapollon et la fin du paganisme égyptien', *B.I.F.A.O.* xi (1914), 163–95 (a complaint *propter res amotas* lodged against his adulterous wife by Horapollo the younger).
[4] As is stated in the entry in the *Souda*, Adler, p. 644. 14. It is generally supposed that this information comes from the *Vita Isidori*: see the attempted reconstruction (in German translation) by R. Asmus, *Das Leben des Philosophen Isidoros von Damaskios aus Damaskos* (Leipzig, 1911), which interpolates with much skill fragments extracted from the *Souda* with the quotations from the *Vita* used by Photius, *Bibliotheca, cod.* n. 181, and especially n. 242. There is naturally a good deal of conjecture in such attributions and reconstructions.

But, the historian's scruples satisfied by these reservations, it remains a fact that there was a great deal of philosophizing going on in Alexandria during this long period, and that philosophical thought and teaching had developed in quite a different atmosphere from that to be found, during the same period, in Athens. The two milieus cannot, of course, be contrasted *toto caelo*. As the Reverend H. D. Saffrey has pointed out again recently,[1] there were close and frequent exchanges between them. There were, as we have just seen, the ties of master and pupil, three of the Alexandrian philosophers having received their training in Athens; ties of origin, two of the Athenian masters, Syrianus and Isidorus, being Alexandrian by birth; ties of family and friendship—Hermias married Aedesia, a relation of Syrianus, the master of Proclus; he was also a close friend of a maternal uncle of Isidorus, the successor of Proclus.

Nevertheless, there were considerable differences between Athens and Alexandria: more than that, there was an element of rivalry, a case of Oxford *v.* Cambridge, Harvard *v.* Yale! Synesius bears witness to it in an amusing fashion. Educated in the school of Hypatia, he visited the famous city of Athens, as a tourist at least. In a letter to his brother he ridicules the decadence of philosophical studies there, represented then by two contemptible 'Plutarchians' (apparently Syrianus and one of his colleagues): 'Athens has no longer anything sublime except the country's famous names. Just as in the case of a victim burnt in the sacrificial fire, there remains nothing but the skin to help us to reconstruct a creature which was once alive. . . . Philosophy has left these precincts. . . .' It is in Egypt now that philosophy flourishes, thanks to the fruitful wisdom of Hypatia![2]

From the Athenian side, Damascius was later to reply to these pleasantries by comparing Isidorus with Hypatia: 'There was a great difference between them, not only in that which distinguishes a man from a woman but still more in that which distinguishes a simple geometer from a true philosopher'[3]—which means perhaps in plain language only that Isidorus knew nothing of mathematics.

---

[1] 'Le Chrétien Jean Philopon et la survivance de l'École d'Alexandrie au VIe siècle', *Revue des Études Grecques*, lxvii (1954), 396–410.
[2] Synesius, *Ep.* cxxxvi; Petavius, p. 272; Fitzgerald, *Letters*, p. 228.
[3] Damascius, *Vita Isidori*, Westermann, § 164, ap. Photius, *Bibl. cod.* 242, p. 346, Bekker B 13 ff. Our interpretation of this passage is that of P. Tannery, *Mémoires Scientifiques*, i (Paris, 1912), 75–76.

It was not only this all too human rivalry that divided the two schools, however. There was also a difference in the orientation of thought, in the spiritual climate—and this was especially noticeable in the conflict between paganism and Christianity. It is well known that in the school in Athens, paganism and Neoplatonism became from generation to generation ever more closely linked— a development that began and can be clearly seen in Plotinus and that was continued by Porphyry and Iamblichus. And as time went on, the Neoplatonists in Athens became increasingly involved with paganism, the whole of paganism, even above all paganism in its most popular, most shady and least rational forms, in theurgy, magic, and the occult sciences. We can understand that to Justinian the closing of the school in Athens must have seemed an essential part of his campaign against the last strongholds of the old religion.[1] Damascius, Simplicius, and his other pupils, preferred exile to conversion and sought refuge with the Sassanid king, Chosroes. We learn, somewhat surprisingly, from the Arab authors that something of their pagan-theurgical philosophy lingered on among the Ṣābians of Ḥarrān until the twelfth century.[2]

In Alexandria, it seems to me, things were different. Admittedly, however active and flourishing the Christian Church, paganism had not been completely eliminated from the great metropolis— certainly not among educated circles.[3] For a long time yet there were to be convinced and ardent pagans. Fanaticism was not the monopoly of Christians; it was to be found equally in the other camp. An historian must take into account the barbarous times, the violent temperament of Egyptians, and the traditional turbulence of Alexandrian life. Zacharias Scholasticus, a lively and sharply observant witness, records for us in his *Life* of Severus of Antioch, the future Monophysite patriarch,[4] a significant episode which occurred about 485–7,[5] nearly a century after the student

[1] E. Stein, *Histoire du Bas-Empire*, ii (Paris-Brussels, 1949), 369–73.

[2] It is time that a competent Arabist gave us a book on this fascinating subject, one more accessible than the old and indigestible work by D. Chwolsohn, *Die Ssabier und der Ssabismus*, (2 vols., St. Petersburg, 1856).

[3] This point has been well brought out by J. Maspéro, the fortunate editor of P. Beaugé 67295, in his paper of 1914; but, carried away by the importance of his document, he did perhaps exaggerate a little the significance of the pagan element in educated circles in Alexandria at the end of the fifth century; cf. the just criticism of Saffrey, op. cit., p. 399; R. Rémondon, 'L'Égypte et la suprême résistance du Christianisme (Vᵉ–VIIᵉ siècles)', B.I.F.A.O. li (1952), 63–78, also follows Maspéro too closely.

[4] Since the work of Mgr. J. Lebon, *Le Monophysisme sévèrien* (Louvain, 1909), the word must be used with care: perhaps we should be content with saying 'anti-Chalcedonian'.

[5] M. A. Kugener, *Revue de l'Orient Chrétien*, v (1900), 205.

Synesius of Cyrene and Alexandrian Neoplatonism

days of Synesius.[1] He describes how pagan students in Alexandria lynched one of their fellows, Paralios, who was about to become a convert to Christianity, for having dared to defame publicly their great goddess Isis.[2] But the same text shows us that at the time there were side by side and, except for such incidents, coexisting without difficulty, groups of pious and charitable Christians, organized into missionary brotherhoods in the service of the Church, called in Alexandrian Greek φιλόπονοι.[3] The professorial body was equally mixed: together with the grammarian Horapollo the younger,[4] a pagan by birth and conviction, Zacharias mentions a professor of rhetoric, Aphthonios, 'who was Christian and had many students'.[5]

It may be objected that this applies to literary studies, the higher teaching of which had flourished in Alexandria,[6] as in Athens and Rome, in an atmosphere of perfect religious neutrality since the middle of the fourth century.[7] But this is just where Alexandria differs from Athens; here the same thing had happened in the philosophical schools. Admittedly, it was not until Joannes Philoponus[8] that teachers of Christianity occupied professorial chairs and definitely assumed the leading positions. But it is a sign of the times that in the same year 529, when the Christian emperor closed the pagan school in Athens, John wrote his treatise *De aeternitate mundi*, against Proclus, in defence of the Christian dogma of the creation of the universe in time. It was the kind of profession of faith that may have helped to spare Alexandrian philosophy the tribulations that overwhelmed its rival in Athens.[9]

But already John's pagan master, Ammonius, had been obliged

---

[1] Which places them about 393–4 and later; Lacombrade, op. cit., p. 38.

[2] Zacharias, *Vita Severi*, ed. M. A. Kugener (*Patrologia Orientalis*, ii), p. 23.

[3] See as well Saffrey, op. cit., p. 403 and the earlier references, ibid., n. 2.

[4] Zacharias, *Vita Severi*, ed. Kugener, p. 15 (cf. pp. 16 and 22): it is, indeed, Horapollo the younger, whom J. Maspéro, following the *Souda* (Z 159, Adler, iii. 615), rightly distinguishes from another Horapollo—the elder, no doubt his grandfather, a grammarian under the emperor Theodosius (op. cit. ii. 408–50). But though he may sometimes be described as 'philosopher' (Stephan. Byz. s.v.; P. Cairo Masp. 67295, i, 14, iii, p. 51) there is no doubt that he was primarily, like his namesake and predecessor, a professor of grammar: Zacharias' evidence is conclusive (the editor, Kugener, notes (p. 15) 'the words "grammarian, grammar" are always represented in the Syriac text (sc. our *Vita*) by the Greek words γραμματικός, γραμματική.')

[5] *Vita*, p. 25.

[6] As the evidence cited from the *Vita Severi* shows, at least for the end of the century.

[7] Cf. my *History of Education . . .*, pp. 322–6.

[8] I refer the reader again to the article by H. D. Saffrey.

[9] This point had already been stressed by P. Tannery in his excellent paper of 1896, *Sur la religion des derniers mathématiciens de l'Antiquité*, reprinted in *Mémoires Scientifiques*, ii. 532.

to compromise with the Christians and to conclude a sort of *modus vivendi* with their patriarch:[1] the pagan Damascius reproached him with it bitterly.[2] Furthermore, even in the preceding generation the Neoplatonist philosophy of Hierocles had been tending gradually closer to the Christian position: for him the *Demiurge* was no longer a subordinate hypostasis (in Plotinus it was the *nous*, the second hypostasis, which fulfilled this function); it was identified with God, the one God, God the Creator, of the Jews and Christians.[3] And Hierocles, like Ammonius, had had Christian pupils—Aeneas of Gaza, for instance, that remarkable exponent of Christianized Neoplatonism.[4] In the light of this tolerant attitude towards the new religion, the fanatically pagan philosophers appear of little consequence,[5] apart from Syrianus and Isidorus who, precisely because they were seeking a more congenial atmosphere for their ideas, left Alexandria for Athens.

The evidence of Synesius, however difficult to assess, is important because it acquaints us with an early stage on this journey of Alexandrian Neoplatonism towards its meeting with Christianity. As far as we can judge from its reflection in Synesius, the teaching of Hypatia had already, during the years 390–400, started a reaction against extremism, against the murkier aspects of paganism in which, as we have seen, the Athenian school had indulged before it sank into the ultimate degeneracy of the Ṣābians referred to by Dimishki and Mas'udi: 'the temple they dedicated to the planet Jupiter was triangular in shape with a pyramidal roof: it was built in green stone and in the middle was an idol of tin, seated on a throne with eight steps: to this a child was sacrificed. . . .'[6]

Naturally, Synesius did not break completely with the occult sciences: he would not have been a man of the *Spätantike* if he had.

---

[1] Damascius, *Vita Isidori*, Westermann, § 292 (cf. 179), i.e. Photius, *Bibl. cod.* 242, p. 352. 11 ff. (Bekker, p. 347. 19).

[2] For the interpretation of these fragmentary and difficult texts, see finally Saffrey, op. cit. pp. 400–1.

[3] If we accept the interpretation of the ideas of Hierocles suggested by K. Praechter, 'Christlich-neuplatonische Beziehungen', *Byzantinische Zeitschrift*, xxi (1912), 1–27.

[4] I have profited from the researches of my pupil Marie Jeanne Turlot on this subject.

[5] J. Maspéro went beyond the scope of his documents by stating, with regard to his Horapollo the younger: 'Son nom est célèbre dans l'histoire de l'École d'Alexandrie' (*B.I.F.A.O.*, 1914, p. 176): once again the evidence proves this 'philosopher' to have been primarily a professor of grammar.

[6] Mas'udi, *Les Prairies d'Or*, iv. 61–71 (Barbier de Meynard); Dimishki, *Cosmography*, pp. 39–48 (Mehren).

Synesius of Cyrene and Alexandrian Neoplatonism 139

Even Theon, Hypatia's father, who was primarily a mathematician, had felt called upon to write a treatise *On Omens, the observation of birds and the voice of ravens*.[1] But Synesius too kept to the more innocent techniques of divination, like oneiromancy. No doubt this was a matter of political prudence,[2] but it also shows a taste for the rational. He knew the classics of occultism, such as *The Chaldaean Oracles* with in particular Porphyry's commentary,[3] but I find nothing in the nature of that theurgical *diadoche* through women of which Marinus tells us in his *Life* of Proclus, who is said to have received his initiation into the rites of the Chaldeans through Asclepigenia, daughter of Plutarch.[4]

We observe, then, in Alexandria a more rational atmosphere. Whereas Athenian Neoplatonism increasingly stressed the occultist tendencies introduced by the first followers of Plotinus, we can see from the philosophical development of Synesius that the Alexandrians reacted against it. Whilst Plutarch accepted and enhanced his legacy from Iamblichus,[5] Synesius broke with him and returned to Porphyry. As I have pointed out before, what counts at the beginning of any philosophical development is its course, its direction, and momentum. To part company with Iamblichus (and on so central a point as theurgy), to revert to Porphyry, was to turn his back on contemporary paganism and go to meet Christianity.[6] It is true that Porphyry was still, or perhaps I should say was already, greatly attracted by these religious blind-alleys of late antiquity, but much less so than Iamblichus and his successors.[7] What Synesius took from Porphyry was not the anti-Christian polemic nor the *Philosophy*

---

[1] Entry in the *Souda*, Θ 205, Adler, ii. 702. Cf. Synesius, *De insomniis*, Terzaghi, 2, p. 146. 9, 10 (Petavius, p. 132B); Fitzgerald, ii. 328.

[2] Synesius, ibid., Terzaghi, 12, p. 169. 14 ff. (Petavius, p. 145A); Fitzgerald, ii. 344: 'To speak of nothing else but those things with which the prisons were lately congested . . .'; ibid., Terzaghi, p. 170. 11 ff. (Petavius, p. 145CD); Fitzgerald, ii. 345: 'The laws of a malicious government do not forbid it . . .' (i.e. oneiromancy).

[3] They are referred to in the *De insomniis*, Terzaghi, 4, p. 151. 16–17 (Petavius, p. 135B); Terzaghi, 7, p. 158. 4–6 (Petavius, p. 138B); Terzaghi, 9, p. 161. 15–16 (Petavius, p. 140D).

[4] Marinus, *Vita Procli* (Fabricius), 28, p. 68.

[5] What remains obscure, in the present state of our knowledge, is (as with the relationship between Porphyry and Iamblichus) the way in which, historically, the tie between Iamblichus and Plutarch was established: was the latter taught by one of the former's pupils (Chrysanthius has been suggested, or Theodorus of Asine: see E. Zeller, *Die Philosophie der Griechen*, III. ii, 4th and 5th eds., p. 805, n. 1)? Or was the succession established through the intervening literature?

[6] See my note in *Revue des Études Grecques*, lxv (1952), 481.

[7] This is well known; see (after J. Bidez, W. Lang, and P. Courcelle), Lacombrade, op. cit., pp. 63, 165, 213.

of the Oracles,[1] but what he could most easily 'infléchir vers la doctrine chrétienne',[2] essentially what was most rational in his work.

The education Synesius received was based on two main disciplines: Aristotelian logic and mathematics. In the former, Porphyry had led the way by writing his famous *Isagoge* to the Categories, and we know the part that Alexandria was to play in the compilation of the *Commentaria in Aristotelem Graeca*. In mathematics, Hypatia continued, as we have seen, the tradition inaugurated by her father Theon, the commentator of Aratos, Euclid, and Ptolemy;[3] she worked in her turn on Diophantes, Apollonius, and on the 'astronomical canon'.[4] We find Synesius himself, the gentleman-farmer, engaged when not hunting on researches of an entirely rational nature. He designed an 'astrolabe', actually a celestial map, a conical projection of the sphere of the stars,[5] and also a 'hydroscope', what we call an aerometer, with a weighted float which allowed the specific gravity of fluids to be measured by a simple grading.[6]

What stage had been reached then in the relationship between pagan and Christian in the school, or philosophical milieu, of Alexandria, when Synesius was a young man? I believe that even then we can speak with Praechter of a *neutral-philosophische Anstalt*.[7] Christian pupils were attending the courses of a pagan professor, in this case Hypatia, as they were to do later in the times of Aeneas of Gaza and Joannes Philoponus. Among Synesius' own contemporaries there was even a cleric, a deacon—he has been tentatively identified with the future Saint Isidore of Pelusium.[8] It was already a very mixed company.

As for Synesius himself, it is even possible that he came of a Christian family; his brother Evoptius, who in all likelihood succeeded to the episcopal seat of Ptolemais, served as his inter-

[1] That J. O'Meara has recently suggested that we should find in the *De regressu animae*, quoted at length by St. Augustine: *Porphyry's Philosophy from Oracles in Augustine* (Paris, 1959).

[2] Lacombrade, op. cit., p. 168; cf. pp. 49, 148, 165–6.

[3] The entry in the *Souda* on Theon already referred to; Lacombrade, op. cit., p. 40.

[4] *Souda*, Y 166, Adler, iv. 644. 3–5: Lacombrade, op. cit., pp. 41–42.

[5] Synesius, *Ad Paeonium*, Terzaghi, pp. 132–42 (Petavius, pp. 307B–313C): the instrument was identified by P. Tannery, *Recherches sur l'histoire de l'astronomie ancienne* (Paris, 1893), pp. 50 ff.

[6] Synesius, *Ep.* xv (Petavius, p. 72); Fitzgerald, p. 99; cf. Lacombrade, op. cit., pp. 42–43.

[7] F. Überweg-F. Praechter, op. cit. i (12th ed.), 635, 638–9; by Praechter also in Pauly-Wissowa, *Realencyclopädie*, s.v. Hypatia, col. 245.

[8] Synesius, *Ep.* cxliii (Petavius, p. 281); for the identification, proposed with every caution, see Lacombrade, op. cit., pp. 54–55.

mediary to the Patriarch Theophilus in 410. . . .[1] I have said how delicate and difficult a task it is to account for Synesius, and to interpret the evidence correctly. But we can do better than multiply tenuous hypotheses. We do possess at least one explicit statement of his, the justly celebrated *Letter 105*. It was written in 410 to his brother, an open letter, intended to be read by the Bishop of Alexandria, and in it Synesius revealed all his unwillingness to accept the episcopal dignity that had just been conferred upon him.[2]

To understand it, we must break away from a much-abused antithesis—Hellenism versus Christianity. It has been said too often that this letter proves that Synesius was still pagan when, much against his will, he was elected bishop. My reply to this has been that we ought not to confuse vocation and conversion.[3] What we hear is Synesius protesting against being called to an unwelcome ecclesiastical appointment; he does not speak of his admission into the bosom of the Church, his baptism.

It is very likely true that he was still unbaptized, but there is nothing odd about that, late baptism of adults still being at that period common practice.[4] The fact that his marriage, which went back to 403,[5] had been solemnized by the 'blessed hand' of Theophilus of Alexandria,[6] suggests that he was at least a catechumen at that date.[7] There is also another document in which we may fathom his religious convictions in the years preceding his election. His *Hymn 3*, composed on his return from the dramatic embassy to Constantinople (399–402),[8] shows him, during his stay in the capital, visiting the shrines of the martyrs (v. 450–70), beseeching God, the God of the Christians, for the grace of baptism (v. 620–1): 'Now at last, let my suppliant soul

---

[1] Id. *Ep.* cv (Petavius, pp. 246 ff.); Fitzgerald, pp. 196–202.
[2] See the excellent commentary on this essential text by Lacombrade, op. laud., pp. 220–8.
[3] *Revue des Études Grecques*, lxv (1952), 477–80.
[4] For the end of the fifth century, see the testimony of Zacharias, *Vita Severi* (ed. Kugener), p. 11. 10.
[5] For this date, Lacombrade, op. cit., p. 137.
[6] Synesius, *Ep.* cv (Petavius, p. 248); Fitzgerald, p. 199: 'God himself, the law of the land, and the blessed hand of Theophilus himself have given me a wife. . . .'
[7] I refer the reader to the argument developed in *Revue des Études Grecques*, lxv (1952), 477, s. 2.
[8] Lacombrade, op. cit., pp. 101, 136, 177; as for the objection raised by P. Lemerle, *Revue de Philologie* (1953), p. 230: 'Mais ces poèmes n'ont-ils pas été retouchés par Synésios devenu évêque' (cf. already Lacombrade, p. 171), it is supported by no positive argument and the probabilities are against it (Lacombrade, p. 194: the brief episcopate of Synesius saw him 'chaque jour absorbé davantage par les contraintes matérielles d'un ministère entièrement voué à l'action militante').

bear the seal of the Father'; σφραγῖδα πατρός—the expression is technical.[1]

Admittedly, this is still only a wish: I readily admit that as a catechumen Synesius was rather a half-hearted Christian, lacking in enthusiasm, if not necessarily in conviction. That he should have been elected bishop nevertheless can be explained easily enough: it was not the religious man who was appointed, but the distinguished citizen, the skilled orator, the astute ambassador, a man able to hold his own with the representatives of the imperial administration and, on top of that, a soldier capable of organizing the resistance against the tribes of the interior. The clergy and the people of Ptolemais saw in Synesius the man to fulfil in those difficult times the role of *defensor plebis* or *civitatis*, That was a *vocatio* in an active sense, in the original and strict sense of the word. We might easily multiply the instances of similar episcopal appointments in the patristic era, imposed upon men for whom ecclesiastical status had none of the *attrait intérieur* which modern spirituality in the St. Sulpice tradition understands as the true test of vocation. Apart from the well-known cases of St. Ambrose and St. Augustine, we remember, for instance, how a nobleman from Lyons was to be appointed head of the church in the city of Arvernes in 470. Aged about forty, like Synesius, and also a man of letters, he had married into the local nobility: already a Christian, but tepid like Synesius, he was chosen for similar, essentially extrinsic, reasons—because he was the son and grandson of a *praefectus praetorio*, was himself a former *praefectus Urbi* and a patrician, son-in-law of a former emperor....[2]

As we can see from his *Letter 105*, Synesius accepted his promotion without enthusiasm: whilst he did not definitely refuse (he said he was ready to bend before the will of Theophilus[3]—which is what he finally did), he betrayed no eagerness to accept a task which appeared to him to be beyond his powers. What was it that he was so reluctant to sacrifice? There was first, to be sure, the gentlemanly life, the pleasures of the hunt, the dogs, the horses[4]—though he was himself the first to say that he was

---

[1] See F. J. Dölger, *Sphragis, eine altchristliche Taufbezeichnung in ihren Beziehungen zur profanen und religiösen Kultur des Altertums* (Paderborn, 1911).
[2] The correspondence of Synesius acquaints us with a less celebrated but analogous case, that of Siderius, a former functionary of the emperor Valens, appointed Bishop of Palaebisca: *Ep.* lxvii (Petavius, p. 209); Fitzgerald, pp. 151–2.
[3] *Ep.* cv (Petavius, p. 250); Fitzgerald, p. 201.   [4] Ibid.

prepared to relinquish all these for the sake of a higher service. Harder to bear was the disruption of his family life; he did not want to be separated from his wife, with whom he would have liked to have more children.[1] But above all there was his ideal of the philosophical life, a life in which he was his own master, free to devote himself to his studies—studies, certainly, directed towards the highest knowledge, contemplation which must in the end lead to God—but it was his own study, his own search for the truth and personal perfection[2]—the cherished activities of his leisure. 'Omnes illae deliciae fugere de manibus', as that other contemplative, St. Augustine,[3] wrote when he too was called to the priesthood against his will—a dignity which he accepted with anguish and tears,[4] feeling that what was demanded of him was the sacrifice of his whole conception of life.

Synesius did not defend himself against the call of the Church simply on the grounds of his own incompetence, like St. Augustine;[5] he also had doctrinal difficulties. He argued that his philosophical certainties, the convictions 'which have entered the soul through knowledge to the point of demonstration', were not opposed strictly speaking to the official doctrine of the Church, but to those 'convictions which are cherished by the common [i.e. Christian] people'.[6] We shall come back to this point later, but we must realize that for Synesius the real obstacle, the true rival in his heart, not to Christianity but to the episcopal office, was not so much the content of his philosophy, his doxography, as Philosophy itself, the classical ideal of the *Bios theoretikos*, the personal search for inner perfection through a life of studious pursuits, which were also those of a gentleman.

I believe that the case of Synesius is one more instance of a very general truth to which I have often drawn attention:[7] what estranged the men of letters of the old aristocracy or for a long time kept them at a distance from Christianity was not, principally, paganism (Synesius was never tempted to worship the ancient gods, to sacrifice to Isis or Hecate); it was the religion of Culture, the classical ideal of the *Paideia*, the legacy of the

---

[1] Ibid. (Petavius, p. 248); Fitzgerald, p. 199.
[2] Ibid. (Petavius, p. 247); Fitzgerald, pp. 197-8.
[3] Augustine, *Ep.* ci. 3, referring to the interrupted composition of his *De musica*.
[4] Possidius, *Vita Augustini*, iv. 2; Pellegrino, p. 52.
[5] Augustine, *Ep.* xxi. 3.
[6] Synesius, *Ep.* cv (Petavius, p. 248); Fitzgerald, p. 200.
[7] Cf. my *MOYCIKOC ANHP, étude sur les scènes de la vie intellectuelle figurant sur les monuments funéraires romains* (Grenoble, 1937), pp. 255-7.

Hellenistisch-römische Kultur. We notice that in Synesius' language the word 'Hellenism' did not have the sense of 'paganism', as it had for Julian the Apostate, but simply of 'culture'.[1]

In this respect his treatise '*Dion* or Apology for his own "*Lebensanschauung*"', to which Kurt Treu's commentary has recently drawn our attention, is particularly important; it is a plea for Greek culture, ἑλληνικὴ διαγωγή, as the most fruitful and generally effective method of training the mind.[2] What strikes me as especially significant in *Dion*, for the light it throws on the intellectual atmosphere of contemporary Alexandria rather than on Synesius' own inner development,[3] is that the discussion is never conducted in religious terms. The fight which Synesius leads against lack of culture, the ἀμαθία, the ἄμουσοι,[4] seems to him to be the common concern, and for the same reason, of both pagans and Christians.[5] Hence the trouble he takes to distinguish the two groups whilst at the same time seeking to unite them. Yes, he says, it is sometimes permissible to do without the help of classical propaedeutics, without that of the Muses, but that is an accomplishment of only quite exceptional minds, like Amous of Nitria, Zoroaster, Hermes Trismegistus, and St. Anthony:[6] two Christian saints—and how typical this is—in the company of two pagan 'saints'.

Amongst the enemies of culture he no doubt also included the monks, but he did nevertheless give these simple, uncouth souls their due. His criticism, in fact, is very delicate. If, for example, he condemns their rigorism in matters of chastity, it is because they sometimes exaggerated and confused the means with the end:[7] even the best friends of the Desert Fathers—and I number myself among them—would hardly dare, on this point,

---

[1] E.g. *Dion*, Terzaghi, 4, p. 245. 10 (Petavius, p. 42B); Fitzgerald, i. 156.

[2] *Dion*, Terzaghi, 9, p. 255. 21 (Petavius, p. 49A); Fitzgerald, i. 165.

[3] Lacombrade, op. cit., p. 139, places the writing of *Dio* between his marriage and his episcopate, in the years 404 and 405.

[4] *Dion*, Terzaghi, 10, p. 259, 19–20 (Petavius, p. 52CD); Terzaghi, 12, p. 264. 16 (Petavius, p. 54B).

[5] I am taking up here, but interpreting in a different way, a remark by U. v. Wilamowitz-Möllendorf, victim of the false Hellenism-Christianity antithesis, in his article 'Die Hymnen des Proklos und Synesios', *Sitzungsberichte* of the Berlin Academy (Philol.-histor. Kl., 14, 1907), pp. 272–95.

[6] *Dion*, Terzaghi, 10, p. 259. 19–20 (Petavius, p. 51BC); there is sometimes a desire here, and above (Terzaghi, 9, p. 255. 13; Petavius, p. 48D) to replace the name Ἀμοῦς, vouched for by all the mss. (insignificant variants, Ἀμοῦν, Ἀμμοῦς) by the Θαμοῦς of Plato, *Phaedrus*, 274d, or even by Plotinus (thus S. A. Naber, 'Ad Synesii epistulas', *Mnemosyne*, 1894, p. 96). Where shall we be if we read in the texts not what they contain, but what we would like them to contain?

[7] *Dion*, Terzaghi, 9, p. 257. 11 f. (Petavius, p. 50A); Fitzgerald, i. 166.

to acquit them entirely. But his real enemies were not the humble Coptic monks, who relaxed after the fatigue of contemplation by weaving baskets[1] (he himself, a Greek and a cultivated man, would relax in a nobler fashion in the company of the Muses),[2] but the pagan philosophers, the hierophants and theurgists that the Athenian followers of Iamblichus had become. The criticism in *Dion*,[3] in which Fitzgerald saw objections of Aristotelian origin levied against Plotinus, was addressed, not against Neoplatonism in general as Theiler maintained, but in a very precise way against Neoplatonism corrupted by the superstitious pagan belief in theurgy. It is an Alexandrian criticism of contemporary Athens, and one which pagans of reason and judgement could share with educated Christians.

What, then, are we to think of the doctrinal misgivings to which Synesius bears witness in his *Letter 105*? They formulate very neatly the problem posed by the emergence of a professional philosophy within the Christian Church. Synesius, like so many of the Christian Neoplatonists from Alexandria who came after him, was in a very different position from the Latin Neoplatonists studied by Pierre Courcelle. As Geffcken observed,[4] such men as Marius Victorinus, those who composed St. Ambrose's circle in Milan, St. Augustine, and later Claudius Mamertus, were not philosophers but theologians, at home with the problems debated by churchmen among themselves, ready to borrow from philosophy—the Neoplatonism of Plotinus and Porphyry—such arguments or concepts which might prove useful in their theological feuds: Victorinus polemicized against the Arian Candidus, St. Augustine against Manichaeism, Mamertus against the naïve fundamentalism of Faustus of Riez.[5] But Synesius and the Alexandrians were first and foremost philosophers. The doctrine they received from their pagan masters, Neoplatonism, was an 'independent' philosophy, like all philosophy worthy of the name. It was not *a priori* either for or against Christianity; as it turned out it was both friend and foe: it suggested satisfactory

---

[1] Ibid., Terzaghi, 7, p. 251. 20 f. (Petavius, p. 46c); Fitzgerald, p. 161.
[2] Ibid., Terzaghi, 8, p. 253. 1 f. (Petavius, p. 47AB); Fitzgerald, p. 162.
[3] Ibid., Terzaghi, 8, p. 254. 10 f. (Petavius, p. 48B); cf. Fitzgerald's notes, pp. 232–4; W. Theiler, *Die chaldäischen Orakel und die Hymnen des Synesios* (Halle, 1942); cf. K. Treu, op. cit. (*T.U.* lxxi), p. 75.
[4] J. Geffcken, *Der Ausgang des griechisch-römischen Heidentums* (2nd ed., Heidelberg, 1929), p. 221.
[5] For the latter, see E. L. Fortin, *Christianisme et culture philosophique au cinquième siècle: la querelle de l'âme humaine en Occident* (Paris, 1959).

solutions for certain problems, but for others it put forward arguments difficult to reconcile with the faith. Like all philosophical systems it could not be integrated into a Christian culture without a patient effort of criticism, reappraisal, and adjustment. In 410 the work had hardly begun.

It is necessary now to say a word about the three difficulties enumerated by Synesius, the future bishop, in *Letter 105*. They are of a kind to reconcile him to the philosophical reader; if hitherto we have tended to treat him with a certain condescension, he now appears to us as a man capable of asking exactly the right questions, even if he was not able to solve them. He dwelt on just those problems which at that time were uppermost in the minds of philosophical Christians and to which for more than a century the Christian Neoplatonists from Alexandria chose to devote themselves with unflagging zeal.

(*a*) 'For my own part', he wrote,[1] 'I can never persuade myself that the soul is of more recent origin than the body.' This is the typical question discussed at the time—*difficillima quaestio*, as St. Augustine was to call it; and when in 419–20 he devoted to it a long treatise in four books, *De anima et eius origine*, he was still loath to commit himself. In the East, another bishop, Nemesius of Emesa, who may well have been writing about the same time as Synesius and had an equally Neoplatonist background, professed openly the doctrine of the pre-existence of the soul. A Latin translation of his work *On the Nature of Man*,[2] was widely read in the West during the Middle Ages when it was attributed to Gregory of Nyssa, and under cover of his authority caused many qualms among the scholastics.

I think that here Synesius was not in opposition to the doctrine of the Church; in any case Nemesius' example shows that the dogma on this particular point was not yet fixed. He was objecting to the theories naïvely formulated by Methodius of Olympus to refute Origen's well-known teaching on the pre-existence of souls. These were difficult for a Platonist to accept, for if the soul were created after the body, as Methodius alleged, the spiritual nature of man would appear to be in some way inferior to his corporeal nature.[3]

---

[1] Synesius, *Ep.* cv (Petavius, p. 248); Fitzgerald, p. 200.
[2] See the excellent English translation by W. Telfer, *The Library of Christian Classics*, iv (London, 1955).
[3] Gregory of Nyssa had already criticized this theory of Methodius in his *De hominis opificio*, 229B–233B.

(*b*) 'Never would I admit', he continues in the same passage, 'that the world, with all its parts, must perish. . . .' The words καὶ τἄλλα μέρη appear to be redundant, but they seem to me to imply a certain reservation: the destruction of at least some parts of the world is difficult to accept—the stars, for instance. This is a major difficulty, arising from the permanence of the laws of nature; is it necessary to recall that in the middle of the thirteenth century St. Thomas Aquinas himself was to admit that 'there is no evidence to demonstrate that the creation of an eternal world is impossible'?

The fact that Synesius did not take up the analogous objection regarding the creation of the world in time was in itself an important concession to Christian theology: as the Cappadocian Fathers had already pointed out, those who admitted that the world had a beginning would soon be led to conclude that it must also have an end.[1]

(*c*) Finally, 'as for the resurrection such as common belief admits it, I see here an ineffable mystery and I am far from sharing the views of the vulgar crowd thereon'. Here again, Synesius is not opposed to Christian dogma as such (he declares himself ready to accept it as a sacred mystery, ἱερόν τι ἀπόρρητον), but to the idea of it in the minds of simple people, which must indeed often have been crude enough. Once more it is the man of letters of the ancient world, with his sensitive and subtle mind, who feels himself offended. One suspects that his objections are still close to those of Celsus for whom the Christians were men of the flesh, not of the soul, who hoped for the resurrection of the body because of their pathetic belief that it would be necessary for them to have eyes, the instruments of sense perception, in order to see God.[2] But Synesius was not against the perpetuation, to a certain extent, of man's whole being. We can refer here to his *De insomniis* where we find a theory of the εἴδωλον, which is original and in which, 'sous l'influence accentuée des idées chrétiennes',[3] he does not hesitate to correct the ideas of his master Porphyry; with a little good will, we can here perceive an outline, by no means crude, of what was to become the orthodox doctrine of the 'glorified body'.

These are, I repeat, precisely the problems to which the

---

[1] St. Basil, *In Hexaëmeron*, i. 4B; Gregory of Nyssa, op. cit., 209B.
[2] Origen, *Contra Celsum*, vii. 36–38; English translation by H. Chadwick, pp. 423–6.
[3] This is the opinion of Lacombrade, op. cit., p. 168.

Christian thinkers who followed Synesius in the Alexandrian tradition of Neoplatonism were to devote their most important works. We need only mention some of their titles. At the end of the fifth century (his ἀκμή was about 490) Aeneas of Gaza, philosopher and rhetorician, former pupil of Hierocles in Alexandria, wrote the dialogue, *Theophrastus or the immortality of the soul and the resurrection of the body*. His friend Zacharias Scholasticus, the biographer of Severus with whom he studied in Alexandria *c*. 485, devoted himself to Synesius' third problem in his *Ammonius or the creation of the world* (so called because it criticized the position of Ammonius, the son of Hermias and the last of the pagan masters of Alexandria). The brother of Zacharias, Procopius of Gaza, challenged the Athenians in his *Refutation of the theological elements in Proclus*. Finally, in 529, as we have seen, Joannes Philoponus published his treatise *On the eternity of the world, against Proclus and his eighteen arguments*. Later he was to write a treatise *On the creation of the world*, a commentary on the first chapters of Genesis, and another one *On the resurrection*.[1]

The questions raised by Synesius take us right to the heart of the Christian philosophy of that time and place, and that he should have raised them is in itself a considerable achievement. But he does not yet seem to have been in a position to answer them. What he suggests are counter-arguments of a practical order which at first sight are a little disquieting. He contemplates, for instance, the possibility of adopting a popularized version of the truth, to conciliate the vulgar and appeal to the common man, whilst at the same time preserving his own 'scientific' convictions. It occurred to me one day, in an argumentative frame of mind, to examine this standpoint against the false picture of St. Augustine at the time of his baptism suggested by P. Alfaric, who argued that Augustine was converted to Neoplatonism rather than the Gospel: 'pour lui le Christ est le Platon des foules.'[2] But we must not be misled: it is a Platonist who is speaking when Synesius uses such phrases as, 'the philosophic mind admits the employment of falsehood. ... I consider that the false may be beneficial to the populace':[3] we should not forget that the word ψεῦδος means 'fiction' rather than 'falsehood'. As for the famous formula which comes at the end of the same passage: 'I can take

---
[1] G. Bardy, in *Dictionnaire de Théologie Catholique*, s.v. Jean Philopon, cols. 835, 837.
[2] *Saint Augustin et la fin de la culture antique*, Retractatio (Paris, 1949), pp. 629-30.
[3] *Ep*. cv, loc. cit.

over the holy office on condition that I can philosophize at home, mythicize in public',[1] φιλοσοφῶν, φιλομυθῶν, it refers us back to the venerable and fruitful part played by the notion of myth in the Platonic tradition.[2] It does not mean for Synesius a double truth, two irreconcilable and contradictory truths, but two presentations of the same doctrine, one scientific, the other suitable for weaker spirits. It is a question of adjusting the intensity of the light to the capacities of the intellectual vision: 'For light is to the truth what the eye is to the mind. Just as the eye would be injured by excess of light, and just as darkness is more helpful to those of weak eyesight',[3] so the myth may be beneficial to the common people. Here again it is not a pagan who is speaking, but a man of letters of the ancient world, with his prejudices, his intellectual pride, his contempt for simple souls, 'the populace', 'the vulgar'.

One would love to know what the patriarch Theophilus replied to these propositions. I am prepared to believe that this pastor, who preached very simple sermons to his flock on the healing of the woman with an issue of blood, or on the good thief, on death and judgement, repentance and sobriety—and who was also a man of action, the spirited antagonist of St. John Chrysostom and of John of Jerusalem—must have thought that this intellectual raised difficulties where none existed and was making mountains out of molehills. We know in any case how the clergy of Ptolemais answered Synesius: 'I listened', he tells us, 'to certain aged priests who averred that God was acting as my shepherd, and one of these said that the Holy Spirit is joyful, and fills with joy those who receive Him; adding that demons disputed the possession of me with God. . . . But . . . none the less the philosopher priest is not neglected by God. . . .'[4] So Synesius gave way. 'I was overcome by God', he says,[5] hoping, as they had promised him, that his entry into orders would not be for him 'a descent from the realm of philosophy, but rather a step upwards to it'.[6]

There was not to be time, however, for the fulfilment of

[1] I have altered Fitzgerald's translation, which misses the pun in the Greek.
[2] There are some excellent observations on this point in K. Treu, op. cit., p. 54; on *Dion*, Terzaghi, 4, p. 245. 14 (Petavius, p. 42C), for the word φιλόμυθος, which comes from Aristotle, reappears several times in Synesius: e.g. *de Providentia*, Terzaghi, i. 2, p. 66. 5 (Petavius, p. 90A).
[3] *Ep.* cv: still the same passage.
[4] *Ep.* lvii, Petavius, p. 194; Fitzgerald, p. 132.
[5] Ibid., Fitzgerald, p. 131.
[6] *Ep.* xcvi, p. 236; Fitzgerald, p. 184.

this dream. As he had feared, no sooner was he ordained than overwhelming responsibilities were thrust upon him. He found himself besieged by the Ausurian barbarians in the episcopal city. He was forced to struggle against a wicked governor, Andronicus, whom in the end he had to excommunicate. In religious matters he had to warn the faithful against the perils of the Arian heresy, which was recurring in the virulent form of Anomoeanism: he had also to resist the encroachments of a neighbouring bishop.[1] In addition there were domestic tragedies: the death of his wife presumably,[2] the deeply felt loss of his three sons. We learn of this from a last letter to his old teacher, Hypatia—a moving letter, revealing despondency and resignation rather than a spirit of Christian hope.[3] No, Synesius did not have time to become a saint. He did not have time to become the Christian philosopher for whom his questions had prepared the way. What he was unable to do, others did after him: Aeneas, Procopius, Zacharias, Joannes Philoponus. But we must not forget that it was with Synesius, the first baptized Neoplatonist, that the Christian Neoplatonism of Alexandria began.

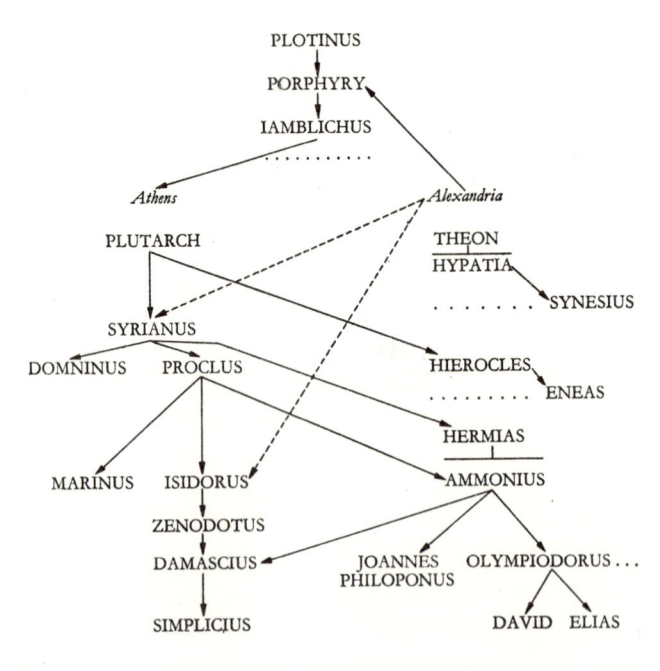

```
                        PLOTINUS
                           |
                        PORPHYRY
                           |
                        IAMBLICHUS
                       ..........
            Athens                  Alexandria
           PLUTARCH                   THEON
                                      HYPATIA
                                      ........ SYNESIUS
           SYRIANUS
    DOMNINUS   PROCLUS              HIEROCLES
                                    ......... ENEAS
                                      HERMIAS
    MARINUS   ISIDORUS               AMMONIUS
             ZENODOTUS
             DAMASCIUS ←   JOANNES    OLYMPIODORUS...
                |         PHILOPONUS
             SIMPLICIUS              DAVID   ELIAS
```

[1] For all this, see Lacombrade, op. cit., pp. 229 ff.
[2] There is no further mention of her after *Ep.* cv of 410.
[3] *Ep.* xvi, Petavius, p. 173; Fitzgerald, pp. 99–100.

VII

Anti-Christian Arguments and Christian Platonism: from Arnobius to St. Ambrose

PIERRE COURCELLE

IN studying the basic elements in the conflict of ideas between Christianity and paganism and their development in the course of the fourth century, it is instructive to compare the work of Ambrose, which dates from the last quarter of the century, with that of Arnobius, which goes back to the first decade. Both present us with an abundance of anti-Christian statements, some of which are in the form of popular sayings, some in the form of intellectual arguments deriving directly or indirectly from Neoplatonism. Between these two writers, however, the methods of Christian apologetics changed considerably.

Arnobius' *Adversus nationes* is directed against an opponent, or sometimes against several opponents, to whom are ascribed all manner of allegations, introduced either by *inquit* or *inquiunt*, or indirectly. If we piece together the truly anti-Christian statements from amongst these we can detect a more or less coherent doctrine and the various stages of an argument. At the beginning of the work the adversary expresses the spirit of this doctrine in three general propositions. 'Ever since the Christians have been on the earth, the world has gone to ruin; many and various scourges have attacked the human race; and the celestial beings themselves, abandoning the care with which hitherto they have watched over our interests, are banished from the regions of the earth.' These three grievances are repeated a few lines farther on in a slightly different form. 'The world has departed from its natural law, the gods are banished to afar, and many afflictions have befallen the generations of men.'[1] These propositions, expressive of popular anger and hatred, were formulated by a few arrogant intellectuals, according to Arnobius, with as much frenzy as if they were pronouncing an oracle.[2]

The new evils, for which the progress of Christianity was held responsible, were carefully enumerated.

> The earth had fallen victim to decay since the Christian religion had been introduced into the world. . . . Epidemics, droughts, wars, famines, locusts, mice, hail and other frightful things had been inflicted upon the human race by the gods, who were exasperated by the insulting and offensive behaviour of the Christians. . . .[3] The shortage of grain, the lack of corn, was worse than had ever been known before. . . .[4] There was no rain, there was an unbelievable famine.[5]

Similar grievances, which belong to all ages, had been mentioned by Tertullian and St. Cyprian.[6] But there were some which were more specific and immediate. Violent earthquakes had imperilled the cities:[7] there had been wars, ruined towns, the invasions of the Germans and the Goths.[8] As Arnobius' Book I appears to have been written in 296–7, there seems little doubt that this refers to the great invasion of the Goths in 269, which was crushed by Claudius II, and to the German invasion of 276, repulsed by Probus: the double threat had been extremely alarming and it was many years before Gaul recovered from the devastation.[9] The anger of the gods against the Christian religion was the only explanation offered for these invasions.[10] And it accounted also for all other calamities: if it were true that the activities of the Christians were harmless, from where did these evils come that had lately been oppressing suffering humanity?[11] It was entirely the fault of the Christians if the gods now unleashed these calamities upon the world and the heavenly beings destroyed the harvests.[12] At the same time, the pagans blamed themselves for neglecting their own cults, which led to the advance of Christian propaganda and aroused the rancour of the gods: the gods were ignored, they cried, and the faithful rarely seen in the temples: the ancient ceremonies were scorned, and the sacred rites of old had succumbed before the superstitions of unheard-of cults. It was no more than just that the human race should be beset by so many difficulties and miseries, and fall victim to so many hardships.[13] For, they say, you practise profane rites and unheard-of cults all over the earth.[14]

Continuing his argument with a rhetorical figure of speech (*praeteritio*) Arnobius avoids identifying these opponents; he does not explain from where they derive their authority or their knowledge, nor does he say why they trembled when they heard the name of Christ yet regarded his disciples as their most hated enemies.[15]

It was to the Christians, rather than Christ, that they took exception, and on whom they heaped all kinds of offensive epithets. They emphasized the enfeebled and obtuse nature of their intelligence, the emptiness of their doctrine,[16] and still more their impiety; for, though the Christians might honour the supreme god they were nevertheless dangerous atheists.[17] Not only did they themselves fail to worship the gods, they even had the impudence to claim that the pagans did not worship the supreme god.[18] The Christians had the audacity to worship a man: 'The gods are hostile to you not because you worship the all-powerful god, but because you allege that a being who was born a man and who died on the cross (a death which would bring shame on the lowest of men) was god, that he still survives to this day, and you address your daily prayers to him.'[19] Apart from stressing the infamous nature of the gallows, it was suggested that a god could not die a violent death; by definition divinity could not be touched by violence.[20]

They found it hard to believe that the Christians were sincere when they worshipped him as a god and the founder of their sect.[21] The assertion that Christ's mission as redeemer was entrusted to him by the Supreme King was not susceptible of proof, they argued.[22] His miracles were no proof of divine mission either: he was a magician and had accomplished them all by a secret art, having stolen the esoteric lore and the names of powerful angels from the Egyptian sanctuaries.[23] But he was a mortal man like anybody else.[24] Indeed, to pretend that he had been a god would not be a fitting motive for neglecting the other gods, who had themselves often cured men of sickness.[25] Aesculapius, for example, restored to health at least those honest people who deserved to be healed.[26] But Christ was an ordinary magician, like so many others from Zoroaster to Apollonius of Tyana, Julian the Chaldean, Baebulus, and the rest.[27] What is more, he was a charlatan.[28]

Whatever else may be said, they went on, it must at least be admitted that there is no truth in the story of his life.[29] The best proof of that is the description of the extraordinary cosmic phenomena which accompanied the death of this so-called god—

the earth shook, the sea drew back, the day grew dark, the sun lost its warmth. Such disorder of the elements was a physical impossibility.[30] But then, the witnesses of these signs were very second-rate people.[31] Their accounts inflated the insignificant events to an inordinate degree.[32] Against them also was the fact that they did not have the prestige of antiquity: the authorities of the pagans were more ancient, more deserving therefore of belief, and closer to the truth.[33] The evangelists did not deserve any credence, because they were ignorant and simple folk;[34] their language was debased and vulgar;[35] the Christian scriptures were strewn with barbarisms, solecisms, and mistakes of all kinds.[36]

The human form of Jesus made it quite impossible to believe that he was a god: 'If Christ were god, why did he appear in human shape, why had he to die a human death?'[37] It was not at all necessary for his mission. 'Could not the Supreme King do what he had decided to do on earth without taking on a human shape?'[38] It was too easy to appeal, as Christians did, to the ineffable mysteries of the divine will, which neither men nor gods could understand.[39] In fact Christ deserved our hatred, because he drove out the other religions and forbade the worship of the gods.[40] His teachings did not deserve to be believed,[41] for he made promises without offering any proof that these promises would be fulfilled.[42]

The Christian faith was scoffed at because of its foolish trust in invisible realities.[43] Arnobius objects that Simon Magus was actually seen falling from the sky, to his own confusion, and that many other miracles had been observed. But his opponents considered that they did not need the help of the Christian Revelation, Arnobius went on; they trusted only in their own wisdom and allowed impostors (men of evil intention whose first desire was to see the name of Christ disappear) to obscure these mighty facts, so that the miracles inspired contempt instead of faith.[44]

Arnobius eventually discloses, as he had promised,[45] the identity of the philosophers who professed these anti-Christian opinions. They were the Hermetists, the Platonists, and the sect of *viri novi*:[46] they regarded Christian doctrine as stupid, though they professed similar ideas themselves.[47] They jeered at the Christians for worshipping God as the father and the lord of the universe, for entrusting to him all their hopes and for fearing from him the annihilation of the soul.[48] They reproached them for believing in the resurrection of the dead, but they did not properly understand the dogma.[49] They blamed them for attempting to provide by their own efforts for the salvation of their souls,[50] and for allowing for the existence of beings who consign souls to the fires of Gehenna.[51]

Arnobius then enters into a long digression, in order to expose and combat the doctrine of the *viri novi* concerning the immortality of the human soul, the daughter of God and impeccable.[52] Whilst the philosophers distinguished three possible ways of salvation—by purification through wisdom, by the theurgical prayers of the oriental magi, and by the Etruscan sacrifices of the Acherontic Books[53]—they refused to admit that Christ himself offered such a way. 'If Christ was sent by God to save unhappy souls from destruction, what of the fate of previous generations, which before his coming were destroyed in their mortal condition?'[54] The very novelty of Christianity, less than 400 years old,[55] was, they argued, a strong objection to its claim to be the way of universal salvation and to replace the ancestral religion by foreign and barbarian rites.[56] Why should the supreme God have waited so long, until so very recently,[57] before sending Christ the saviour down from heaven? Moreover, if Christ came to save the human race, as was said, why did he not free all men with equal generosity?[58] It would have been enough to ordain salvation for everybody. If God were powerful, merciful, and a saviour, let him change our understanding and make us believe in his promises in spite of ourselves.[59] It was scandalous that non-Christians should find themselves denied the possibility of salvation: 'If I do not become a Christian, is there then for me no hope of salvation?'[60] It was also pointed out ironically that Christ apparently did not save even his own followers, let alone the infidels: 'Why, if you are the servants of the almighty God and if, according to your own belief, he watches over your safety and salvation, why then does he allow you to suffer so much persecution, so many trials and torments?'[61]

In Book III, Arnobius presents a new set of objections to Christianity. It is incomprehensible that the Christians cut themselves off from the syncretistic religions: 'If you have holy things so much at heart, why do you not honour and worship other gods with us, why do you not share your rites in common with those of your fellow countrymen?'[62] That is why the pagans refused to read the Christian scriptures and thought it right that the senate should destroy them: they undermined the respect due to the old national traditions.[63]

The Christians were criticized for worshipping a male god,[64] and assuming that the divinity had a bodily shape,[65] as Jews and Sadducees did in their writings.[66] It was no use for Christians to refer to the forms of certain pagan gods; these were not in fact artisans but only represented as such because they were the patrons of various arts and teachers of various crafts.[67] Also, the myths, in which the Christians saw nothing but their lack of morality, were understandable on account of their value as total[68] or partial[69] allegories. Finally, they charged the Christians with having no temples, statues, or effigies of their divinity, no altars on which to offer sacrifices, incense, libations, and sacred meals.[70]

As we have seen, the *Adversus nationes* is, from beginning to end, a reply to anti-Christian arguments which, in Book II at least, are not of a popular but of a philosophical character. I have shown elsewhere, through the close parallels which exist between the texts, that the reasoning is that of Porphyry, the author of the two great works *Against the Christians* and *On the Return of the Soul*. The doctrine of the soul professed, according to Arnobius, by the *viri novi* is none other than that of the 'sages' to whom Porphyry attributed the discovery of a philosophical way of salvation, superior to the theurgical methods of the magi, the way of the Etruscans, and, naturally, to the way of Christ. As opposed to the magi, who sought the purification of the 'pneumatic' soul, the way of the 'sages' achieved the purification of the 'intellectual' soul, so that the soul, daughter of God, could return by herself and without hindrance to her Father's dwelling.

The point worth noting is that whilst Arnobius deployed all the resources of his vehemence and irony against the mad pride of his opponents, he reminds them at the same time that 'their dear Plato' ('Plato vester . . ., ut eum potissimum nominem') actually held theories which were very close to the Christian dogmas. These pagan philosophers, for all their imputations against the Christians, did themselves watch over the salvation of their souls, either by refraining from passion, or by using the theurgical formulas of prayers. Arnobius insisted on Plato's insight, on the fact that he was not far from the truth, as if his authority were equally acceptable to Hermetists, *Platonici* and the 'others'. He praises the *prudentia* of Plato who, in the *De animae immortalitate* (the *Phaedo*), whilst upholding the immortality and incorporeity of the soul, asserted at the same time, in spite of the apparent contradiction, that souls are cast into rivers of fire. Plato must have had a presentiment of the Christian doctrine (or of what Arnobius claimed to be Christian doctrine) according to which the soul was liable either to be annihilated or, if it had earned it, to become immortal.[71]

None the less, it might be asked whether Arnobius was in fact attempting to outline a synthesis between Platonist philosophy and the Christian revelation, as Eusebius of Caesarea or Theodoret of Cyrrhus did in Greek.[72] My answer is that it is much more likely that his tactics were to use his opponents' weapons against themselves, to turn against them the authorities they claimed as their own.[73] For sarcasm was the soul of Arnobius' polemical gifts.

The political victory of the Christian empire did not immediately put an end to the controversies, which were still very much alive at the close of the century. The pagans, it is true, had henceforth to take great care. Macrobius' commentary on the *Dream of Scipio*, for instance, did not betray any specifically anti-Christian purpose, although the beginning of his *Saturnales* indicated the survival of a group in Rome still greatly influenced by Porphyrean Hellenism, even if it did not dare to attack the victorious Christians openly.[74] To understand how both the anti-Christian polemic and the Christian position had developed by this time, one of the most useful witnesses is certainly St. Ambrose.[75] He had known personally the aristocrats for whom religious conservatism went hand in hand with the ancestral and national traditions; he describes their psychology.[76] His controversy with Symmachus over the Victory altar is too well known to be repeated at length. Symmachus maintained in his *Relatio* that a people, like each individual, received from the divine intelligence its own guardian spirit appointed by destiny. He asserted that throughout the whole of the national history this spirit had manifested itself, and that cults handed down from generation to generation ought to be continued.[77] In the form of a prosopopaeia, he makes Rome say:

Emperors, most excellent of men, fathers of the country, respect my old age: I have attained it thanks to my pious rites. Let me perform the ancestral ceremonies, for I have no reason to regret them. Let me live according to my custom, for I am free. This religion has subjected the universe to my laws, these sacrifices drove Hannibal from my walls and the Senonians from the Capitol. Was I saved only for reproaches in my great age?'[78]

Symmachus advocated a syncretism according to which there were all kinds of ways and all kinds of philosophies which helped to penetrate the mystery of divinity. He claimed toleration on this account,[79] but conceded implicitly that Christianity could be one of these ways. Ambrose, however, was not deceived. He recognized the essentially Porphyrean doctrine, which conceded that Christ was a 'sage' among others,[80] but not that he was a God, for God does not die and Christ died on the cross.[81]

We unfortunately no longer possess the treatise in several books in which Ambrose contrasted the *sacramentum regenerationis* with Platonic philosophy. All that we know is that it was an attack on those Neoplatonists who presented the teachings of Christ as a kind of counterfeit Platonism.[82] Far from inclining towards a synthesis, they insisted on the two dogmas most difficult to reconcile with the Christian faith. Firstly, on the question of the deity, they upheld polytheism, in which beneath the supreme God, the creator of souls, there were secondary gods, creators of bodies. Secondly, with regard to man, they insisted on metempsychosis.[83]

Since the *De philosophia* is lost, we can only piece together various remarks referring to the anti-Christian polemic from the surviving works of Ambrose; there are objections raised directly by the pagans,[83a] or else by Christians susceptible to their arguments.

Many of the criticisms were of an exegetical nature, attacking the Judaeo-Christian Revelation. The stories of Genesis, for instance, gave rise to the following dilemmas: Did God know or did he not that Adam would disobey his orders? If it is said that he did not know, that is inconsistent with the divine power. If he knew and nevertheless gave his orders, knowing that they would be disobeyed, it does not behove the divinity to issue superfluous injunctions.[84] This objection, notes Ambrose, is made by rationalist pagans as well as by certain heretics who rebel against the Old Testament. Others seized on the story of Abraham. 'How can you set up Abraham as a model, when he had a son by his maidservant? How could such a hero, many of whose deeds we admire, have committed this offence? . . . He was already conversing with God when he went in unto his servant!'[85] David was also assailed: was he not a murderer, an adulterer?

'What? The Christians attach so much importance to a clear conscience, they put faith to the fore, they venerate religion, they teach chastity; yet their masters committed murders and adulteries! This David, from whose house, you say, Christ chose to be born, celebrated his murders and adulteries in his songs. As the master, so the pupils.'[86] How could God have chosen such a man as king and made him victorious over many nations?[87]

Furthermore the New Testament, they say, does not agree with the Old Testament. Circumcision was thought to be useful in the Old Testament, where Abraham first received the divine oracle commanding its practice. But it is repudiated as useless in the New Testament.[88] And why should the seal of the divine covenant be put upon a shameful organ? How can the maker of our bodies desire such a thing, that no sooner are we born than his work should be circumcised, mutilated, and covered with blood: that a part should be cut off that the ordainer of all things saw fit to make at the same time as all the other members? Either this part of the body is against nature, and all men alike ought not to have this thing against nature, or else it is in accord with nature and it is not proper to amputate what was created in accordance with natural perfection. Furthermore, if God was proposing to call a great many men to practise this religion, he would have attracted many more if he had not discouraged a good number of them by the danger or disgrace of circumcision: to pagans, in fact, the circumcised are objects of derision.[89]

A similar line of reasoning was employed to emphasize the incompatibility of the Old and New Testaments: Why is it that, although God gave the Law to Moses, most of the tenets of the Law are now abandoned by the Gospels? How could there be one founder of both Testaments when what was allowed in the Law was no longer permitted in the Gospel—such as physical circumcision, which is a non-rational sign. How do we account for the contradiction that circumcision, formerly believed to be a mark of piety, is now considered a sign of godlessness? Again, observance of the Law required that the Sabbath should be a day of rest and the penalty for gathering wood on that day was death. Now one can fetch and carry and go about one's business without incurring any penalty. The precepts of the law are, for the most part, no longer accepted.[90] And when the Old Testament commanded that shoes should be worn to eat of the lamb, why did Jesus tell his disciples to go barefoot?[91] In the same vein, they observe ironically that the just who lived before Christ must have had to remain for a very long time without their reward, waiting for the day of judgement to come.[92]

It seemed impossible to accept the idea of an incarnate Son of God,[93] or of a newborn God.[94] They made a joke of Luke's verse in which it was said that Jesus was 'supposed' to be the son of Joseph,[95] and in the genealogy in St. Matthew they discovered several women of ill-repute.[96] The discrepancies between the synoptic Gospels were also emphasized. Who complained about the annointing of Christ's feet, his disciples or a pharisee?[97] Did Christ meet two men at Gerasa or only one?[98] There were discrepancies too in the accounts of the signs accompanying the crucifixion,[99] and the witnesses were at odds with one another about what happened at the resurrection.[100]

Every effort was made to discredit Jesus himself and his teaching. He proved himself lacking in foresight and power when he chose Judas as an apostle, without suspecting that he was going to betray him.[101] When he promised the eleven a place in his father's house, there was nothing to prove that he meant humanity in general.[102] To say, as he did, 'Salute no man by the way', was a harsh and haughty precept, unbecoming in a master who was supposed to be gentle and meek: the pagans did not hesitate to salute Christians.[103] As for the Apostles, they were being even more harsh when they forbade little children to come unto him.[104]

The whole Judaeo-Christian morality was challenged. Its precepts were deplorable. For example, 'An eye for an eye, a tooth for a tooth', and, 'If thy right hand offend thee, cut it off'.[105] The doctrine of sin and forgiveness, moreover, was senseless. For one thing, man was not responsible for his mistakes: his decisions and his actions were excusable because he acted under the compulsion of necessity; nobody was voluntarily wicked, not even the murderer Cain.[106] This necessity was a result of our *nativitas*, of the position of the stars at the time of our birth.[107] The idea of forgiveness is inadmissible: God cannot be angered and then forgive, for the deity is immutable.[108] In any case, what need is there for forgiveness? 'Why baptize me? I have never sinned.'[109]

The precepts of asceticism were particularly odious and, they said, unheard of even within the Judaeo-Christian tradition. 'Why, bishop, do you forbid us to have earrings and bracelets when Rebecca received such things as a gift and you exhort us to be like Rebecca?'[110] Fasting too was a novelty.[111] And to give alms was contrary to the divine will; if God had reduced a person to poverty it was a sign of his displeasure.[112] Virginity, they maintained, was not at all the monopoly of the Christians, as the Christians seemed to imagine: the Vestal virgins and the priestesses of Pallas were the equals of the Christian virgins and their virginity was dedicated to the well-being of the state.[113] The Pythagorean philosophy of silence also trained virgins, who had behaved heroically in refusing to betray a secret.[114] As for chastity in marriage, it was beyond human endurance, insupportable, a torture.[115] Violent reproaches were levied against aristocrats, like Paulinus of Nola, who, not content with renouncing conjugal life, dispose of their fortunes and become monks, exchanging their social position and responsibilities for the monastic life: it was intolerable that a man of so great a family, of such nobility, of such character, gifted with so much eloquence, should leave the senate and break the order of succession.[116] . . . Many conversions had an ulterior motive, they added: some might simulate Christianity for a time in order either to secure a young girl from her parents, or a job. These people did not shrink from genuflexions designed to deceive the public authorities; they put on Christianity like a borrowed garment.[117]

From the philosophical point of view, the pagans directed their arguments above all against the Christian conception of the afterlife. The most disputed doctrine was that of the resurrection of the body, a stumbling-block to Athenians since the days when Paul preached on the Areopagus.[118] 'How are the dead raised up? And with what body do they come? What was rotten cannot become fresh again, nor scattered limbs be reunited, nor what was consumed be restored. . . . Men swallowed by the sea, men torn and devoured by wild beasts, cannot be given back by the earth.'[119] Though the pagans were united in denying the resurrection, which to them belonged in the realm of poetic myth,[120] they were divided on the question of the eventual fate of the human soul. Some believed it to be mortal.[121] But others, dreading the thought of its destruction, believed in metensomatosis.[122] 'Souls', they said, 'are common to men and to beasts. The highest reward, for the souls of the great philosophers, is to migrate into the bees or the nightingales; they who have nourished the human race on their words, then charm it with the sweetness of their honey or the beauty of their song.'[123] The famous story of Circe was given a philosophical meaning: each man becomes the animal for which his aptitudes have fitted him.[124] One of the few passages of the *De philosophia* which has survived, thanks to St. Augustine, is concerned with just this question of metempsychosis. Ambrose is scolding Plato:

> I am astonished that so great a philosopher, who attributes to the soul the power to receive immortality, should enclose it in owls or frogs, and also confine it within ferocious wild beasts, even though in the *Timaeus* he refers to it as the work of God, made by God along with the immortal beings; whereas the body, he assures us, does not appear to be the work of the supreme God, since the flesh of man does not differ in its nature from the flesh of beasts.[125]

It is surprising that Ambrose is never mentioned in Stettner's work on metempsychosis.[125a] The views expressed in these three quotations appear to have a certain unity and probably derive from some commentary on Plato according to which philosophical souls are changed into bees and nightingales, and the rest into frogs, owls, and wild beasts. Various elements of a classification of this kind are to be found scattered throughout Plato's work. In the *Phaedo* men who had practised the social and civic virtues of temperance and justice become bees.[126] In the tenth book of the *Republic*, Er the Pamphylian declares that he had seen the soul of Thamyras choosing the life of a nightingale and that of Ajax the life of a lion.[127] Wild beasts reappear in the *Timaeus* as the final resting-place for those who had had no use for philosophy, but were wholly $Θυμός$.[128]

Already, several of these elements come together in Plotinus: singing birds, bees, wild beasts.[129] But Ambrose was certainly not following Plotinus here. For the latter still accepted metensomatosis in the strict sense and does not say a word about frogs and owls. Ambrose's source on the contrary furnished an allegorical interpretation of the Circe episode: the metamorphoses acclaimed by the poets meant only that the soul, by its own conduct, might be reduced to the level of a particular beast. One such interpretation of the Circe myth, attempting to prove that, in spite of Plotinus, Plato had never said that the human soul did in practice enter the body of an animal, was the work of Porphyry, who believed, nevertheless, in the doctrine of metempsychosis and contested the Christian dogma of the resurrection of the body.[130] He was followed on this point by Iamblichus who, as we learn from Nemesius, wrote a book called, 'Metensomatosis does not

Anti-Christian Arguments and Christian Platonism 163

take place from men into reasonless beasts nor from reasonless beasts into men, but from beasts into beasts and from men into men'.[131] Nemesius himself adopted this view, which prevailed among the majority of the later Neoplatonists[132] and was known and accepted by Latins as well;[133] even some ecclesiastical writers believed that they had found in the scriptures texts to support it.[134] But Ambrose did not only reject metensomatosis in the sense of mythological metamorphoses into the bodies of animals. He denied the very idea of metempsychosis, that is the passage of the human soul after death into the body of another human being leading a brutish life of one kind or another. For the human soul, created in the image of God and destined to have dominion over the animals, could not possibly, in as much as it was rational, be transformed into an animal. It was really the view of Porphyry and the later Neoplatonists, too, that St. Ambrose was condemning.

Some of his observations allow us at least to find our bearings as far as his sources are concerned. His argument depends in fact on making Plato contradict himself. On the one hand, Plato argued that the soul passed from body to body, including the bodies of wild animals, frogs, and owls. On the other hand, he said in the *Timaeus* that the soul was an immortal being, the work of the Demiurge, whilst the body was the work of inferior deities. These views were incompatible because the value attached to the soul was different in either case. Ambrose concluded that it was more coherent to reject the whole doctrine of metempsychosis, in whatever form, and to affirm that the body was the work of the supreme God, just as much as the soul.

Ambrose's source was no doubt some Christian apologist, for a series of similar texts—the passage from the *Phaedo* on palingenesis and the passage from the *Timaeus*—are used by Tertullian,[135] and the same exposition of the *Timaeus* provided Chalcidius[136] and St. Augustine[137] with the opportunity to consider the question of metempsychosis in general.

On the other hand, the two examples of the frog and the owl are not invented either; they also are traditional. I have no doubt that we would seek in vain for any mention of these two animals in Plato[137a] or in the works of his numerous pagan commentators. But the Christian apologist Aeneas of Gaza indicated, as a possible end of metensomatosis, on the same level as ants and wasps, the frog: it was the body reserved for the garrulous, for men like

Cleon.[138] In this context Aeneas of Gaza mentioned two birds—the nightingale, which comes directly from Plato's *Republic*, (620a), and the jackdaw (κολοιός).[139] The satirical origin of the choice of the latter bird is obvious from Lucian's *The Cock*, which was a direct attack on the doctrine of metensomatosis.[140] The cock with the human voice tells us that he is the last incarnation of Pythagoras and humorously narrates the whole posthumous history of the philosopher. His two most recent incarnations were precisely the jackdaw and the frog.[141] The reason why these two creatures appear together, immediately preceding the cock, is because they stand for the type of malicious or pretentious chatterbox.[142] Later in Lucian the frog and the jackdaw appear again together, the former being related to the profession of the sycophants, the latter to that of the Sophists.[143] What he was trying to show, as he had already warned the reader, was that the doctrine of metempsychosis consisted of no more than empty and idle chatter, and that Pythagoras would have done better to practise his own precept of silence.[144] Gregory of Nyssa also said that Pythagoras chattered like frogs and jackdaws when he was expounding his views on metensomatosis.[144a]

It seems to me very likely that the passage from Ambrose's *De philosophia* is to be explained in terms of this satirical tradition. It may be a little surprising that he should use, together with the frog, *noctua* (instead of *monedula*) as an equivalent of κολοιός. But I think that either he or the apologist he was following resorted to this approximate translation because the jackdaw may have been considered to be in some way related to the owl (as the French words *le choucas* and *la chouette* suggest).[145] In any case, the contexts of Lucian, Gregory of Nyssa, and Ambrose show us that these creatures were chosen to exemplify extreme cases and to show how absurd and 'monstrous' such a doctrine was.[146]

We may add that the immediate context of the passage in Aeneas of Gaza concerning the frog expresses views very close to those apparently held by Ambrose himself. It is not enough, he says, to deny with Porphyry and Iamblichus that a man can be turned into a bird of prey (ἰκτῖνος). It is also necessary to say—as Syrianus and Proclus did against Porphyry and Iamblichus—that the predatory soul cannot even become a man with the soul of a bird of prey.[147] The object of the two Christian apologists is naturally to forbid—even if Syrianus and Proclus never thought of doing such a thing—every possible form of reincarnation other than the return of the soul into its own body at the resurrection of the dead.

It will be observed that Ambrose is here attempting to show that the human soul has nothing in common with that of beasts.[148] He is completely opposed in this respect to the reasoning of Arnobius, who confuted the Neoplatonists with their own doctrine of metempsychosis. Criticizing them for exalting the human soul for being close to the divinity by its νοῦς and λόγος, he reduced man to the level of the other animals, as Montaigne was to do in his turn in *l'Apologie de Sebond*.[149] Ambrose maintained, on the contrary, the dominion of man over the animals and the pre-eminence of the human soul. But if their objectives differed, their polemical methods were of the same order. To judge from the fragment of his *De philosophia*, Ambrose was ready enough to use once more the old weapons forged by the sceptic Lucian against pythagorized Platonism.

The researches of the last ten years have shown more than anything else how deeply imbued with Platonism Ambrose was. I pointed out in 1950 how he did not hesitate in his sermons, *De Isaac* and *De bono mortis*, to follow closely and consistently several treatises from the *Enneads*.[150] Since then, Father Solignac has succeeded in proving a similar relationship between the *De Jacob* of Ambrose and the Plotinian treatise *On Happiness*.[151] Important contributions have also been made by Taormina and Hadot,[152] and it is particularly evident that Ambrose was influenced by the later exegetes of the *Phaedo*, especially by those discussed by Porphyry in *De regressu animae*.[153] It is not at all impossible that he had obtained his knowledge of Neoplatonism from certain Greek Fathers.[154] He even seems to have appreciated Macrobius' commentary on *The Dream of Scipio* as soon as it was published, though it issued from the pagan circles around Symmachus.[155] He preferred, as more easily compatible with Christianity, Plotinus' moral teaching to his metaphysical theories, and he suppressed allusions which were too flagrantly pagan, but he was nevertheless so imbued with their doctrine and metaphorical vocabulary that he was capable of truly Neoplatonist lapses on such questions as the pre-existence and descent of souls.[156] The work of synthesis, which had hardly begun with Arnobius,[157] had been carried a long way by Ambrose, almost recklessly far.

It is certainly not my intention to question recent progress in patristic studies. But the present inquiry does offer one important corrective. The same Ambrose who bears witness to such a strong desire for a synthesis also knew, when a doctrine appeared to him clearly incompatible with the Christian faith, how to reject it without hesitation and to pursue it with the most cruel irony.

NOTES

1. Arnobius, *Adversus Nationes*, i. 1, ed. C. Marchesi, in *Corpus Paravianum* (Turin, 1953), p. 1, 1: 'Quoniam comperi nonnullos, qui se plurimum sapere suis persuasionibus credunt, insanire, bacchari et uelut quiddam promptum ex oraculo dicere: "postquam esse in mundo Christiana gens coepit, terrarum orbem perisse, multiformibus malis affectum esse genus humanum, ipsos etiam caelites derelictis curis sollemnibus, quibus quondam solebant inuisere res nostras, terrarum ab regionibus exterminatos", statui pro captu ac mediocritate sermonis contraire inuidiae et calumniosas dissoluere criminationes.... Neque enim negauerim ualidissimam esse accusationem istam hostilibusque condignos odiis nos esse, si apud nos esse constiterit causas, per quas suis mundus aberrauit ab legibus, exterminati sunt dii longe, examina tanta maerorum mortalium inportata sunt saeculis'; iii. 11, p. 169, 17: 'res perditas inuenietis humanas et abiecisse clauum deos.... Nam nobis quidem cur irascantur non habent' (cf. in Augustine the expressions *ruit mundus, pereunt omnia, Roma perit*: see my articles, 'Propos antichrétiens rapportés par S. Augustin', *Recherches Augustiniennes*, i (1958), 180, nn. 162, 168, 171; 'Critiques exégétiques et arguments antichrétiens rapportés par Ambrosiaster', in *Vigiliae Christianae* xiii (1959), pp. 133–69). The *abiecisse clauum* indicates that the gods reject their providential rudder, which explains in the preceding text the *derelictis curis*; it is not a question, as MacCracken believes, of abandoning sacrifices.

2. The words *insanire, bacchari*, seem to be chosen with a view to evoking the oracular delirium.

3. Arnobius, i. 3, p. 4. 13: '... dicitur inuectam esse labem terris, postquam religio Christiana intulit se mundo.... "Sed pestilentias, inquiunt, et siccitates, bella, frugum inopiam, locustas, mures et grandines resque alias noxias, quibus negotia incursantur humana, dii nobis inportant iniuriis uestris atque offensionibus exasperati"' (cf. Augustine, my article, p. 181, n. 169, the proposition *antequam ista doctrina per mundum praedicaretur*); iv. 24, p. 229. 2: 'miseriarum omnium causas, quibus genus, ut dicitis, iamdudum afflictatur humanum' (cf. Augustine, my article, p. 181, n. 173: '*Roma ... afflicta est*').

4. Ibid., i. 3, p. 5. 9: 'Penuria, inquit, frugum et angustiae frumentariae artius nos habent.... Casus frequentissimi grandinis accidunt atque adterunt cuncta.... Difficiles pluuiae sata faciunt emori et sterilitatem indicunt terris. ... Pestilentiae contagia urunt genus humanum.... Ab locustis, a muribus genus omne acciditur atque adroditur frugum.'

5. Ibid. i. 9, p. 10. 11: 'Non pluit, inquit, caelum et frumentorum inopia

nescio qua laboramus' (cf. Augustine, my article, p. 179, n. 155: '*Non pluit...
pluuia defit*').

6. Tertullian, *Apol.* xl; *Ad Nat.* i. 9; Cyprian, *Ad Demetrianum*, ii, C.S.E.L. iii. 1, p. 252. 7.

7. Arnobius, p. 6. 8: 'Terrarum ualidissimis motibus tremefactae nutant usque ad periculum ciuitates'; cf. Cyprian, *Epist. ad Firmilianum*, lxxv. 10, C.S.E.L. iii. 2, p. 816. 18: 'Ante uiginti enim et duos fere annos temporibus post Alexandrum imperatorem . . . terrae etiam motus plurimi et frequentes extiterunt, ut per Cappadociam et per Pontum multa subruerent, quaedam etiam ciuitates in profundum receptae dirupti soli hiatu deuorarentur, ut ex hoc persecutio quoque grauis aduersum nos nominis fieret' (events of the year 235; cf. M. Besnier, *L'Empire romain de l'avènement des Sevères au Concile de Nicée* (Paris, 1937), p. 145. I do not agree therefore with W. Kroll, 'Die Zeit des Cornelius Labeo', in *Rheinisches Museum*, lxxi (1916), 321, that the source is Tertullian.

8. Arnobius, i. 4, p. 6. 21: 'Nobis obiectare consuestis bellorum frequentium causas, uastationes urbium, Germanorum et Scythicas inruptiones'; i. 16, p. 14. 10: 'Quanquam istud quod dicitur quale sit explicabili non potest conprehensione cognosci. Si Alamannos, Persas, Scythas idcirco uoluerunt deuinci, quod habitarent et degerent in eorum gentibus Christiani, quemadmodum Romanis tribuere uictoriam, cum habitarent et degerent in eorum quoque gentibus Christiani?'

9. See my *Histoire littéraire des grandes invasions germaniques* (Paris, 1948), p. 9.

10. Arnobius, i. 6, p. 8. 1: 'Ista quae dicitis bella religionis nostrae ob inuidiam commoueri'; iv. 24, p. 229. 9: '. . . ut in inuidiam iaciantur nostram labores generis humani et commoditates quibus uiuitur imminutae' (cf. Augustine, my article, p. 179, n. 158: 'humanarum rerum felicitas defessa ac *deminuta*').

11. Ibid. i. 7, p. 8. 22: 'Sed si per uos, inquiunt, nihil rebus incommodatur humanis, unde sunt haec mala, quibus urgetur et premitur iamdudum miseranda mortalitas?'

12. Ibid. i. 13, p. 12. 20: 'Christianorum, inquiunt, causa mala omnia di serunt et interitus comparatur ab superis frugibus.' The *inquiunt* is taken up, p. 13. 7, by the singular: 'ei qui nos arguit' (cf. Augustine, my article, p. 179, n. 155: '*Causa Christiani sunt*').

13. Ibid. i. 24, p. 20. 1: 'Negleguntur dii, clamitant, atque in templis iam raritas summa est, iacent antiquae derisui caerimoniae et sacrorum quondam ueterrimi ritus religionum nouarum superstitionibus occiderunt, et merito humanum genus tot miseriarum angustiis premitur, tot laborum excruciatur aerumnis: et homines, brutum genus et quod situm sub lumine est caecitate ingenita nequeuntes uidere, audent adseuerare furiosi quod uos credere non erubescitis sani' (the phrase *et homines* is not very clear; A.-J. Festugière 'Arnobiana', in *Vigiliae Christianae*, vi (1952), 219, rightly understands it as a reflection of Arnobius); iii. 24, p. 182. 9: 'Tutelatoribus, inquit, supplicat diis nemo, et idcirco singuli familiaribus officiis atque auxiliis desunt'; vii. 48, p. 408. 1: 'Nisi forte aliquis dicet, minoribus et consequentibus saeculis

idcirco dei talis defuisse custodiam, quod impiis iam moribus et inprobabilibus uiueretur' (cf. Augustine, my article, p. 179, n. 158 and p. 181, n. 174: '*deseruerunt; dii praesules*').

14. Ibid. i. 25, p. 20. 22: 'Religiones, inquiunt, impias atque inauditos cultus terrarum in orbe tractatis'; iv. 27, p. 234. 10: 'audetis salua uerecundia dicere, aut esse nos impios aut uos pios'; iv. 30, p. 236. 21: 'nos impios et inreligiosos uocatis, uos contra et deorum contenditis esse cultores.'

15. Ibid. i. 27, p. 22. 8: 'Nondum est locus ut explicemus, omnes isti qui nos damnant qui sint uel unde sint, quantum possint uel nouerint, cur ad Christi paueant mentionem, discipulos cur eius inimicos habent et inuisos' (cf. Augustine, my article, p. 154, n. 26: 'quamuis audeant Christianos, Christum non audent reprehendere'; and n. 27: 'quantum sit illud nomen').

16. Ibid. i. 28, p. 23. 12: 'Nos hebetes, stolidi, fatui, obtunsi pronuntiamur et bruti, qui dedidimus nos deo, cuius nutu et arbitrio omne quod est constat?'; ii. 6, p. 70, 19: 'Nisi forte obtunsi et fatui uidentur hi uobis, qui per orbem iam totum conspirant et coeunt in istius credulitatis adsensum?' (cf. Augustine, my article, p. 151, n. 9: '*hebetem*').

17. Ibid. i. 29, p. 24. 24: 'Ergone impiae religionis sumus apud uos rei, et quod caput rerum et columen uenerabilibus adimus obsequiis, ut conuicio utamur uestro, infausti et athei nuncupamur?'

18. Ibid. i. 34, p. 28. 19: 'Sed frustra, inquit, nos falso et calumnioso incessitis et adpetitis crimine, tamquam eamus infitias esse deum maiorem, cum a nobis et Iuppiter nominetur et optimus habeatur et maximus cumque illi augustissimas sedes et Capitolia constituerimus immania.'

19. Ibid. i. 36, p. 30. 1: 'Sed non, inquit, idcirco dii uobis infesti sunt, quod omnipotentem colatis deum, sed quod hominem natum et, quod personis infame est uilibus, crucis supplicio interemptum et deum fuisse contenditis et superesse adhuc creditis et cotidianis supplicationibus adoratis'; i. 41, p. 36. 3: 'Et tamen, o isti, qui hominem nos colere morte functum ignominiosa ridetis, nonne Liberum et uos patrem membratim ab Titanis dissipatum fanorum consecratione mactatis?' (cf. Augustine, my article, p. 156, nn. 40–41: '*crucifixum colamus*' and already in Tertullian, *Apol.* xxi. 3, ed. Waltzing (Budé), p. 47: 'Sed et uulgus iam sciunt Christum, hominem utique aliquem, qualem Iudaei iudicauerunt: quo facilius quis nos hominis cultores existimauerit'; Lactantius, *Inst.* iv. 16. 1, p. 337. 9: 'Venio nunc ad ipsam passionem, quae uelut obprobrium nobis obiectari solet, quod et hominem et ab hominibus insigni supplicio adfectum et cruciatum colamus.'

20. Arnobius, i. 40, p. 35. 6: 'Sed patibulo adfixus interiit.—Quid istud ad causam? Neque enim qualitas et deformitas mortis dicta eius immutat aut facta, aut eo minor uidebitur disciplinarum eius auctoritas, quia uinculis corporis non naturali dissolutione digressus est, sed ui inlata decessit.'

21. Ibid. i. 42, p. 37. 8: 'Infitiaturos arbitramini nos esse, quam maxime illum ab nobis coli et praesidem nostri corporis nuncupari?'; ii. 60, p. 136. 11: 'Christus licet uobis inuitis deus.'

22. Ibid. i. 42, p. 37. 10: 'Ergone, inquiet aliquis furens iratus et percitus, deus ille est Christus? Deus, respondebimus, et interiorum potentiarum deus

et quod magis infidos acerbissimis doloribus torqueat, rei maximae causa a summo rege ad nos missus. Postulabit forsitan insanior et furiosior factus, an se ita res habeat, quemadmodum dicimus, comprobari' (cf. Augustine, my article, p. 160, n. 55). We should no doubt read *inferiorum* for *interiorum*; cf. A.-J. Festugière, 'Arnobiana', p. 220.

23. Ibid. i. 43, p. 37. 24: 'Occursurus forsitan rursus est cum aliis multis calumniosis illis et puerilibus uocibus: "Magus fuit, clandestinis artibus omnia illa perfecit, Aegyptiorum ex adytis angelorum potentium nomina et remotas furatus est disciplinas"' (cf. Eusebius of Caesarea, *Demonstratio*, iii. 6, *P.G.* xxii. 232B, where he refers to a similar charge against Jesus: Ἀλλὰ διδασκάλοις αὐτὸν φῂς προσεσχηκέναι πλάνοις, μηδὲ λαθεῖν αὐτὸν τὰ σοφὰ τῶν Αἰγυπτίων, καὶ τῶν πάλαι παρ' αὐτοῖς λεγομένων τὰ ἀπόρρητα, παρ' ὧν συλλεξάμενον, ἄνδρα τοιοῦτον οἷον ὁ λόγος παρίστησιν, ἀποδειχθῆναι; Augustine, my article, p. 155, nn.27 and 31; J. Barbel, *Christos Angelos*, Theoph. 3 (Bonn, 1941), 219 et seq.)

24. Ibid. i. 45, p. 39. 6: 'Quid dicitis o iterum? Ergo ille mortalis aut unus fuit e nobis, cuius imperium, cuius uocem popularibus et cotidianis uerbis missam ualetudines, morbi, febres atque alia corporum cruciamenta fugiebant?'

25. Ibid. i. 48, p. 42. 10: 'Sed frustra, inquit nescio quis, tantum adrogas Christo, cum saepe alios sciamus et scierimus deos et laborantibus plurimis dedisse medicinas et multorum hominum morbos ualetudinesque curasse' (cf. Augustine, my article, p. 160, n. 56).

26. Ibid. i. 49, p. 44. 6: '... cum Aesculapium ipsum datorem, ut praedicant, sanitatis, quoad illis superfuit uita, et precibus fatigarent et inuitarent miserrimis uotis.... Nisi forte dicetis, opem bonis ab diis ferri, malorum miserias despici.'

27. Ibid. i. 52, p. 48. 1: 'Age nunc ueniat quaeso per igneam zonam magus interiore ab orbe Zoroastres....' There are then cited successively Zoroaster, the Bactrian, Armenius Zostriani nepos, Er the Pamphylian, Apollonius of Tyana, Damigeron, Dardanus, Belus, Julian the Chaldean, Baebulus (for these people see MacCracken's commentary, p. 294, nn. 260 et seq.; on Apollonius of Tyana see Augustine, my article, p. 152, n. 19, and p. 161, n. 57).

28. Ibid. i. 53, p. 49. 3: 'Nihil, ut remini, magicum, nihil humanum, praestigiosum aut subdolum, nihil fraudis delituit in Christo, derideatis licet ex more atque in lasciuiam dissoluamini cachinnorum.'

29. Ibid. i. 55, p. 50. 12: 'Quodsi falsa, ut dicitis, historia illa rerum est, unde tam breui tempore totus mundus ista religione completus est?' (cf. Augustine, my article, p. 156, nn. 37–38).

30. Ibid. i. 53, p. 49. 15: 'Nouitate rerum exterrita uniuersa mundi sunt elementa turbata, tellus mota contremuit, mare funditus refusum est, aer globis inuolutus est tenebrarum, igneus orbis solis tepefacto ardore deriguit. Quid enim restabat ut fieret, postquam deus est cognitus is, qui esse iamdudum unus iudicabatur e nobis? Sed non creditis gesta haec.' MacCracken, p. 295, n. 271, observed, like many others, the omission, as compared with the

evangelistic texts, of the resurrection of many of the dead, but he also noticed the additions—the sea flowing back, the sun losing its warmth. Dramatization to add to the wonder of it all? I would say rather that Arnobius was here following not the evangelistic texts but an anti-Christian source arguing the physical impossibility of such a disorder of the four elements (the same kind of argument as that in Augustine, my article, p. 168, n. 94); the additions were voluntary, in view of the argument.

31. Ibid. i. 54, p. 49. 26: 'Quinam isti sint fortasse quaeritis?'

32. Ibid. i. 56, p. 51. 5: 'Sed conscriptores nostri mendaciter ista prompserunt, extulere in immensum exigua gesta et angustas res satis ambitioso dilatauere praeconio'; i. 57, p. 52. 13: 'Quidquid dicere de nostris conscriptoribus intenderitis, et de uestris haec dicta paribus sumite atque habetote momentis.'

33. Ibid. i. 57, p. 52. 19: 'Sed antiquiora, inquitis, nostra sunt ac per hoc fidei et ueritatis plenissima' (cf. Ambrosiaster, my 'Critiques exégétiques et arguments antichrétiens rapportés par Ambrosiaster', in *Vigiliae Christianae*, xiii (1959), 161, n. 151).

34. Ibid. i. 58, p. 53. 7: 'Sed ab indoctis hominibus et rudibus scripta sunt et idcirco non sunt facili auditione credenda.'

35. Ibid. i. 58, p. 53. 11: 'Triuialis et sordidus sermo est.'

36. Ibid. i. 59, p. 53. 22: 'Barbarismis, soloecismis obsitae sunt, inquit, res uestrae et uitiorum deformitate pollutae' (cf. Augustine, my article, p. 176, n. 144).

37. Ibid. i. 60, p. 56. 20: 'Sed si deus, inquiunt, fuit Christus, cur forma est in hominis uisus et cur more est interemptus humano?'; i. 62, p. 58. 1: 'Sed more est hominis interemptus.'

38. Ibid. i. 61, p. 57. 12: 'Quid enim, dicit, rex summus ea quae in mundo facienda esse decreuerat sine homine simulato non quibat efficere?' (cf. Augustine, my article, p. 160, n. 56).

39. Ibid. i. 63, p. 59. 1: 'Quae sunt ista, inquies, clausa atque obscura mysteria? Quae nulli nec homines scire nec ipsi, qui appellantur dii mundi, parte queunt aliqua suspicionis atque opinationis attingere, nisi quos ipse dignatus est cognitionis tantae inpertire muneribus et in abditos recessus thesauri interioris inducere.' A.-J. Festugière, 'Arnobiana', p. 222, thinks that the phrase *quae nulli* is Arnobius' reply to the question of his opponent, which seems likely.

40. Ibid. ii. 2, p. 67. 3: 'At enim odio dignus est, quod ex orbe religiones expulit, quod ad deorum cultum prohibuit accedi.—Ergone ille religionis extinctor et impietatis auctor arguitur, qui ueram in orbe religionem induxit . . .?'; ii. 3, p. 68. 3: 'Sed minoribus supplicare diis homines uetuit' (cf. Augustine, my article, p. 155, n. 32, where the contrary point of view is put).

41. Ibid. ii. 4, p. 68. 18: 'Non credimus, inquitis, uera esse quae dicit.'

42. Ibid. ii. 4, p. 68. 22: 'Sed et ipse quae pollicetur non probat' (cf. Origen, *Contra Celsum*, ii. 10).

43. Ibid. ii. 8, p. 73. 19: 'Ridere nostram fidem consuestis atque ipsam credulitatem facetiis iocularibus lancinare. . . . Quid? Illa de rebus ab humana cognitione sepositis, quae conscribitis ipsi, quae lectitatis, oculata uidistis inspectione et manibus tractata tenuistis? Nonne uestrum quicumque est huic uel illi credit auctoribus?' (cf. Augustine, my article, p. 151, nn. 8, 10, 11).

44. Ibid. ii. 12, p. 79. 17: 'Quae omnia uos gesta neque scitis neque scire uoluistis neque umquam uobis necessaria iudicastis, ac dum uestris fiditis cordibus et quod typhus est sapientiam uocatis, dedistis circumscriptoribus locum, illis, inquam, noxiis, quorum nomen interest obsolefieri Christianum, superfundendi caligines atque obscurandi res tantas, eripiendae uobis fidei subiciendique contemptus.' The *circumscriptores*, according to Festugière, 'Arnobiana', p. 226, would designate the evil demons.

45. See above, n. 15.

46. Arnobius, ii. 13, p. 80. 11: 'Vos, uos appello qui Mercurium, qui Platonem Pythagoramque sectamini, uosque ceteros, qui estis unius mentis et per easdem uias placitorum inceditis unitate'; on these three groups, cf. A.-J. Festugière, 'La Doctrine des "Viri noui" sur l'origine et le sort des âmes d'après Arnobe', ii. 11–66, in *Mémorial Lagrange* (Paris, 1940), p. 99, n. 1.

47. Ibid. ii. 13, p. 80. 4: 'Interea tamen o isti, qui admiramini, qui stupetis doctorum et philosophiae scita, ita non iniustissimum ducitis inequitare, inludere tanquam stulta nobis et bruta dicentibus, cum uel ea uel talia repperiamini et uos dicere quae nobis dici pronuntiarique ridetis?'

48. Ibid. ii. 13, p. 80. 14: 'Audetis ridere nos, quod patrem rerum ac dominum ueneramur et colimus quodque illi dedamus et permittamus spes nostras'; ii. 32, p. 104. 10: 'quid est quod a uobis tamquam bruti et stolidi iudicemur, si propter hos metus liberatori dedidimus et mancipauimus nos Deo?' This last grievance comes from the *uiri noui*, of whom it is said, p. 74. 29: 'uos uestrarum animarum salutem in ipsis uobis reponitis.'

49. Ibid. ii. 13, p. 80. 20: 'Audetis ridere nos, quod mortuorum dicamus resurrectionem futuram, quam quidem nos dicere confitemur, sed a uobis aliter quam sentiamus audiri' (cf. Augustine, my article, pp. 163–70).

50. Ibid. ii. 13, p. 81. 3: 'Audetis ridere nos, quod animarum nostrarum prouideamus saluti, id est ipsi nobis.'

51. Ibid. ii. 14, p. 81. 14: 'Audetis ridere nos, cum gehennas dicimus et inextinguibiles quosdam ignes, in quos animas deici ab earum hostibus inimicisque cognouimus'; p. 82. 19: 'Animae nescientes Deum per longissimi temporis cruciatum consumentur igni fero, in quem illas iacient quidam crudeliter saeui et ante Christum incogniti et ab solo sciente detecti' (which shows Arnobius has in mind the Christian demons). Festugière, 'Arnobiana', p. 227, is quite right in thinking that the *hostes* were the demons, not the passions.

52. Cf. Festugière, 'La Doctrine des "Viri noui"', pp. 97–132.

53. Arnobius, ii. 62, p. 138. 5 et seq.

54. Ibid. ii. 63, p. 139. 11: 'Sed si, inquiunt, Christus in hoc missus a Deo

est, ut infelices animas ab interitionis exitio liberaret, quid *saecula* commeruerunt priora, quae *ante ipsius aduentum* mortalitatis condicione consumpta sunt? Potestis enim scire, *quid* sit *cum* eis *animis actum* priscorum ueterrimorumque mortalium?' (cf. Augustine, my article, p. 160, n. 55, and p. 185, n. 190: '*Quid egerunt* tot *saeculorum* homines *ante Christum* . . . *quid*, inquit, *actum de* tam innumeris *animis* quae omnino in culpa nulla sunt, siquidem is cui credi posset nondum *aduentum* suum hominibus commodaret?').

55. Ibid. ii. 71, p. 149. 20: 'Ante quadringentos annos religio, inquit, uestra non fuit.' On the necessity of not correcting *quadringentos* into *trecentos* see Zeno of Verona, 'Tractatus', i. 5. 4, *P.L.* xi. 304A: 'Cum ante annos ferme quadringentos uel eo amplius apostolicum hoc operetur edictum, quo et uiuaciores fuere homines et rarissimi Christiani . . .'; and MacCracken's commentary, i. 344, n. 440.

56. Ibid. ii. 66, p. 143. 21: 'Nam quod nobis obiectare consuestis, nouellam esse religionem nostram et ante dies natam propemodum paucos neque nos oportuisse antiquam et patriam linquere et in barbaros ritus peregrinosque traduci, ratione istud intenditur nulla'; ii. 69, p. 146, 17: 'Sed nouellum nomen est nostrum et ante dies paucos religio est nata quam sequimur'; ii. 72, p. 151. 7: 'At religiones uestrae multis annis praecedunt nostram, et eo sunt ueriores quod uetustatis auctoritate munitae sunt.'

57. Ibid. ii. 74, p. 153. 12: 'Et quid, inquit, est uisum deo regi ac principi, ut ante horas, quemadmodum dicitur, pauculas sospitator ad uos Christus caeli ex arcibus mitteretur?'; ii. 75, p. 154. 15: 'Tu opponas et referas: "Cur tam sero emissus est sospitator?"' (cf. Augustine, my article, p. 159, n. 54: 'Quare non ante uenit Christus?').

58. Ibid. ii. 64, p. 140. 14: 'Sed si generis Christus humani, ut inquitis, conseruator aduenit, quor omnino non omnes aequali munificentia liberat?'

59. Ibid. ii. 65, 141. 20: 'Immo, inquit, si Deus est potens, misericors, conseruator, conuertat nobis mentes et inuitos faciat suis pollicitationibus credere.'

60. Ibid. ii. 65, p. 142. 14: 'Christianus ergo ni fuero, spem salutis habere non potero?' (the same argument drawn from the rectitude of pagans is in Augustine, my article, p. 171, nn. 111–13).

61. Ibid. ii. 76, p. 155. 17: 'Cur ergo, inquit, si omnipotenti seruitis Deo et eum habere confiditis salutis atque incolumitatis uestrae curam, cur persecutiones patitur perpeti uos tantas atque omnia genera poenarum et suppliciorum subire?'

62. Ibid. iii. 2, p. 160. 1: 'Nunc ad ordinem reuertamur a quo sumus necessario paulo ante digressi, ne diutius interrupta defensio palmam criminis comprobati calumniatoribus concessisse dicatur. Subiciunt enim haec: "Si uobis diuina res cordi est, cur alios nobiscum neque deos colitis neque adoratis nec cum uestris gentibus communia sacra miscetis et religionum coniungitis ritus?"'; I do not think it is necessary to read *nostris* for *uestris*, as Axelson suggests, but I doubt whether we need assume, like Festugière ('Arnobiana', p. 233), that *uestris gentibus* refers to the Jews, not the Romans.

It is more likely that, as is customary with Arnobius, the second proposition is redundant in view of the first, except for the reproachful implication—you lack solidarity with your own nation.

63. Ibid. iii. 7, p. 165. 1: 'Sed quid aucupia uerborum splendoremque sermonis peti ab hoc dicam, cum sciam esse non paucos, qui auersentur et fugiant libros de hoc eius nec in aurem uelint admittere lectionem opinionum suarum praesumpta uincentem, cumque alios audiam mussitare indignanter et dicere, oportere statui per senatum, aboleantur ut haec scripta quibus Christiana religio comprobetur et uetustatis opprimatur auctoritas'?; iv. 36, p. 244. 20: 'Nam nostra quidem scripta cur ignibus meruerunt dari? Cur immaniter conuenticula dirui, in quibus summus oratur Deus, pax cunctis et uenia postulatur magistratibus, exercitibus, regibus, familiaribus, inimicis?'

64. Ibid. iii. 8, p. 165. 15: 'Ac ne tamen et nobis inconsideratus aliquis calumniam moueat, tamquam deum quem colimus marem esse credamus, ea scilicet causa, quod eum cum loquimur pronuntiamus genere masculino....' This criticism perhaps specially concerned Christ.

65. Ibid. iii. 12, p. 170. 4: 'Neque quisquam Iudaeicas in hoc loco nobis opponat et Sadducaei generis fabulas, tamquam formas tribuamus et nos Deo: hoc enim putatur in eorum litteris dici et uelut re certa atque auctoritate firmari: quae aut nihil ad nos attinent nec ex aliqua portione quicquam habent commune nobiscum, aut si sunt, ⟨ut⟩ creditur, sociae, quaerendi sunt uobis altioris intellegentiae doctores, per quos possitis addiscere, quibus modis conueniat litterarum illarum nubes atque inuolucra relaxare.'

66. Ibid. iii. 15, p. 173. 22. Arnobius retorted that these anti-Christians, while deriding Egyptian zoolatry, in a way practise it themselves, for their idols have the features of humans, that is to say of animate beings: 'Hocine est illud fastidium uestrum, sapientia haec adrogans, qua despuitis nos ut rudes atque omnem scientiam remini rerum uobis diuinarum patere? Aegyptiorum ridetis aenigmata, quod mutorum animantium formas diuinis inseruerint causis easdemque quod species multo ture accipiant et reliquo caerimoniarum paratu: uos effigies hominum tamquam deorum ueneramini potestates nec pudet his ora terreni animalis imponere, erroris alios et stultitiae condemnare et in erroris eiusdem similitudine ac uitio deprehendi.' On the meaning of *Aegyptiorum aenigmata* cf. Festugière, 'Arnobiana', p. 235.

67. Ibid. iii. 22, p. 179. 11: 'Sed erras, inquis, et falleris; non enim ipsi opifices dii sunt, sed ingeniis hominum subiciunt has artes atque, ut uita sit instructior, tradunt scienda mortalibus.... Dii ergo sunt artifices primi, siue quod ipsi, ut dicitis, subdunt scientiam mentibus, siue quod immortales et geniti numquam genus omne terrenum uetustate temporis antecedunt.... Nisi forte hoc dicitis, deos artifices non esse, sed eos his artibus praesidere, curare, immo sub illorum posita esse tutela omnia quae administramus, quae gerimus, atque ut bene ac feliciter cedant, illorum prouisione curari.'

68. Ibid. v. 32, p. 290. 1: 'Sed erras, inquit, et laberis satisque te esse imperitum, indoctum ac rusticum ipsa rerum insectatione demonstras. Nam omnes istae historiae, quae tibi turpes uidentur atque ad labem pertinere diuinam, mysteria in se continent sancta, rationes miras atque altas nec quas facile quiuis possit ingenii uiuacitate pernoscere. Neque enim quod scriptum

est atque in prima est positum uerborum fronte, id significatur et dicitur, sed allegoricis sensibus et subditiuis intelleguntur omnia illa secretis.'

69. Ibid. v. 36, p. 295. 3: 'Nisi forte dicetis non toto in historiae corpore allegorias has esse, ceterum partes alias esse communiter scriptas, alias uero dupliciter et ambifaria obtentione uelatas.'

70. Ibid. vi. 1, p. 307. 1: 'Nunc quoniam summatim ostendimus, quam impias de diis uestris opinionum constitueritis infamias, sequitur ut de templis, de simulacris etiam sacrificiisque dicamus deque alia serie quae his rebus adnexa est et uicina copulatione coniuncta. In hac enim consuestis parte crimen nobis maximum impietatis adfigere, quod neque aedes sacras uenerationis ad officia construamus, non deorum alicuius simulacrum constituamus aut formam, non altaria fabricemus, non aras, non caesorum sanguinem animantium demus, non tura neque fruges salsas, non denique uinum liquens paterarum infusionibus inferamus'; vii. 1, p. 343. 1: 'Quid ergo, dixerit quispiam, sacrificia censetis nulla esse omnino facienda?'; vii. 15, p. 359. 4: 'Quid ergo, inquiet aliquis, honorem diis dandum nullum esse omnino censetis?' (cf. Augustine, my article, p. 163, n. 67, on the victims and the incense).

71. For all this see my article 'Les Sages de Porphyre et les "Viri novi" d'Arnobe', in *Revue des Études Latines*, xxxi (1953), 257–71, notably the references on pp. 261–2.

72. On the 'Graecarum Affectionum Curatio' of Theodoret, see P. Canivet, *Histoire d'une entreprise apologétique au Ve siècle* (Paris, no date [1959]).

73. An hypothesis very well formulated, but at once abandoned, by A.-J. Festugière, 'Arnobiana', in *Vigiliae Christianae*, vi (1952), 212: 'Celui-ci combattrait donc la thèse des opposants par l'*auctoritas* même sur laquelle cette thèse se fonde; il montrerait que les textes indiqués se retournent contre ceux qui les allèguent.... Tout ce que nous savons des méthodes de travail des polémistes anciens nous autorise à penser qu'Arnobe prend son bien chez ceux-là même qu'il attaque. Cette hypothèse me semblait séduisante, quand j'ai été arrêté par deux autres observations....' These observations do not seem to me personally to ruin the hypothesis.

74. Cf. my *Lettres grecques en Occident, de Macrobe à Cassiodore*, 2nd edn. (Paris, 1948), pp. 3–36; E. Türk, *Macrobius und die Quellen seiner Saturnalien* (Diss. Freiburg, 1962).

75. His statements should, of course, be compared with those of other witnesses. For Augustine see my article previously referred to; for Ambrosiaster see my article 'Critiques exégétiques et arguments antichrétiens rapportés par Ambrosiaster', in *Vigiliae Christianae*, xiii (1959), 133–69. I found nothing on this particular subject in J. Mesot, 'Die Heidenbekehrung bei Ambrosius von Mailand', *Neue Zeitschrift für Missionswissenschaft*, supplementum 7, Schöneck/Beckenried (Schweiz), 1958, which nevertheless contains an excellent disquisition, pp. 56–68.

76. Ambrose, *In Psalm.* cxviii. 16. 45, *C.S.E.L.* lxii, p. 377. 5: 'Sunt etiam qui, dum maiorum suorum statum secuntur, ueluti digna conuersatione contenti nec errores quidem patrios existimant declinandos, ut fide mutandam

Notes

perfidiam non arbitrentur, cum in melius mutare propositum non leuitas, sed uirtus, neque culpa, sed gratia sit.'

77. Symmachus, *Relatio*, c. 8, ed. Lavarenne (in vol. iii of the *Oeuvres* of Prudentius), p. 109: 'Suus cuique mos, suus ritus est: uarios custodes urbibus cultus mens diuina distribuit; ut animae nascentibus, ita populis fatales genii diuiduntur. Accedit utilitas, quae maxime homini deos adserit. Nam cum ratio omnis in operto sit, unde rectius quam de memoria atque documentis rerum secundarum cognitio uenit numinum? Iam si longa aetas auctoritatem religionibus faciat, seruanda est tot saeculis fides et sequendi sunt nobis parentes, qui secuti sunt feliciter suos.' On the hermetic and Neoplatonist theory of the guardian spirit see *Hermetica*, ii. 16. 14, ed. Nock and Festugière, ii, p. 236. 13; Porphyry ap. Proclus, *In Tim*. 24a, ed. Diehl, iii, p. 152, 15; Iamblichus, *De Mysteriis*, v. 25. 3; Rutilius Namatianus, *De Reditu suo*, i. 15–18; Martianus Capella, *De nuptiis Mercurii et Philologiae*, ii. 152; Prudentius, *Contra Symmachum*, ii. 71, pp. 370–487, rejects it, but it is taken up again and christianized by Gregory of Nazianzus, *Poemata Dogmatica*, viii, v. 25, *P.G.* xxxvii. 440, and by Pseudo-Chrysostom, *P.G* lix. 756. On the guardian spirit of Rome see F. Cumont, 'Les Anges du paganisme romain', in *Revue de l'Histoire des Religions*, lxxii (1915), 159–82; J.-P. Callu, *Genio populi Romani* (Paris, 1960), pp. 105–12; J. Doignon, 'Perspectives ambrosiennes. Ss Gervais et Protais, génies de Milan', in *Revue des Études Augustiniennes*, ii, 1956, 313–34.

78. Ibid., c. 9, p. 109: 'Optimi principum, patres patriae, reueremini annos meos, in quos me pius ritus adduxit! utar *caerimoniis* auitis, neque enim paenitet! Viuam meo more, quia libera sum! Hic *cultus* in leges meas orbem redegit, *haec sacra Hannibalem a moenibus, a Capitolio Senonas reppulerunt*. Ad hoc ergo seruata sum, ut longaeua reprehendar?' (cf. Ambrose, *Epist. ad Valentinianum*, xviii. 4; ibid., p. 119: 'In prima propositione, flebili Roma questu sermonis illacrimat, ueteres, ut ait, *cultus ceremoniarum* requirens. "*Haec sacra*, inquit, *Hannibalem a moenibus, a Capitolio Senonas reppulerunt*."'

79. Symmachus, *Relatio*, c. 10, p. 110: 'Ergo diis patriis, *diis* indigetibus *pacem rogamus*. Aequum est, quidquid omnes colunt, unum putari. Eadem spectamus astra, commune caelum est, idem nos mundus inuoluit: quid interest, qua quisque prudentia uerum *requirat*? *Vno itinere non potest perueniri ad tam grande secretum*' (cf. Maximus of Madaura, *Epist. ad Augustinum* 16, *C.S.E.L.* xxxiv. 1, p. 39. 13: 'Dii te seruent, per quos et eorum atque cunctorum mortalium communem patrem uniuersi mortales, quos terra sustinet, mille modis concordi discordia ueneramur et colimus'; Longinianus, *Epist. ad Augustinum* ccxxxiv. 2, *C.S.E.L.* lvii, p. 520. 10: 'Via est in Deum melior . . . qua purgati antiquorum sacrorum piis praeceptis expiationibusque purissimis et abstemiis obseruationibus decocti anima et corpore constantes deproperant'). Augustine, *Solil*. i. 13. 23, ed. Labriolle, p. 70: 'Sed *non* ad eam [sapientiam] *una uia peruenitur*'; *Retract*. i. 4. 3, ed. Bardy, p. 290: 'Item quod dixi: "Ad sapientiae coniunctionem *non una uia peruenirí*", non bene sonat; quasi alia uia sit praeter Christum qui dixit: "Ego sum uia" (*Ioh*. xiv. 6). Vitanda ergo erat haec offensio aurium religiosarum, quamuis alia sit illa uniuersalis uia, aliae autem uiae, de quibus et in Psalmo canimus: "Vias tuas, Domine, notas fac mihi et semitas tuas doce me" (*Ps*. xxiv. 4). Et in eo, quod

ibi dictum est: "penitus ista sensibilia fugienda" (*Solil.* i. 14. 24), cauendum fuit, ne putaremur Porphyrii falsi philosophi tenere sententiam, qua dixit "omne corpus fugiendum'"; cf. Porphyry, *De regressu animae*, ed. Bidez, pp. 42* et sqq.

80. On this Porphyrean doctrine, referred to notably in Augustine's *De consensu evangelistarum*, see my article, pp. 155-8, and 'Saint Augustin "photinien" à Milan', in *Ricerche di storia religiosa*, i (1954), 63-71. On the various ways envisaged see Porphyry, *De regressu animae*, ed. Bidez, p. 42* (Augustine, *Civ. Dei*, x. 32, 1).

81. Ambrose, *Epist.* xviii. 8-9, p. 121: ' "*Vno*, inquit, *itinere non potest perueniri ad tam grande secretum.*" Quod uos ignoratis, id nos Dei uoce cognouimus. Et quod uos suspicionibus *quaeritis*, nos ex ipsa sapientia Dei et ueritate compertum habemus. Non congruunt igitur uestra nobiscum. Vos "*pacem diis*" uestris ab imperatoribus obsecratis, nos ipsis imperatoribus a Christo "*pacem rogamus*". Vos manuum uestrarum adoratis opera, nos iniuriam ducimus omne quod fieri potest Deum putari. Non uult se Deus in lapidibus coli. Denique etiam ipsi philosophi uestri ista riserunt. Quod si uos ideo Christum Deum negatis, quia illum mortuum esse non creditis (nescitis enim quod mors illa carnis fuerit, non diuinitatis, quae fecit ut credentium iam nemo moriatur), quid uobis imprudentius, qui contumeliose colitis, et honorifice derogatis; uestrum enim Deum lignum putatis; o contumeliosa reuerentia! Christum mori potuisse non creditis; o honorifica peruicacia!'; on the difficulties of this text see *P.L.* xvi. 1015C, n. 23; Lavarenne, p. 121, n. 6; but the meaning becomes clear in the light of the anti-Christian statements referred to by Augustine; cf. my article, pp. 156-7, nn. 40-46; cf. also Ambrose, *In Ps.* xliii. 72, *C.S.E.L.* lxiv, p. 313. 1: 'Est enim et confusionis gloria, ut si in multos gentiles incidas uel philosophos et illi tibi obiciant crucem Christi et uerbo respondere non possis nec quisquam audiat salutaria uerba referentem.'

82. Augustine, *Epist. ad Paulinum Nolanum*, xxxi. 8, *C.S.E.L.* xxxiv. 2, p. 8. 2 (written about 396): 'Libros beatissimi Ambrosii credo habere sanctitatem tuam; eos autem multum desidero, quos aduersus nonnullos inperitissimos et superbissimos, qui de Platonis libris Dominum profecisse contendunt, diligentissime et copiosissime scripsit.'

83. Text quoted below, n. 125.

83a. It is certain that the pagans heard the sermons of Ambrose; cf. Ambrose, *in Ps.* xxxvi. 61, *C.S.E.L.* lxiv, p. 118. 25: 'Si quis ex gentibus ueniens sermonem audiat nostrum.'

84. Ambrose, *De paradiso*, viii. 38, *C.S.E.L.* xxxii. 1, p. 294. 9: 'Iterum quaestio: "Sciebat praeuaricaturum Deus Adam mandata sua an nesciebat? Si nesciebat, non est ista diuinae potestatis adsertio; si autem sciebat et nihilominus sciens neglegenda mandauit, non est Dei aliquid superfluum praecipere. Superfluo autem praecepit primoplasto illi Adae quod eum nouerat minime seruaturum. Nihil autem Deus superfluo facit; ergo non est scriptura ex Deo." Hoc enim obiciunt qui uetus non recipiunt testamentum et has interserunt quaestiones. . . . Nam et ipse dominus Iesus elegit Iudam, quem proditorem sciebat. Quem si per inprudentiam electum putant, diuinae de-

Notes

rogant potestati. . . . Conticescant igitur repugnatores isti ueteris testamenti. Sed quoniam etiam gentilibus si forte istud obiecerint, respondendum uidetur, qui exemplum non accipiunt, rationem exigunt, accipiant etiam ipsi qua ratione Dei filius uel praeuaricaturo mandauerit uel elegerit proditurum. . . . Nunc autem uterque redarguitur atque reconuincitur.' Before considering the pagans Ambrose alluded to Apelles, whose *Syllogisms* he knew from Origen's commentary on Genesis, according to A. Harnack, *Die gnostischen Quellen Hippolyts in seiner Hauptschrift gegen die Häretiker*, in *Texte und Untersuchungen*, vi. 3 (Leipzig, 1890), 116–20.

85. Ambrose, *De Abraham*, i. 4, 22, *C.S.E.L.* xxxii. 1, p. 517. 7 (referring to Genesis xvi): 'Sed fortasse dicat aliquis: "Quomodo Abraham nobis imitandum proponis, cum de ancilla susceperit filium? Aut quid sibi hoc uult esse, ut tantus uir huic errori fuerit obnoxius, cuius tanta opera miramur?" . . . Mouere tamen aliquos potest quod iam cum Deo loquebatur et ad ancillam introiuit. . . . Et tu peccasti, cum gentilis esses: habes excusationem. . . . Fecisti gentilis adulterium.' Ambrose recognized, p. 517. 11, that 'locum hunc . . . plerique uadosum putant'.

86. Ambrose, *Apologia prophetae Dauid*, i. 6. 27, *C.S.E.L.* xxxii. 2, p. 316. 18: 'Arguis quod unum occiderit' (referring to Goliath); ii. 2. 5, p. 361. 24: 'Gentili dico, Iudaeo dico, Christiano dico. Et ideo mihi tripertito distinguendus uidetur esse tractatus, unus aduersus gentiles, alius aduersus Iudaeos, tertius apud Christianos. Primus igitur aduersus gentiles mihi sermo est, qui plerumque obiectare consuerunt: "Ecce quomodo Christiani innocentiam sequuntur, fidem praeferunt, religionem uenerantur, castitatem docent, quorum principes et homicidia et adulteria fecisse produntur? Ipse Dauid, de cuius genere, ut dicitis, nasci Christus elegit, ipse et homicidia sua et adulteria decantauit. Quales possunt esse discipuli, quorum tales magistri sunt?"'

87. Ibid. ii. 3. 20, p. 369. 3: 'Miramini quod Dauid regem fecerit uictoremque multarum gentium? . . . Haec aduersus gentiles.'

88. *De Abraham*, i. 4. 29, p. 524. 3: 'Quo loci *plerosque moueri* scio. Si enim bona est *circumcisio*, hodieque teneri debuit; *si inutilis*, mandari non debuit. Sed cum apostolus dixerit Paulus quia "*Abraham* signum *accepit* circumcisionis" (*Rom.* iv. 11) utique signum non ipsa res, sed alterius est rei, hoc est non ueritas, sed indicium ueritatis.'

Epist. ad Constantium, lxxii. 1, *P.L.* xvi. 1297C (ed. of 1880): 'Non mediocris *plerosque mouet* quaestio, qua causa *circumcisio* et Veteris Testamenti auctoritate quasi utilis imperetur et Noui Testamenti magisterio *quasi inutilis* repudietur (*Act.* xv. 10), cum praesertim *Abraham* primus oraculum circumcisionis celebrandae *acceperit* (*Gen.* xvii. 10).'

Cf. Ambrosiaster, my article, p. 157, n. 135, and Augustine, pp. 162–3.

89. Ambrose, *Epist. ad Constantium*, 3, *P.L.* xvi. 1298A: 'Cur uero signum Testamenti diuini in ea datur parte membrorum, quae uisu inhonestior aestimatur? Aut qua gratia ipse operator corporis nostri in ipso nostrae generationis exordio circumcidi uoluit opus suum et uulnerari et cruentari, et abscidi partem quam uelut necessariam qui omnia disposuit ordinate cum caeteris membris faciendam putauit? Aut enim praeter naturam est haec portio corporis nostri, et non oportuit habere omnes homines, quod esset praeter naturam; aut secundum naturam est, et non decuit amputari, quod secundum naturae perfectionem creatum foret; cum praesertim alieni a

portione Domini Dei nostri id praecipue irridere soliti sint. Deinde cum propositum sit Deo, ut frequenter ipse testificatus est, plures ad sacrae obseruantiam prouocare religionis, quanto magis inuitarentur, si non aliqui circumcisionis ipsius aut periculo aut opprobrio reuocarentur.... Duplex est accusatio: una quae irrogatur a gentilibus, altera quae ab iis, qui de populo Dei sunt, aestimatur. Vehementior autem gentilium, qui uiros circumcisione signatos etiam opprobrio et illusione dignos arbitrantur. Sed etiam ipsorum sapientissimi quique ita circumcisionem approbant, ut electos suos erga cognoscenda et celebranda mysteria circumcidendos putent.... Haec aduersum eos dicta sint, qui nulla nobis unitate fidei sociantur.' Here Ambrose makes the point that the priests of Egypt and the Magi are circumcised and that it is customary practice among the Ethiopians, the Arabs, and the Phoenicians. These anti-Christian arguments reappear in chapters 6, 18, and 27, where they are refuted. Cf. Barnabas, *Epist.* ix. 6, ed. Funk, p. 29.

90. Ambrose, *Epist. ad Irenaeum*, lxxiv. 1, *P.L.* xvi, 1308C: 'Sunt enim qui dicant: "Cum legem Deus Moysi dederit, quid causae est ut pleraque in lege sint, quae per euangelium iam uacuata uidentur? Et quomodo unus utriusque conditor Testamenti, cum id quod licebat in lege, per euangelium coeperit non licere: ut est circumcisio corporalis, quae licet etiam tunc signo data sit, ut circumcisionis spiritalis ueritas teneretur, tamen qua ratione in ipso signo fuit? Cur ista diuersitas aestimatur, ut tunc circumcidi pietas crederetur, nunc impietas iudicetur? Deinde sabbati diem feriatum esse debere obseruabatur ex lege, ita ut, si quis onus aliquod lignorum portasset, mortis fieret reus (*Num.* xv. 35), nunc autem diem ipsum et oneribus subeundis et negotiis obeundis sine poena aduertimus deputari. Et pleraque praecepta sunt legis, quae praesenti tempore cessare uidentur."'

91. Ambrose, *In Lucam*, vii. 57, xxxii. 4, p. 305. 16: 'Quod si quem mouet, qua ratione in Aegypto calciati iubentur edere agnum (*Exod.* xii. 11 sqq.), apostoli autem sine calciamentis ad praedicandum diriguntur (*Luc.* x. 4; xxii. 35.'

92. Ambrose, *De bono mortis*, x. 46, *C.S.E.L.* xxxii. 1, p. 742. 3: 'Denique et scriptura habitacula illa animarum "promptaria" (*Esdras*, iv. 7. 32) nuncupauit, quae occurrens querellae humanae, eo quod iusti qui praecesserunt uideantur usque ad iudicii diem per plurimum scilicet temporis debita sibi remuneratione fraudari, mirabiliter ait coronae esse similem iudicii diem ...'

93. Ambrose, *Apol. Dauid*, ii. 5. 30, p. 377. 16: 'Qui tamen hoc obiciunt, quod Dei filius carnem suscipere non potuerit, si gentiles, quomodo, qui deos suos, quoniam homines fuisse negare non possunt, humana specie uisos esse testantur?'

94. Ambrose, *In Lucam*, ii. 44, p. 66. 10: 'Istum igitur paruulum, quem tu quasi uilem, qui infidelis es, arbitraris, magi ex Oriente uenientes tam longo spatio sequebantur.'

95. Ibid. iii. 2, p. 98. 11: 'Neminem mouere debet quod ita scriptum est: "Qui putabatur esse filius Ioseph" (*Luc.* iii. 23).'

96. Ibid. iii. 17, p. 110. 17: 'Plerique etiam mirantur, cur Thamar mulieris famosae, ut illis uidetur, Matthaeus conmemorationem in dominica generatione contexendam putauerit, cur etiam Ruth, cur eius quoque mulieris, quae

Notes

Uriae uxor fuit et occiso marito in Dauid nuptias conmigrauit, cum praesertim Sarrae et Rebeccae et Rachel, sanctarum feminarum, nusquam fecerit mentionem.'

97. Ibid. vi. 13, p. 236. 1.

98. Ibid. vi. 44, p. 249. 10; cf. also pp. 295. 1, 349. 1, 499. 18, 252. 6: 'Sed dicit aliqui: "Cur hoc a Deo permittitur diabolo?"'

99. Ibid. x. 129, p. 504. 15.

100. Ibid. x. 147, p. 510. 24: 'Magna oritur hoc loco plerisque quaestio'; 511. 12: 'Quomodo ergo soluendum, nisi quattuor euangelistas de diuersis quattuor putes dixisse temporibus, ut et personas alias mulierum et alias conicias uisiones? . . . ne quem spinosae interpretationis in fine offendat asperitas.'

101. Text quoted above, n. 84. On the complaint of *imperitia* in Augustine see my article, p. 151, n. 9; and in Ambrosiaster, my article, p. 145, n. 71, and p. 148, n. 82.

102. Ambrose, *De bono mortis*, xii. 54, p. 749. 1: 'Sed dicis quia solis discipulis loquebatur, quod ipsis solis spoponderit multas mansiones: igitur undecim tantum discipulis praeparabat.'

103. Ambrose, *In Lucam*, vii. 62, p. 308. 12: ' "Et neminem salutaueritis in uia" (*Luc*. x. 4). Fortasse quibusdam hoc durum et superbum nec mansueti et humilis domini praecepto conuenire uideatur, quod ille qui etiam accubitionis loco praecepit esse cedendum hoc loco mandet discipulis: "Neminem salutaueritis in uia", cum iste conmunis sit usus gratiae. Sic inferiores superiorum sibi fauorem conciliare consuerunt, gentiles quoque cum Christianis habent huiusmodi officiorum conmercia (cf. *Matth*. v. 47). Quomodo Dominus hunc usum humanitatis auellit?'

104. Ibid. viii. 60, p. 421. 6.

105. Ambrose, *De paradiso*, xii. 58, p. 318. 7: 'Sed etiam gentilis si quis scripturas accipiat, legit: "Oculum pro oculo, dentem pro dente" (*Leuit*. xxiv. 20), legit etiam: "Si scandalizauerit te dextera tua, abscide illam' (*Matth*. v. 30), non intellegit sensum, non aduertit diuini sermonis arcana, peius labitur quam si non legisset.'

106. Ambrose, *De Caïn et Abel*, ii. 9. 27, p. 401. 22: 'Nam qui peccatum suum ad quandam referunt, ut gentiles adserunt, decreti aut operis sui necessitatem diuina arguere uidentur, quasi ipsorum uis causa peccati sit; qui enim necessitate aliqua coactus occiderit quasi inuitus occidit. Ea uero quae a nobis sunt excusationem non habent, quae autem praeter nos sunt excusabilia sunt.' Cf. Ambrosiaster, my article, pp. 167 sqq.

107. Ambrose, *De interpellatione Iob et Dauid*, iii. 5. 12, C.S.E.L. xxxii. 2, p. 255. 13: 'Ponunt autem in caelum os suum qui sibi criminum auctoritates natiuitatis putant quadam necessitate deferri. Hi nec caelo nec terris parcere solent, ut cursu quodam stellarum arbitrentur uitam hominis gubernari. Nihil prouidentiae, nihil bonis moribus relinquunt'; *De excessu fratris*, ii. 86. 1, C.S.E.L. lxxiii, p. 296: 'De solis cursu caelique ratione philosophi disputant et sunt, qui putant his esse credendum, cum, quid loquantur, ignorent. Neque enim caelum ascenderunt, axen dimensi mundi oculis perscrutati

sunt, quia nullus eorum cum Deo in principio fuit'; *In Ps.* xxxvi. 28. 2, *C.S.E.L.* lxiv, p. 93. 16: 'Est quidam diues in uerbis, ut sunt philosophi istius mundi de sacrilegiis disputantes, de motu siderum, de stella Iouis ac Saturni, de generationibus hominum, de simulacrorum cultu, de geometria et dialectica. Philosophi ergo in sermone diuites sunt, fidei inopes, ueritatis exsortes. Et sunt plerique simplices domini sacerdotes, in sermone pauperes, abstinentia et uirtute sublimes. Illi multis locuntur perfidiam, isti paucis fidem asserunt; illi suos amittunt cotidie sacerdotes, hic pauper populus adquirit ecclesiae numeroque credentium'; i. 22. 3, p. 17. 8: 'Chaldaei sunt qui siderum cursus uanae studio superstitionis explorant et impiae serunt gentilitatis errores.'

108. Ambrose, *De paenitentia*, v. 21. 1, *C.S.E.L.* lxxiii, p. 129 (concerning *Ps.* lxxvi. 9–10): 'Sed aiunt ideo se ista adserere, ne mutabilem Deum facere uideantur, si his, quibus fuerit iratus, ignoscat. Quid ergo? Repudiabimus diuina oracula et istorum opiniones sequemur?'

109. Ambrose, *De sacramentis*, iii. 3. 13, *C.S.E.L.* lxxiii, p. 44: 'Sunt quidam —scio certe aliquem fuisse, qui diceret—cum illi diceremus: "In hac aetate magis baptizari debes", dicebat ille: "Quare baptizor? Non habeo peccatum, numquid peccatum contraxi?"'; cf. Augustine, my article, p. 171, nn. 111–13.

110. Ambrose, *De Abraham*, ix. 89, p. 560. 5: 'Fortasse audientes haec, filiae, quae ad gratiam Domini tenditis, et uos prouocemini, ut habeatis inaures et uirias, et dicatis: "Quomodo prohibes hoc, episcope, ut habeamus quod Rebecca accepit pro munere et hortaris ut similes simus Rebeccae?" Sed non has inaures Rebecca habebat et uirias, quae lites in ecclesia serere solent, quae labuntur frequenter.'

111. Ambrose, *De Helia et ieiunio*, iv. 6, *C.S.E.L.* xxxii. 2, p. 415. 4: 'Itaque ne terrenum quis aut nouellum putet esse ieiunium, primus usus mundi a ieiunio coepit.'

112. Ambrose, *De Nabuthae*, viii. 40, *C.S.E.L.* xxxii. 2, p. 490. 8: 'Sed fortasse dicas quod uulgo soletis dicere: "Non debemus donare ei cui Deus ita maledixit, ut eum egere uellet"'; cf. vi. 28, p. 482, 15: 'Ditem dicunt gentiles inferi praesulem, arbitrum mortis; ditem appellant et diuitem, quod nisi mortem diues inferre non nouerit, cui regnum de mortuis, cui sedes inferna sint.'

113. Ambrose, *De uirginibus*, i. 4. 14–15, *P.L.* xvi. 203B–C: 'Hoc solo tamen naturae parilis conuicia declinamus, quod uirginitas affectatur a gentibus, sed consecrata uiolatur, incursatur a barbaris, nescitur a reliquis. Quis mihi praetendit Vestae uirgines et Palladis sacerdotes? Qualis ista est non morum pudicitia, sed annorum.' The comparison of the Vestals and the Christian virgins is also the theme of Ambrose's reply, *Epist.* xviii. 11–12, p. 122, to Symmachus, *Relatio*, 11, p. 110, which stresses, in favour of maintaining the fiscal immunity of the Vestals, their 'saluti publicae dicata uirginitas'; cf. Augustine, *Epist. ad Maximum Madaurensem*, xvii. 4, *C.S.E.L.* xxxiv. 1, p. 43. 9: 'Quod autem dicis eo nostris uestra sacra praeponi, quod uos publice colitis deos, nos autem secretioribus conuenticulis utimur, primo illud a te quaero, quo modo oblitus sis Liberum illum, quem paucorum sacratorum oculis committendum putatis.'

114. Ambrose, *De uirginibus*, i. 4. 17, *P.L.* xvi. 204B: 'Videamus ne forte aliquam uel philosophiae praecepta formauerint, quae magisterium sibi omnium solet uindicare uirtutum. Pythagorea quaedam una ex uirginibus celebratur fabula, cum a tyranno cogeretur secretum prodere, ne quid in se ad extorquendam confessionem uel tormentis liceret, morsu linguam abscidisse atque in tyranni faciem despuisse, ut qui interrogandi finem non faciebat, non haberet quam interrogaret. Eadem tamen forti animo, sed tumenti utero exemplum taciturnitatis et proluuium castitatis, uicta est cupiditatibus, quae tormentis uinci nequiuit. . . . Quanto nostrae uirgines fortiores, quae uincunt etiam quas non uident potestates, quibus non tantum de carne et sanguine, sed etiam de ipso mundi principe saeculique rectore uictoria est!' This, it seems, concerns Leaena, glorified by Plutarch in particular, *De garrulitate*, c. 8; Cicero, *De gloria*, fragm. 12 Müller; but derided by Lactantius, *Inst.* i. 20. 3, *C.S.E.L.* xix, p. 72. 13 (meretrix). Ambrose's direct source must have been Athanasius, as Michel Aubineau pointed out in 'Les écrits de S. Athanase sur la virginité' in *Revue d'Ascétique et de Mystique*, xxxi (1955), 166 (as opposed to Faller, ed. of *De virginibus* in *Florilegium patristicum*, xxxi (1933), 26, n. 2).

115. Ambrose, *De Abraham*, ii. 4. 17, p. 576. 19: 'Nonne dicit: "Putaui rem faciliorem castimoniam sequi: supra umeros meos, supra uires meas est. Rarus cui ista iungantur. Vale castitas, recede, recede de finibus sensuum meorum. Recurre cito eo unde uenisti. Non sustineo praesentiam tuam, adfligor grauibus quaestionibus, dum tenendam te arbitror, quam tenere non possum."'

116. Ambrose, *Epist. ad Sabinum*, lviii. 3, *P.L.* xvi. 1229A: 'Haec ubi audierint proceres uiri, quae loquentur? "Ex illa familia, illa prosapia, illa indole, tanta praeditum eloquentia migrasse a senatu, interceptam familiae nobis successionem." Et cum ipsi capita et supercilia sua radant, si quando Isidis suscipiunt sacra, si forte Christianus uir attentior sacrosanctae religioni uestem mutauerit, indignum facinus appellant.' Cf. Augustine, my article, p. 171, nn. 108-10.

117. Ambrose, *In Ps.* cxviii. 20. 48, *C.S.E.L.* lxii, p. 468. 21: 'Quanti foris confessi sunt et intus negauerunt! Namque uxoris ducendae gratia, quae gentili uiro a Christianis parentibus negabatur, simulata ad tempus fide plerique produntur quod foris confessi sunt intus negasse. . . . Venit quis in ecclesiam, dum honorem affectat sub imperatoribus Christianis, simulata mente orationem deferre se fingit, inclinatur et solo sternitur qui genu mentis non flexerit'; cxviii. 3. 22, p. 53. 25: 'Inrepsit aegritudo ueteri fermento, eo quod non exuimus uel gentilem uel Iudaicam suffusionem, cum primum ueniremus ad ecclesiam. . . . Superuestiuit ergo se aliquis, non expoliauit: serpit grauior aegritudo'; *Epist.* xvii. 7, ed. Lavarenne, p. 115: 'Ipsis gentilibus displicere consueuit praeuaricantis affectus; libere enim debet defendere unusquisque fidele mentis suae et seruare propositum.'

118. Ambrose, *In Lucam*, vi. 105, p. 279. 2: 'Qui enim tractat debet audientium considerare personas, ne prius inrideatur, quam audiatur. Quando enim Athenienses crederent quia "Verbum caro factum est" et de spiritu uirgo concepit, qui inridebant quia resurrectionem audierant mortuorum?'

119. Ibid. vii. 129, p. 338. 15: 'Gentes huius mundi quaerunt, quomodo resurgant mortui et quali corpore ueniant'; *De excessu fratris*, ii. 54. 1, p. 277: 'Quid dubitas de corpore corpus resurgere?'; ii. 57. 1, p. 279: 'Sed incredibile tibi uidetur, ut mortui reuiuescant'; ii. 55. 1, p. 278: 'Sed miraris quemadmodum putrefacta solidentur, dispersa coeant, absumpta reparentur' (cf. p. 314. 7); ii. 58. 1, p. 280: 'Sequitur illud, quod gentiles plerumque perturbat, quomodo fieri possit, ut quos mare absorbuerit, ferae dilacerauerint, bestiae deuorauerint, terra restituat.' Cf. Athenagoras, *De resurrectione*, 4, *P.G.* vi. 982A sqq.; Ambrosiaster, my article, pp. 135, n. 15; 164, n. 163; Augustine, my article, pp. 163–6.

120. Ambrose, *De excessu fratris*, ii. 70. 1, p. 287: 'Quod si ueteres sapientes satis hydri dentibus (cf. Virg. *Georg.* ii. 140–2) in regione Thebana inhorruisse armatorum segetem crediderunt, cum utique alterius naturae semina certum sit in naturam uerti alteram nequiuisse nec partum suis discordem fuisse seminibus, ut ex serpente homines nascerentur, ut caro ex dentibus gigneretur, quanto magis utique credendum est, quaecumque seminata sint, in suam naturam resurgere ... carnem de carne, os de ossibus, sanguinem de sanguine, umorem de umore reparari. Potestis ergo, gentiles, reformationem negare naturae, qui mutationem potestis adserere? Potestis non credere oraculis, non euangelio, non prophetis, qui fabulis inanibus creditis?'

121. Ambrose, *De excessu fratris*, i. 71. 1, p. 245: 'Certe si illi sibi aliqua solacia reppererunt, qui finem sensus defectumque naturae mortem arbitrati sunt, quanto magis nos, quibus meliora post mortem *praemia* bonorum *factorum conscientia* pollicetur! Habent gentiles solacia sua, quia requiem malorum omnium mortem existimant, et, ut uitae fructu carent, ita etiam caruisse se putant omni sensu et dolore poenarum, quas in hac uita graues et adsiduas sustinemus'; *De obitu Valentiniani*, 45. 1, *C.S.E.L.* lxxiii, p. 351: 'Quod si gentes, quae spem resurrectionis non habent, hoc uno se consolantur, quo dicant, quod nullus post mortem sensus sit defunctorum ac per hoc nullus remaneat sensus doloris, quanto magis nos consolationem recipere debemus ...'; *De bono mortis*, iv. 13, *C.S.E.L.* xxxii. 1, p. 714. 13: 'Quomodo mors mala si aut secundum gentiles sensu caret. ... Vbi enim nullus sensus, nullus utique iniuriae dolor, quia dolor sensus est'; *Epist. ad Ecclesiam Vercellensem*, lxiii. 17, *P.L.* xvi. 1245C: 'Denique Epicurei dicunt assertores uoluptatis, quia mors nihil ad nos; quod enim dissoluitur, insensibile est; quod autem insensibile, nihil ad nos. Quo demonstrant corpore se tantum, non mente uiuere ... nihil reliquiarum superesse animae, cum ipsum corpus non statim resoluatur. Prius ergo dissoluitur anima quam corpus.' Cf. Cicero ap. Macrobius, *In Somn. Scip.* i. 4. 2, p. 478. 19: 'Sapientibus *conscientia* ipsa *factorum* egregiorum amplissimum uirtutis est *praemium*'.

122. Ambrose, *De excessu fra.ris*, ii. 50. 1, p. 275: 'Gentiles plerumque se consolantur uiri uel de communitate aerumnae uel de iure naturae uel de inmortalitate animae. Quibus utinam sermo constaret ac non miseram animam in uaria portentorum ludibria formasque transfunderent! Quid igitur facere nos oportet, quorum stipendium resurrectio est? Cuius gratiam quoniam negare plerique non possunt, fidem abnuunt'; ii. 65. 1, p. 285: 'Illud mirum quod, cum resurrectionem non credant, tamen ne genus pereat humanum,

clementi quadam benignitate prospiciunt et ideo transire ac demigrare in corpora dicunt animas, ne mundus intereat. Sed quid sit difficilius, ipsi adserant, transire animas an redire, sua repetere an noua quaerere?'; ii. 131. 1, p. 323: 'Sed uidero quid uos de uobis, gentes, opinionis habeatis; neque enim mirum debet uideri, quod creditis uos in bestias posse mutari, qui bestias adoratis. Ego tamen malim de uestro merito melius iudicetis, ut non inter coetus ferarum, sed inter angelorum consortia uos credatis futuros.'

123. Ambrose, *De bono mortis*, x. 45, p. 741, 16: 'Sed Hesdrae usus sum scriptis, ut cognoscant gentiles ea quae in philosophiae libris mirantur translata de nostris. Atque utinam non superflua his et inutilia miscuissent, ut dicerent animas hominum pariter ac bestiarum esse communes earumque summum praemium, si magnorum philosophorum animae in apes aut luscinias demigrarent, ut qui ante hominum genus sermone pauissent postea mellis dulcedine aut cantus suauitate mulcerent. Satis fuerat dixisse illis quod liberatae animae de corporibus Ἀιδην peterent, id est locum qui non uideretur, quem locum latine infernum dicimus.' On the etymology of Hades, which goes back to Plato, *Crat.* 404 b, *Phaedo* 80 d and 81 d, *Gorgias* 493 b, cf. Plotinus, *Enn.* vi. 4, 16, 36, ed. Bréhier, p. 198: Τὸ δὲ εἰς ᾅδου γίνεσθαι, εἰ μὲν ἐν τῷ ἀϊδεῖ, τὸ χωρὶς λέγεται; Hermes, *Asclepius*, 17, ed. Festugière, ii, p. 317. 1: 'Ab eo itaque, quod uisu priuentur, graece Ἀίδης, ab eo quod in imo sphaerae sint, *Latine Inferi* nuncupantur; Chalcidius, *In Tim.* cxxxiii: 'Nonnulli regionem hanc nostram Ἀιδην merito, quod sit ἀειδής, hoc est obscura, cognominatam putant.'

124. Ambrose, *De excessu fratris*, ii. 126. 1, p. 320: 'Quid philosophi ipsi genus post mortem aliquod reppererunt, quo nos uti magis quam resurgere delectabit? Et illi quidem, qui dicunt animas inmortales esse, non satis mulcere me possunt, cum pro parte me redimunt. Nam quae potest esse gratia, ubi non totus euasi, quae uita, si in me opus Dei occidat, quae iustitia, si naturae finis mors sit erranti iustoue communis, quae ueritas, ut, "quia ipsa se moueat" et semper moueatur anima, inmortalis esse credatur—quod nobis in corpore commune cum bestiis, ante corpus, quid geratur, incertum—nec ex contrariis colligatur ueritas, sed destruatur? An uero illorum sententia placet, qui nostras animas, ubi ex hoc corpore emigrauerint, in corpora ferarum uariarumque animantium transire conmemorant? At certe haec Circaeis medicamentorum inlecebris conposita esse ludibria poetarum ipsi philosophi disserere solent, nec tam illos, qui perpessi ista simulentur, quam sensus eorum, qui ista confinxerint, uelut Circeo poculo ferunt in uaria bestiarum monstra conuersos. Quid enim tam simile prodigii quam homines credere in habitus ferarum potuisse mutari? Quanto maioris est prodigii gubernatricem hominis animam aduersam humano generi bestiarum suscipere naturam capacemque rationis ad inrationabile animal posse transire quam corporis effigies esse mutatas? Vos ipsi haec destruitis, qui docetis. Nam magicis incantata carminibus portentosae huius conuersionis genera tradidistis. Ludunt haec poetae, reprehendunt philosophi, et quae putant ficta de uiuentibus, haec arbitrantur uera de mortuis. Illi autem, qui ista finxerunt, non suam probare fabulam, sed philosophorum errores inridere uoluerunt, qui putant, quod illa anima, quae miti humilique proposito iracundiam uincere, patientiam adsumere, cruore abstinere consueuerat,

eadem frementi motu leonis incensa irae inpatiens (cf. *Aen.* vii. 15) effrena rabie sitire sanguinem caedemque possit expetere, et illa, quae "populorum" fremitus uarios "regali" quodam consilio temperabat et rationabili uoce "mulcebat" (*Aen.* i. 148–53), eadem se inter deuia atque deserta ritu "luporum" patiatur "ululare" (*Aen.* vii. 18), aut quae iniusto sub onere gemens duros aratri labores questu miserabili mugiebat, eadem postea in figuram hominis conmutata "leui cornua quaerat in fronte" (*Buc.* vi. 48–51), uel illa, quam praepetes prius pennae usque ad alta caeli per sublime aeris alarum remigiis euehebant, eadem postea uolatus iam non suos requirat et se humani doleat corporis grauitate pigrescere (*Aen.* vi. 14–19). Hinc fortasse et illum Icarum perdidistis, quod persuasionibus uestris inductus adulescens prius auem se fuisse fortasse crediderat (Ov. *Metam.* viii. 223). Hinc etiam senes plerique decepti sunt, ut graui inmorerentur dolori, cygneis male creduli fabulis, dum putant modulis se mulcendo flebilibus albentem "molli pluma" mutare canitiem (*Aen.* x. 189–92; *Metam.* ii. 367). Haec quam incredibilia, quam deformia! ... Quid uero praestantius, quam ut opus Dei iudices non perire et secundum imaginem et similitudinem Dei factos transferri non posse in effigies bestiarum, cum utique ad similitudinem Dei non corporis sit imago, sed ratio? Nam quemadmodum homo, cui subiecta sunt animantium genera ceterarum, in subiectum sibi animal meliore sui parte demigret?' See my article 'Les Pères de l'Église devant les Enfers virgiliens', in *Archives d'Histoire Doctrinale et Littéraire du Moyen-âge*, xxii (1955), 5, 74.

125. Ambrose, *De philosophia*, ap. Augustine, *Contra Iulianum Pelagianum*, ii. 7. 19–20, P.L. xliv. 686: 'An forte ipsum quoque Ambrosium scisse ac docuisse dubitabis Deum esse hominum conditorem, et animae et corporis? Audi ergo quod dicat in libro "De philosophia" contra Platonem philosophum, qui hominum animas reuolui in bestias asseuerat, et animarum tantum modo Deum opinatur auctorem, corpora autem diis minoribus facienda decernit. Ergo sanctus Ambrosius: "Miror, inquit, tantum philosophum, quomodo animam, cui potestatem conferendae immortalitatis attribuit, in noctuis includat aut ranulis, feritate quoque induat bestiarum, cum in Timaeo eam Dei opus esse memorauerit, inter immortalia a Deo factam; corpus autem non uideri opus summi Dei asserit, quia natura carnis humanae nihil a natura corporis bestialis differt. Si ergo digna est quae Dei opus esse credatur, quomodo indigna est, quae Dei opere uestiatur?" Ecce non solum animam, quod et illi dicunt, uerum etiam corpus, quod illi negant, contra Platonicos Dei opus esse defendit Ambrosius.'

125a. W. Stettner, *Die Seelenwanderung bei Griechen und Römern*, in *Tübinger Beiträge zur Altertumswissenschaft*, xxii (Stuttgart–Berlin, 1934).

126. Plato, *Phaedo*, 82 a–b, ed. Robin, p. 43 (after mentioning the ass, the wolf, the falcon, and the kite): Οὐκοῦν εὐδαιμονέστατοι, ἔφη, καὶ τούτων εἰσὶ καὶ εἰς βέλτιστον τόπον ἰόντες οἱ τὴν δημοτικὴν καὶ πολιτικὴν ἀρετὴν ἐπιτετηδευκότες, ἣν δὴ καλοῦσι σωφροσύνην τε καὶ δικαιοσύνην, ἐξ ἔθους τε καὶ μελέτης γεγονυῖαν ἄνευ φιλοσοφίας τε καὶ νοῦ;—Πῇ δὴ οὗτοι εὐδαιμονέστατοι; —Ὅτι τούτους εἰκός ἐστιν εἰς τοιοῦτον πάλιν ἀφικνεῖσθαι πολιτικὸν καὶ ἥμερον γένος, ἤ που μελιττῶν ἢ σφηκῶν ἢ μυρμήκων. ...

127. Plato, *Republic*, x. 620 a–b, ed. Chambry, p. 122: Ἰδεῖν δὲ τὴν Θαμύρου

ἀηδόνος ἑλομένην ... Εἰκοστὴν δὲ λαχοῦσαν ψυχὴν ἑλέσθαι λέοντος βίον· εἶναι δὲ τὴν Αἴαντος τοῦ Τελαμωνίου φεύγουσαν ἄνθρωπον γενέσθαι, μεμνημένην τῆς τῶν ὅπλων κρίσεως. Then are mentioned the metamorphoses of Orpheus into a swan, Agamemnon into an eagle, Thersites into a monkey. Cf. also Proclus, *In rempublicam*, 620 a, ed. Kroll, ii, p. 312. 25 : κύκνοι καὶ ἀηδόνες ἀπὸ τῶν ταῖς Μούσαις γεγόνασιν κατόχων, ἀετοὶ καὶ λέοντες ἀπὸ τῶν ἡρωικῶν. ... Οἷον ἀπὸ τῆς Ὀρφέως ζωῆς καὶ τῆς Θαμύρου ζωὴν ἐνδεικνύμενος μουσικὴν μέν τινα πάντως.

128. Plato, *Timaeus*, 91 e, ed. Rivaud, p. 227: Τὸ δ' αὖ πέζον καὶ θηριῶδες γέγονεν ἐκ τῶν μηδὲν προσχρωμένων φιλοσοφίᾳ μηδὲ ἀθρούντων τῆς περὶ τὸν οὐρανὸν φύσεως πέρι μηδέν, διὰ τὸ μηκέτι ταῖς ἐν τῇ κεφαλῇ χρῆσθαι, ἀλλὰ τοῖς περὶ τὰ στήθη τῆς ψυχῆς ἡγεμόσιν ἕπεσθαι μέρεσιν. This phrase follows the mention of birds and precedes that of reptiles, fish, molluscs.

129. Plotinus, *Enneads*, iii. 4. 2. 17, ed. Henry–Schwyzer, i, p. 311 : Ὅσοι δὲ αἰσθήσει μόνον ἔζησαν, ζῷα· ἀλλ' εἰ μὲν αἰσθήσεις μετὰ θυμοῦ, τὰ ἄγρια, καὶ ἡ διαφορὰ ἡ ἐν τούτοις τὸ διάφορον τῶν τοιούτων ποιεῖ. ... Τοὺς δὲ φιλομούσους μέν, καθαρίους δὲ τὰ ἄλλα, εἰς τὰ ᾠδικά. ... Ὁ δ' ἧττον πολιτικῆς μετέχων πολιτικὸν ζῷον, μέλιττα ἢ τὰ τοιαῦτα; cf. iv. 3. 12. 39.

130. Porphyry *ap*. Stobaeus, *Ecloga*, i. 49. 60, ed. Wachsmuth (Berlin, 1884), pp. 445. 15 to 448. 3. This passage is translated in part and commented on by F. Buffière, *Les Mythes d'Homère et la pensée grecque* (Paris, 1956), pp. 506–20. Cf. F. Cumont, *Lux perpetua* (Paris, 1949), p. 203. See also the texts of Augustine quoted below, n. 133.

131. Nemesius of Emesa, *De natura hominis*, 2, P.G. xl. 584A (ed. Matthaei, p. 117): Γέγραπται γοῦν αὐτῷ μονόβιβλον ἐπίγραφον· Ὅτι οὐκ ἀπ' ἀνθρώπων εἰς ζῷα ἄλογα οὐδὲ ἀπὸ ζῴων ἀλόγων εἰς ἀνθρώπους αἱ μετενσωματώσεις γίνονται, ἀλλὰ ἀπὸ ζῴων εἰς ζῷα καὶ ἀπὸ ἀνθρώπων εἰς ἀνθρώπους.

132. *Hermetica*, x. 19–20, 22, ed. Festugière, p. 123. 3 and p. 124.4; Proclus, *In Timaeum*, ed. E. Diehl, iii, p. 295. 30; *In rempublicam*, ed. G. Kroll, ii, p. 336. 28; Sallust, *De diis*, xx, ed. Nock, p. 34. 26; Hermias, *In Phaedrum*, ed. Couvreur, p. 170. 16; Olympiodorus, *In Phaedonem*, ed. Norvin, p. 166. 24. Cf. E. Zeller, *Die Philosophie der Griechen*, 5th edn., iii. 2. 2 (Leipzig, 1923), pp. 712–16, and my *Lettres grecques en Occident, de Macrobe à Cassiodore*, 2nd edn. (Paris, 1948), p. 290.

133. Besides the text of Chalcidius quoted below, n. 136, cf. Boethius, *Philosophiae Consolatio*, iv, pr. 3. 15. 41, ed. Bieler, C.C. xciv, p. 71 : 'Hoc igitur modo quicquid a bono deficit esse desistit. Quo fit ut mali desinant esse quod fuerant. Sed fuisse homines adhuc ipsa humani corporis reliqua species ostentat; quare uersi in malitiam humanam quoque amisere naturam. Sed cum ultra homines quemque prouehere sola probitas possit, necesse est ut quos ab humana condicione deiecit infra homines merito detrudat improbitas; euenit igitur ut quem transformatum uitiis uideas hominem aestimare non possis. Auaritia feruet alienarum opum uiolentus ereptor: lupi similem dixeris. Ferox atque inquies linguam litigiis exercet: cani comparabis. Insidiator occultus subripuisse fraudibus gaudet: uulpeculis exaequetur. Irae intemperans fremit: leonis animum gestare credatur. Pauidus ac fugax non metuenda formidat: ceruis similis habeatur. Segnis ac stupidus torpet: asinum uiuit.

Leuis atque inconstans studia permutat: nihil auibus differt. Foedis immundisque libidinibus immergitur: sordidae suis uoluptate detinetur. Ita fit ut qui probitate deserta homo esse desierit, cum in diuinam condicionem transire non possit, uertatur in beluam.' This passage, which is followed by a poem on the episode of Circe, is directly opposed to the views of Claudian, *In Rufinum*, ii. 482–9, *M.G.H. A.a.* x, p. 52, which accepts the passage of human souls into the bodies of animals. The Porphyrean interpretation clearly had the backing of Augustine, *Civ. Dei*, x. 30; cf. Porphyry, *De regressu*, fragm. xi. 1, ed. Bidez, p. 38*: 'Nam Platonem animas hominum post mortem reuolui usque ad corpora bestiarum scripsisse certissimum est. Hanc sententiam Porphyrii doctor tenuit et Plotinus. Porphyrio tamen iure displicuit.... Puduit scilicet illud credere, *ne mater fortasse* filium in *mulam* reuoluta uectaret.... Quanto, inquam, honestius creditur reuerti animas ad corpora propria quam reuerti totiens ad diuersa! Verumtamen, ut dixi, ex magna parte correctus est in hac opinione Porphyrius, ut saltem in solos homines humanas animas praecipitari posse sentiret, beluinos autem carceres euertere minime dubitaret'; xi. 2, p. 47* (= *Civ. Dei*, xii. 27): 'Cum suo Platone aliisque Platonicis sentit eos, qui inmoderate atque inhoneste uixerint, propter luendas poenas ad corpora redire mortalia, Plato quidem bestiarum, Porphyrius tantummodo ad hominum'; xi, 5, p. 41* (= *Civ. Dei*, xiii. 19): 'Vt Christo aduersaretur, resurrectionem incorruptibilium corporum negans, non solum sine terrenis, sed sine ullis omnino corporibus eas adseruit in sempiternum esse uicturas'; xi. 3, p. 41* (= *Civ. Dei*, xxii. 13): 'Ut fidem resurrectionis inludant.' The passage from Augustine concerning the mule cannot be a fragment of Porphyry as Bidez believed, *Vie de Porphyre*, p. 38*. 16, but must derive from the same satirical tradition as Tertullian, *Apologeticum*, xlviii. 1, ed. Waltzing, p. 101: 'Si quis philosophus affirmet, ut ait Laberius de sententia Pythagorae, hominem fieri ex *mulo*, colubram ex muliere... nonne consensum mouebit et fidem infiget, ut etiam ab animalibus abstinendum propterea persuasum quis habeat, *ne forte* bubulam de aliquo proauo suo obsonet?' The distinction between moral and physical metamorphosis had already been expressed by Cicero, *De officiis*, iii. 20. 82: 'Quid enim interest utrum ex homine se conuertat quis in beluam an hominis figura inmanitatem gerat beluae?' Cf. L. Alfonsi, *Studi Boeziani*, in *Aevum*, xxv (1951), pp. 143, 146, who sees this as the source of the passage in the *Consolatio* of Boethius.

134. Origen, *De principiis*, i. 18. 1, *G.C.S.* v, p. 104. 8: 'Ἡ ψυχὴ ἀπορρέουσα τοῦ καλοῦ καὶ τῇ κακίᾳ προσκλινομένη καὶ ἐπὶ πλεῖον ἐν ταύτῃ γινομένη, εἰ μὴ ὑποστρέφοι, ὑπὸ τῆς ἀνοίας ἀποκτηνοῦται καὶ ὑπὸ τῆς πονηρίας ἀποθηριοῦται... καὶ αἱρεῖται πρὸς τὸ ἀλογωθῆναι καὶ τὸν ἔνυδρον, ἵν' οὕτως εἴπω, βίον καὶ τάχα κατ' ἀξίαν τῆς ἐπὶ πλεῖον ἀποπτώσεως τῆς κακίας ἐνδύεται σῶμα ⟨τοι⟩οῦδε ἢ τοιοῦδε ἀλόγου ζῴου. His views are summarized by Jerome, *Epist. ad Auitum*, cxxiv. 4. 3, *C.S.E.L.* lvi, p. 100. 19: 'Angelum siue animam siue daemonem, quos unius adserit esse naturae, sed diuersarum uoluntatum, pro magnitudine neglegentiae et stultitiae *iumentum* posse fieri et pro dolore poenarum et ignis ardore magis eligere, ut brutum animal sit et in aquis habitet ac fluctibus, et corpus adsumere huius uel illius pecoris, ut nobis non solum quadrupedum, sed et piscium corpora sint timenda. Et ad extremum, ne teneretur

Pythagorici dogmatis reus, qui adserit μετεμψύχωσιν, post tam nefandam disputationem, qua lectoris animum uulnerauit: "Haec, inquit, iuxta nostram sententiam non sint dogmata, sed quaesita tantum atque proiecta, ne penitus intractata uiderentur."' The comparison of a man with a *iumentum* shows that Origen was undoubtedly referring to Psalm xlviii. 13, and that he is aimed at directly by Augustine, *De genesi ad litteram*, vii. 9, *C.S.E.L.* xxviii, p. 208. 1: 'Deinde cauendum est, ne quaedam translatio animae fieri a pecore in hominem posse credatur,—quod ueritati fideique catholicae omnino contrarium est,—si concesserimus inrationalem animam ueluti materiem subiacere, unde rationalis anima fiat. Sic enim fiet, ut, si haec in melius commutata erit hominis, illa quoque in deterius commutata sit pecoris. De quo ludibrio quorundam philosophorum etiam eorum posteri erubuerunt nec eos hoc sensisse, sed non recte intellectos esse dixerunt. Et credo ita esse, uelut si quisquam etiam de scripturis nostris hoc sentiat, ubi dictum est: "Homo in honore positus non intellexit: conparatus est pecoribus insensatis et similis factus est eis." . . . Neque enim non omnes haeretici scripturas catholicas legunt nec ob aliud sunt haeretici, nisi quod eas non bene intellegentes suas falsas opiniones contra earum ueritatem peruicaciter adserunt. Sed quoquo modo se habeat uel hon habeat opinio philosophorum de reuolutionibus animarum, catholicae tamen fidei non conuenit credere animas pecorum in homines uel hominum in pecora transmigrare. Fieri sane homines uitae genere pecoribus similes et ipsae res humanae clamant et scriptura testatur. Vnde est illud, quod commemoraui: "Homo in honore positus non intellexit; conparatus est iumentis insensatis et similis factus est eis" (*Ps.* xlviii. 13), sed in hac uita utique, non post mortem. . . . Quid enim adferunt argumenti philosophi, qui putant hominum animas in pecora uel pecorum in homines post mortem posse transferri? Hoc certe, quod morum similitudo ad id trahat, uelut auaros in formicas, rapaces in miluos, saeuos ac superbos in leones, sectatores inmundae uoluptatis in sues et si qua similia. Haec quippe adserunt nec adtendunt per hanc rationem nullo modo fieri posse, ut pecoris anima post mortem in hominem transferatur. Nullo modo enim porcus similior erit homini quam porco; et cum mansuescunt leones, canibus uel etiam ouibus fiunt similiores quam hominibus. Cum igitur a pecorum moribus pecora non recedunt et quae aliquantulum ceteris dissimilia fiunt, similiora sunt tamen suo generi quam humano longeque plus ab hominibus quam a pecoribus differunt, nunquam erunt hominum animae istae, si ea, quae similiora sunt, trahunt. . . . Unde procliuius et ipse crediderim, quod etiam eorum posteri sectatores, illos homines, qui haec primitus in suis libris posuerunt, in hac uita potius intellegi uoluisse quadam peruersitate morum ac turpitudine homines pecorum similes fieri ac sic quodam modo in pecora commutari, ut hoc dedecore obiecto eos a cupiditatum prauitate reuocarent.' Metensomatosis is also denounced, among the heretics, by a colleague of Ambrose: Philastrius of Brescia, *Diuersarum hereseon liber*, cxxiv (96), *C.C.* ix, p. 287): 'Alia est heresis quae dicit animas uenenariorum, sceleratorum et homicidarum et aliorum talium transire in daemonas ac pecudes et bestias et serpentes. . . . Si quis autem hoc ita putauerit fieri, paganitatis et uanitatis filosoforum quam Christianitatis uidetur habere consortium. . . . Animae itaque natura non uertitur in naturam alteram, sed . . . non aliis morum causa nisi pecudibus cognoscitur comparanda, non natura, sed moribus, ut scriptum est.'

135. Tertullian, *De anima*, xxiii. 5, ed. Waszink, p. 31. 30: 'Doleo bona fide Platonem omnium haereticorum condimentarium fuisse. Illius est enim et in Phaedone, quod animae hinc euntes sint illuc, et inde huc (*Phaedo* 70 c); item in Timaeo quod "genimina Dei delegata sibi mortalium genitura accepto initio animae immortali mortale ei circumgelauerint corpus" (*Timaeus* 69 c: Καὶ τῶν μὲν θείων αὐτὸς γίγνεται δημιουργός, τῶν δὲ θνητῶν τὴν γένεσιν τοῖς ἑαυτοῦ γεννήμασιν δημιουργεῖν προσέταξεν. Οἱ δὲ μιμούμενοι παραλαβόντες ἀρχὴν ψυχῆς ἀθάνατον τὸ μετὰ τοῦτο θνητὸν σῶμα αὐτῇ περιετόρνευσαν).' The debt to the *Phaedo* is still more clear in *De Anima*, xxviii. 1, p. 39. 25: 'Quis ille nunc *uetus sermo apud memoriam Platonis de animarum reciproco discursu; quod hinc abeuntes sint illuc et rursus huc ueniant et dehinc ita habeat rursus ex mortuis effici uiuos?* (*Phaedo* 70 c: Παλαιὸς μὲν οὖν ἔστι τις λόγος οὗ μεμνήμεθα, ὡς εἰσὶν ἐνθένδε ἀφικόμεναι ἐκεῖ, καὶ πάλιν γε δεῦρο ἀφικνοῦνται καὶ γίγνονται ἐκ τῶν τεθνεώτων). Pythagoricus, ut uolunt quidam, diuinum Albinus existimat, Mercurii forsitan Aegyptii.' On *Tim.* 41 cd and 69 c, cf. Arnobius, *Adv. nat.* ii. 52, p. 126. 12.

136. Chalcidius, *In Timaeum* (42 c), c. cxcvi, ed. Mullach, p. 222: 'Sed Plato non putat rationabilem animam uultum atque os ratione carentis animalis induere, sed ad uitiorum reliquias accedente corpore, incorporationem, auctis animae uitiis, efferari ex instituto uitae prioris, et iracundum quidem hominem eundemque fortem prouehi usque ad feritatem leonis, ferum uero et eundem rapacem ad proximam luporum naturae similitudinem peruenire, caeterorum item. Sed cum sit reditus animis ad fortunam priorem, hoc uero fieri non potest, nisi prius reditus factus erit purus ad clemens et homine dignum institutum, rationabilis porro consilii correctio, quae poenitudo est, non proueniat in iis, quae sine ratione uiuunt, anima quondam hominis nequaquam transit ad bestias iuxta Platonem'; cxcix: 'Deinde iubet factis a se diis, id est stellis, *fingere humana corpora* (42 d) animarum competentium receptacula. . . .'

137. Augustine, *Civ. Dei*, xii. 27. 1, *C.C.* xlviii, p. 383: 'Ita sane Plato minores et a summo Deo factos deos effectores esse uoluit animalium ceterorum, ut inmortalem partem ab ipso sumerent, ipsi uero mortalem attexerent (cf. *Timaeus* 41 c–42 d; also *Civ. Dei*, x. 31. 8; xii. 25. 7; xiii. 18. 45). Proinde animarum nostrarum eos creatores noluit esse, sed corporum. Unde quoniam Porphyrius propter animae purgationem dicit corpus omne fugiendum simulque cum suo Platone aliisque Platonicis sentit eos, qui inmoderate atque inhoneste uixerint, propter luendas poenas ad corpora redire mortalia, Plato quidem etiam bestiarum, Porphyrius tantummodo ad hominum, sequitur eos, ut dicant deos istos, quos a nobis uolunt quasi parentes et conditores nostros coli, nihil esse aliud quam fabros compedum carcerumue nostrorum, nec institutores, sed inclusores adligatoresque nostros ergastulis aerumnosis et grauissimis uinculis. Aut ergo desinant Platonici poenas animarum ex istis corporibus comminari, aut eos nobis deos colendos non praedicent, quorum in nobis operationem, ut quantum possumus fugiamus et euadamus, hortantur.'

Notes

137a. Plato, *Phaedo* 109b, names frogs (cf. *Theaet.* 161c; 167b) and ants, but not in connexion with metensomatosis.

138. Aeneas of Gaza, *Theophrastus*, ed. Boissonade (Paris, 1836), p. 15 (*P.G.* lxxxv. 897A: Ὁ δὲ δὴ βάτραχος καὶ Κλέων ἦν (θαμὰ γὰρ βοῶσιν ἀμφότεροι). Cf. H. Dörrie,'Kontroversen um die Seelenwanderung im kaiserzeitlichen Platonismus', in *Hermes*, lxxxv (1957), 433, n. 2. Cf. Alex. Aphrod., *De anima*, ed. I. Bruns (*C.A.G., Supplementum Aristotelicum*, ii. 1, p. 27. 21): Ἔτι τε πῶς οὐκ ἄτοπον τὸ τὸν ἄνθρωπον λέγειν τῶν βατράχων καὶ τῶν τυχόντων ζῴων διαφέρειν μὴ τῇ τῆς ψυχῆς δυνάμει, ἀλλὰ ὀργανικῷ τινι σώματι; Οὐδέν τε διοίσει τῆς ὑπό τινων λεγομένης μετεμψυχώσεως ἥδε ἡ δόξα, εἰ μὴ παρὰ τὰς τῆς ψυχῆς δυνάμεις, ἀλλὰ παρὰ τὰ ὄργανα ἡ τῶν ζῴων καὶ τῶν ἐνεργειῶν αὐτῶν γίνεται διαφορά. Ἡ αὐτὴ μὲν γὰρ ἐν πᾶσι τοῖς ἐμψύχοις ἔσται ψυχή, κατὰ δὲ τὰς τῶν σωμάτων διαφόρως ἐνεργήσει. Κἀκεῖνοι λέγουσιν. Seruius, *In Aen.* vi. 724: 'Non esse in animis dissimilitudinem, sed in corporibus. ...'

139. Ibid., p. 10, *P.G.* lxxxv. 888B: Αὖθις δὲ εἰς ὀρνέου φύσιν μετατιθεμένη, κολοιὸς ἢ ἀηδὼν ὀφθεῖσα, εἰς ἀέρα διέπτη.

140. I cannot understand how M. Caster, in *Lucien et la pensée religieuse de son temps* (Paris, 1937), pp. 292–3, can say that Lucian offered no direct criticism of reincarnation. On the seven reincarnations of Pythagoras into animals see his *Vera historia* 21, ed. Dindorf (Didot), p. 292.

141. Lucian, *Somnium seu Gallus*, 20, p. 500: Εἶτα βασιλεύς, εἶτα πένης καὶ μετ' ὀλίγον σατράπης, εἶτα ἵππος καὶ κολοιὸς καὶ βάτραχος καὶ ἄλλα μυρία. ... Τὰ τελευταῖα δὲ ἀλεκτρυών.

142. For the jackdaw cf. Aristophanes, *Knights*, v. 1020: Πολλοὶ γὰρ μίσει σφε κατακρώζουσι κολοιοί. For the frogs cf. Ovid, *Metam.* vi. 374 (on the shepherds metamorphosed by Leto):

> Sed nunc quoque turpes
> litibus exercent linguas pulsoque pudore,
> quamuis sint sub aqua, sub aqua maledicere tentant.
> Vox quoque iam rauca est inflataque colla tumescunt,
> ipsaque dilatant patulos conuicia rictus.
> Terga caput tangunt; colla intercepta uidentur;
> spina uiret; uenter, pars maxima corporis, albet,
> limosoque nouae saliunt in gurgite ranae.

Seruius, *In Georg.* iii. 431, ed. Thilo–Hagen, iii. 1, p. 310. 9: 'ranis ... loquacibus*, ideo quia ex hominibus factae sunt, ut dicit Ouidius.' Augustine, *Enarr. in Ps.* lxxvii. 27, *C.C.*, xxxix, p. 1087: 'Rana est loquacissima uanitas.'

143. Lucian, *Gallus*, 26–27, p. 503: Ἵππος δὲ ἢ κύων ἢ ἰχθὺς ἢ βάτραχος ὁπότε γένοιο, πῶς ἔφερες ἐκείνην τὴν διατριβήν;—Μακρὸν τοῦτον ἀνακινεῖς τὸν λόγον καὶ οὐ τοῦ παρόντος καιροῦ· πλὴν τό γε κεφάλαιον, οὐδείς ὅστις οὐκ ἀπραγμονέστερος τῶν βίων ἔδοξέ μοι τοῦ ἀνθρωπείου μόναις ταῖς φυσικαῖς ἐπιθυμίαις καὶ χρείαις ξυμμεμετρημένος· τελώνην δὲ ἵππον ἢ συκοφάντην βάτραχον ἢ σοφιστὴν κολοιὸν ἢ ὀψοποιὸν κώνωπα ἢ κίναιδον ἀλεκτρυόνα ἢ ὅσα ὑμεῖς ἐννοεῖτε, οὐκ ἂν ἴδοις ἐν ἐκείνοις.

144. Ibid. 4, p. 493: ... δυ' ἤδη μοι τετηρηκέναι δοκῶ πάνυ ἐν σοὶ ἀλλότρια τοῦ

Πυθαγόρου.—Τὰ ποῖα;—Ἓν μὲν ὅτι λάλος εἶ καὶ κρακτικός, ὁ δὲ σιωπᾶν ἐς πέντε ὅλα ἔτη, οἶμαι, παρῄνει. ... Ὥστε ἢ ἐψεῦσθαί σοι ἀνάγκη καὶ ἄλλῳ εἶναι ἢ Πυθαγόρᾳ ὄντι παρανενομηκέναι....

144a. Gregory of Nyssa, *De hominis opificio*, 28, *P.G.* xliv. 232A: Οἱ ... πρεσβυτέραν τῆς ἐν σαρκὶ ζωῆς τὴν πολιτείαν τῶν ψυχῶν δογματίζοντες, οὔ μοι δοκοῦσι τῶν Ἑλληνικῶν καθαρεύειν δογμάτων, τῶν περὶ τῆς μετενσωματώσεως αὐτοῖς μεμυθολογημένων. Εἰ γάρ τις ἀκριβῶς ἐξετάσειε, πρὸς τοῦτο κατὰ πᾶσαν ἀνάγκην τὸν λόγον αὐτοῖς εὑρήσει κατασυρόμενον, ὄν φασί τινα τῶν παρ' ἐκείνοις σοφῶν εἰρηκέναι, ὅτι ἀνὴρ γέγονεν ὁ αὐτός, καὶ γυναικὸς σῶμα μετημφιάσατο, καὶ μετ' ὀρνέων ἀνέπτη καὶ θάμνος ἔφυ, καὶ τὸν ἔνυδρον ἔλαχε βίον. Οὐ πόρρω τῆς ἀληθείας κατά γε τὴν ἐμὴν κρίσιν φερόμενος ὁ περὶ αὐτοῦ ταῦτα λέγων. Ὄντως γὰρ βατράχων τινῶν ἢ κολοιῶν φλυαρίας, ἢ ἀλογίας ἰχθύων ἢ δρυῶν ἀναισθησίας ἄξια τὰ τοιαῦτα δόγματα, τὸ μίαν ψυχὴν λέγειν διὰ τοσούτων ἐλθεῖν. Τῆς δὲ τοιαύτης ἀτοπίας αὕτη ἐστὶν ἡ αἰτία, τὸ προϋφεστάναι τὰς ψυχὰς οἴεσθαι. Δι' ἀκολούθου γὰρ ἡ ἀρχὴ τοῦ τοιούτου δόγματος ἐπὶ τὸ προσεχές τε καὶ παρακείμενον τὸν λόγον προάγουσα, μέχρι τούτου τερατευομένη διέξεισιν. Cf. *In Cant. hom.*[4] *P.G.* xliv, 833B, on frogs, and n. 134: 'τὸν ἔνυδρον, ἵν' οὕτως εἴπω, βίον.'

145. Cf. Gregory of Nyssa *ap*. Dionysius Exiguus, *De creatione hominis*, c. 29, *P.L.* lxvii. 396D: 'Vere namque *ranarum coruorumque* (!) garrulitatibus et irrationabilitate piscium et arborum insensibilitate digna haec eorum dogmata comprobantur, quae unam animam per tot res pertransire confirmant. Ineptiae huius haec causa est, quod ante subsistere animas arbitrantur. Consequenter enim principium dogmatis eorum in anteriora tendens ac promouens, usque ad haec *monstra* delabitur.' If my conjecture appears unacceptable we might look at Tertullian, *De Anima*, xxxii. 5, ed. Waszink, p. 45. 4, where the owl is referred to, in connexion with metensomatosis, as being incapable of seeing the light of the sun (whereas the eagle (*Rep.* 620 b) can look straight at it). On the metamorphosis of Nyctimene into an owl see Ovid, *Metam*. ii. 593; Hyginus, *Fabula*, cciv, ed. J. H. Rose (Leiden, 1934), p. 142; Lactantius Placidus, *In Statii Thebaida*, iii. 507, ed. R. Jahnke (Leipzig, 1898), p. 172. 20; A. Westermann, *Mythographi* (Brunswick, 1843), p. 348; Seruius, *In Georg.* i. 403, p. 208. 26. The darkness, according to the Mythographers, helped Nyctimene to hide his shame.

146. In Lucian, *Gallus* 2–4, pp. 491–3: Εἶτά σοι τέρας εἶναι δοκεῖ τὸ τοιοῦτον, εἰ ὁμόφωνος ὑμῖν εἰμι; —Πῶς γὰρ οὐ τέρας; ... Τοῦτ' αὖ μακρῷ ἐκείνου τερατωδέστερον, ἀλεκτρυὼν φιλόσοφος; in Gregory of Nyssa, cited above, nn. 144a–145: τερατευομένη = *monstra*. In Ambrose, see above, n. 124: 'illos ... in uaria bestiarum *monstra* conuersos. Quid enim tam *simile prodigii quam homines credere in habitus ferarum potuisse* mutari? *Quanto maioris est prodigii* gubernatricem hominis animam aduersam humano generi bestiarum suscipere naturam.... *Portentosae* huius conuersionis genera tradidistis.' Eusebius, *Praep. Ev.* xiii. 16, ed. Mras, ii, p. 237. 1, relates the Platonist record concerning metensomatosis to Egyptian zoolatry.

147.

Aeneas of Gaza: 893A	Aeneas of Gaza: 896C	Ambrose
(Porphyry's theory)	(Syrianus and Proclus)	(above, n. 124)
Ἐρυθριῶντες τὸν Πλά-	Τὴν πρὸς ἁρπαγὴν παρεσκευ-	'Quid enim tam simile

τωνος ὄνον καὶ λύκον καὶ ἰκτῖνον καὶ κατανοήσαντες ὡς ἄλλη μὲν λογικῆς ψυχῆς ἡ οὐσία, ἄλλη δ' ἀλόγου.... Οὐ γὰρ τὸ λογικὸν τῇ ψυχῇ συμβεβηκὸς ὡς μεταχωρεῖν, ἀλλ' οὐσίας διαφορὰ βεβαίως ἱδρυμένη· καὶ ὅλως ἀδύνατον τὸν λόγον εἰς ἀλογίαν μετατίθεσθαι ... οὐκ εἰς ὄνον φασίν, ἀλλ' ὀνώδη ἄνθρωπον ἀναβιῶναι τὸν ἄνθρωπον· οὐδ' εἰς λέοντα, ἀλλ' εἰς λεοντώδη ἄνθρωπον. Οὐ γὰρ τὴν φύσιν, ἀλλὰ τὴν τῶν σωμάτων μορφὴν μεταμπίσχεσθαι. ἀσμένην ψυχὴν οὐκ εἰς ἰκτῖνον μεταβάλλουσιν· ἄλογον γὰρ εἰς ἄλογον τὴν λογικὴν μετατίθεσθαι. Οὐδ' εἰς ἰκτινώδη ἄνθρωπον ἐκπέμπουσιν· ἄτοπον γὰρ εἰ πλεονεξίας αἰτία γίγνεται κόλασις. Ἀλλὰ τὸν μὲν ἰκτῖνον λέγουσι τὴν ἑαυτοῦ ψυχὴν ἔχειν τὴν ἄλογον, τὴν δὲ ἀνθρωπείαν ταύτῃ συνδεδέσθαι, καὶ παραμένειν καὶ συμπέτεσθαι. Καὶ οὗτος τῆς τιμωρίας ὁ τρόπος. —Καινότερον μὲν τὸ εὕρημα, ἀλλ' ἔτι μᾶλλον καταγέλαστον. prodigii quam homines in habitus ferarum potuisse mutari? Quanto maioris est prodigii gubernatricem hominis animam aduersam humano generi suscipere naturam *capacemque rationis ad inrationabile animal* posse transire quam corporis effigies esse mutatas?'

On Porphyry's assertion that the rational soul cannot in its nature enter into the body of an animal, and the controversies which ensued, see the excellent account by H. Dörrie, 'Kontroversen um die Seelenwanderung im kaiserzeitlichen Platonismus', in *Hermes*, lxxxv (1957), 414–35; 'Porphyrios "Symmikta Zetemata"', in *Zetemata. Monographien zur klassischen Altertumswissenschaft*, xx (Munich, 1959), 147–51. On metensomatosis in Proclus, cf. P. Courcelle, 'Témoins nouveaux de la "région de dissemblance",' in *Bibliothèque de l'École des Chartes*, t. cxviii, 1960, pp. 25–36.

148. See above, n. 123: 'Utinam non superflua his et inutilia miscuissent, ut dicerent animas hominum pariter ac bestiarum esse communes'; n. 124: 'quod nobis in corpore commune cum bestiis.'

149. Arnobius, *Aduersus nationes*, ii. 16, 2nd edn., Marchesi (Turin, 1953), p. 85. 14: 'Quod si et illud est uerum, quod in mysteriis secretioribus dicitur, in pecudes atque alias beluas ire animas improborum, postquam sunt humanis corporibus seiunctae, manifestius comprobatur uicinos nos esse neque interuallis longioribus disparatos. Siquidem res eadem nobis et illis est una, per quam esse animantia dicimur et motum agitare uitalem.—Sed rationales nos sumus et intelligentia uincimus genus omne mutorum.—Crederem istud uerissime dici, si cum ratione et consilio cuncti homines uiuerent. . . .' Cf. Montaigne, *Essais*, ii. 12, ed. Strowsky, ii (Bordeaux, 1909), 156 et seq.

150. P. Courcelle, 'Plotin et S. Ambroise', in *Revue de Philologie*, lxxvi (1950), 29–56; *Recherches sur les Confessions de S. Augustin*, Paris, de Boccard, 1950, pp. 93–138.

151. A. Solignac, 'Nouveaux parallèles entre S. Ambroise et Plotin : Le "De Jacob et vita beata" et le Περὶ εὐδαιμονίας (Enn. i. 4)', in *Archives de Philosophie*, xx (1956), 148–56.

152. L. Taormina, 'Sant'Ambrogio e Plotino', in *Miscellanea di studi di letteratura cristiana antica*, iv (Catania, 1953), 41–85; P. Hadot, 'Platon et Plotin dans trois sermons de S. Ambroise', in *Revue des Études Latines*, xxxiv (1956), 202–20.

153. P. Courcelle, 'Nouveaux aspects du platonisme chez S. Ambroise', in *Revue des Études Latines*, xxxiv (1956), 220–6.

154. See particularly in this sense W. Theiler, in *Gnomon*, xxv (1953), 115 et seq.

155. Courcelle, op. cit., p. 232–9. Cf. 'La Postérité chrétienne du "Songe de Scipion" ', in *Revue des Études Latines*, xxxvi (1958), 224–8; 'De Platon à Saint Ambroise par Apulée (Parallèles textuels entre le "De excessu fratris" et le "De Platone")', in *Revue de Philologie*, lxxxvii (1961), pp. 15–28; 'L'humanisme chrétien de Saint Ambroise', in *Orpheus*, ix (1962), pp. 21–34.

156. Courcelle, 'Quelques symboles funéraires du néo-platonisme latin', in *Revue des Études Anciennes*, xlvi (1944), 65–93; 'La Colle et le clou de l'âme dans la tradition néo-platonicienne et chrétienne (Phédon 82 e; 83 d)', in *Revue Belge de Philologie et d'Histoire*, xxxvi (1958), 72–95; ' "Trames ueritatis", la fortune patristique d'une métaphore platonicienne (Phédon 66 b)', in *Mélanges offerts à E. Gilson* (Toronto–Paris, 1959), pp. 203–10.

157. See above, p. 157.

VIII

The Pagan Revival in the West at the End of the Fourth Century[1]

HERBERT BLOCH

IN one of the sermons in which he tries to elucidate the Song of Songs, St. Bernard of Clairvaux says: 'Habet mundus iste noctes suas, et non paucas' ('this world of ours has its nights, and not a few of them').[2] We ourselves have been passing through such a period of darkness for nearly half a century, uncertain even now whether the present respite will end in a true dawn or whether it is just another ὕποπτος ἀνοκωχή—in Thucydides' words—of the kind that intervened between 1918 and 1939. But in times like ours it becomes easier to understand kindred periods in which long-established traditions and values disintegrate, in which one crisis precipitates another, until an era comes to an end.

There has been no more momentous breakdown in the history of mankind than the one which marks the end of the ancient world and the final conflict between paganism and Christianity, a conflict which culminates and comes to a dramatic conclusion at the end of the fourth century. 'Victrix causa deis placuit, sed victa Catoni': without pleading the cause of the pagans, let us consider it here *sub specie aeternitatis*, trying to understand what the last pagans of the West accomplished in these decisive years of the eighties and early nineties of the fourth century and in the aftermath of their catastrophe.

One of the most notable phenomena of fourth-century history is the speed with which the recently persecuted Church, supported by the newly christianized government, shifted from defence to attack. One generation after the proclamation of the edict of tolerance by Constantine in 312, his son Constans could

---
[1] While a lecture by its very nature does not require a full documentation, the author has in this case a special reason for dispensing with elaborate footnotes: he can—and does expressly—refer to an earlier detailed treatment of some of the problems here discussed: 'A New Document of the Last Pagan Revival in the West', *Harvard Theological Review*, xxxviii (1945), 199-244 (= *A New Document*). I wish to thank Miss Bettie L. Forte and Dr. Chester F. Natunewicz, Fellows of the American Academy in Rome, for their help in improving the style of this paper. Cf. the Addenda below, p. 217.

[2] *Serm. in Cantica Canticorum*, lxxv. 10 (Migne, P.L. clxxxiii. 1149).

decree in 341 the abrogation of pagan sacrifices. While this act proved to be premature and had to be modified in the following year 342 on account of the powerful pagan opposition, it still ushered in a period of increasing pressure at the end of which the pagan cause succumbed.[1]

The pagan resistance was undoubtedly widespread, but its core in the West was the Roman senate which, after Rome had ceased to be the capital of the Roman empire, assumed once more in Roman history a conspicuous role.[2] Unencumbered by the emperor and his court, the leaders of the senate, which to the superficial observer may give the impression of a city council rather than the senate of the Roman empire, met the challenge with more spirit than their predecessors had mustered for centuries. While they were unable to stem the tide which was to engulf the empire within a short time, they became the guardians of the Roman heritage and thus did more to earn the title of Roman senators than thousands of members of that body before them.

One of the fateful characteristics of the Roman heritage was that it included the state religion; hence safeguarding the Roman tradition involved by necessity the defence of the old religion. In 356 Constantius prohibited all sacrifices and ordered the closing of the pagan temples.[3] However, in the following year the emperor showed himself in Rome, and from Ammianus Marcellinus' unforgettable description of this visit (XVI. x) we know that Constantius, for all his haughty bearing, was enthralled by the greatness of Rome. Although he preserved in front of the Romans the same immovable countenance which he displayed in the provinces, moving his eyes neither right nor left as if he were a statue (the hieratic pose so well illustrated by the magnificent colossal bronze head in the Palazzo dei Conservatori) (Fig. 1), he was so overawed by what he saw that he limited himself to the removal of the altar in front of the statue of Victoria in the Curia. Otherwise he did not interfere with the pagan majority of the senate.[4]

---

[1] A. Piganiol, *Histoire Romaine*, iv. 2: *L'Empire chrétien* (325–395) (Paris, 1947), p. 79; O. Seeck, *Regesten der Kaiser und Päpste für die Jahre 311 bis 476 n. Chr.* (Stuttgart, 1919), p. 191.

[2] Cf. F. Klingner, 'Vom Geistesleben im Rom des ausgehenden Altertums' (1941), *Römische Geisteswelt* (3rd ed.) (München, 1956), p. 484.

[3] *Cod. Theod.* XVI. x. 6 and 4; cf. Piganiol, op. cit., p. 96, n. 44.

[4] Cf. A. Alföldi, 'A Festival of Isis in Rome under the Christian Emperors of the IVth Century', *Diss. Pannon.*, ser. 2. vii (1937), 33 f.

The brief pagan reaction under Constantius' successor Julian was centred in the Greek East. Still, it must have benefited also the pagans of the West. Praetextatus, the outstanding leader of the pagan aristocracy, became proconsul of Achaia, a notable distinction in view of the emperor's philhellenism.[1]

A policy of tolerance prevailed under Julian's successors Jovian and Valentinian I. In 367 or 368 Praetextatus as *praefectus urbi* restored the *Porticus Deorum Consentium* and its *sacrosancta simulacra* on the *Forum Romanum* (Fig. 2). This is to our knowledge the last pagan religious monument dedicated by an official in the city of Rome. We shall see later the special significance of the choice of this shrine.[2]

A continuity of the policy of Jovian and Valentinian I seemed to be assured when Gratian succeeded his father Valentinian I in 375, because Gratian's tutor was Ausonius whose inclinations toward the ideals of the pagan majority of the senate were generally known.[3] Yet another influence made itself felt upon the young emperor with steadily increasing vigour: there appeared on the stage the great antagonist of the pagan aristocracy, St. Ambrose, who had been elevated to the see of Milan a year before Gratian took the purple. Henceforth it was he who to a large extent determined the religious policy of the last scions of the house of Valentinian I and after them of Theodosius.[4] In this conflict between Ambrose and his opponents both sides comported themselves with remarkable dignity, in contrast for instance to the riots and bloodshed which accompanied the last controversy between pagans and Christians in Alexandria. The all-important reason for their restraint was the stature and background of both Ambrose and the pagan leaders. They were social equals, and Ambrose had held high office in the state before becoming the most eminent spokesman of the Roman Church in his time.[5] It is an irony of history that it was Ambrose's

---

[1] Ammianus Marcellinus, xxii. vii. 6; E. Groag, 'Die Reichsbeamten von Achaia in spätrömischer Zeit', *Diss. Pannon.*, ser. 1. xiv (1946), 45–48.

[2] *C.I.L.* vi. 102 = Dessau, *I.L.S.* 4003; Platner and Ashby, *A Topographical Dictionary of Ancient Rome* (1929), pp. 421 f.; Bloch, *A New Document*, pp. 204, 208. Cf. below, pp. 209 f.

[3] Alföldi, *A Festival of Isis*, p. 36. The same scholar has emphasized the negative aspects of Ausonius' powerful position in *A Conflict of Ideas in the Late Roman Empire* (Oxford, 1952), pp. 87 f.

[4] Piganiol, op. cit., p. 194 with earlier literature.

[5] He was *consularis Aemiliae et Liguriae* at the time of his elevation to the bishopric: Paulinus, *Vita s. Ambrosii*, v (Migne, *P.L.* xiv. 30). Cf. F. H. Dudden, *The Life and Times of St. Ambrose*, i (Oxford, 1935), 61 f.

distinguished adversary Symmachus himself who as *praefectus urbi* in 384 recommended St. Augustine to him as teacher of rhetoric in Milan.[1] Thus Gratian was swayed by Ambrose's authority when he renounced, apparently in 379, the title of *pontifex maximus*.[2] Simultaneously he proclaimed Theodosius emperor to rule the East. In the same year the imperial busts disappear from the *vota publica* coins, a series of coins decorated with representations pertaining to the festival of Isis called *navigium Isidis*, as we now know thanks to Professor Alföldi.[3]

In 382 the emperor Gratian, by withdrawing the funds which had been used to maintain the public cult until then, inflicted a decisive blow on the ancient religion. At the same time the altar of Victoria, which presumably had been restored to its place by Julian, was again removed from the Curia. It was this act which the pagan leaders seized upon as a symbol of the threat not only to their religion but to Roman tradition as a whole. Hence the famous debate between Symmachus and St. Ambrose, and particularly Symmachus' contribution, the third *relatio*, transcends the question of the altar and becomes a stirring document of the clash between two ages. The debate occurred in 384 after Gratian's death when conditions at the court of his successor Valentinian II seemed more propitious to the pagan cause and the two pagan leaders Praetextatus and Symmachus held the highest offices in Italy, the *praefectura praetorio Italiae* and the *praefectura urbis*, respectively. In 382 a delegation of the senate, sent to protest against the withdrawal of the funds and the removal of the altar, had not even been received by Gratian; two years later Valentinian listened to Symmachus' address with sympathy, but under pressure from Ambrose the senate's petition was once more rejected.[4]

The arguments of Symmachus are very significant. He scrupulously abstains from anything that could be construed as an attack on Christianity. Live and let live is his motto: 'suus enim cuique mos, suus ritus est' ('everyone has his custom, his religion') (*Rel.* iii. 8). Or 'uno itinere non potest perveniri ad tam

---

[1] Aug. *Confess.* v. xiii (23); H. I. Marrou, *Saint Augustin et la fin de la culture antique* (Paris, 1938), p. 3. Klingner, loc. cit., p. 503.

[2] Alföldi, *A Festival of Isis*, pp. 36 f.; Piganiol, op. cit., p. 228, n. 181.

[3] *A Festival of Isis*, pp. 36 f.

[4] For the text of *Relatio* iii cf. Symmachus, ed. O. Seeck, *Mon. Germ. Hist.*, *Auct. Antiquiss.* vi (1883), 280–3. See also J. Wytzes, *Der Streit um den Altar der Viktoria* (Amsterdam, 1936); Klingner, loc. cit., pp. 509 f.; Bloch, *A New Document*, pp. 213–15, 219 f.; Piganiol, op. cit., pp. 245 f.

grande secretum' ('one cannot reach so great a secret by one way alone') (ibid. 10). He emphasizes the 'instituta maiorum': 'repetimus igitur religionum statum, qui rei publicae diu profuit' ('we ask for the restoration of the cult in its former condition which has been salutary to the Roman state for so long') (ibid. 3). And at one point he says: 'consuetudinis amor magnus est' ('the love of habit is great') (ibid. 4). But habit has here almost the meaning of tradition, as it is to tradition that Roma, whom the speaker introduces, ultimately appeals in her plea for tolerance.

The severe setback which the pagan aristocracy suffered in the controversy about the altar of Victoria represents the climax in the drama of the last fight of the pagans, and the subsequent death of their great leader Praetextatus in the same year—he was *consul designatus* for the year 385—further deepened their sense of defeat. Symmachus, under the impact of this blow, resigned his office.[1] The third leader of the pagan senate, Symmachus' relative Virius Nicomachus Flavianus, had retired into private life shortly before for reasons not connected with the pagan opposition.

There followed a period of respite for the pagans which was interrupted by the march of the usurper Maximus into Italy. Symmachus badly compromised himself by addressing a panegyric to Maximus early in 388 shortly before the pretender was vanquished by Theodosius, who generously pardoned Symmachus as well as the other followers of Maximus.

While residing in Milan, Theodosius, like Gratian before him, fell under the spell of St. Ambrose, though he did not submit without a struggle.[2] In 388 the Christians of Callinicum in Mesopotamia had burnt a Jewish synagogue at the instigation of their bishop. When Theodosius ordered the bishop to rebuild the synagogue and failed to heed sufficiently the protests and threats of Ambrose, he was publicly rebuked in the cathedral. While the emperor yielded to Ambrose in this case, he went out of his way to be gracious to the senate when he visited Rome during the summer of 389. Nicomachus Flavianus became *praefectus praetorio Italiae* in the following year. Subsequently two pagans were designated consuls for 391, Symmachus in the West and Tatian in the East.

[1] Cf. *A New Document*, pp. 216 f., where in n. 43 also St. Jerome's comments on the death of Praetextatus are discussed.
[2] About Ambrose's relationship with Theodosius see *A New Document*, pp. 220–4.

Yet in the year 390 an event occurred which, though unrelated to the conflict between pagans and Christians, precipitated the final doom of the pagan cause. In retaliation for the slaying of the commander of the garrison of Thessalonica, Theodosius, determined to make an example, ordered a wholesale massacre among the population of Thessalonica which was promptly executed, and thousands of innocent people lost their lives. Although Theodosius himself repented this outrage, Ambrose demanded public penance from the emperor before readmitting him to communion at Christmas. The effect of this whole experience on Theodosius was profound: in the realization of his guilt, he must have regarded the forgiveness granted him finally by the Church as a means of redemption.[1]

He demonstrated his gratitude by resuming with new zeal the offensive against paganism where Gratian had left it in 382. On 24 February 391, only two months after his reconciliation with the Church, he issued a law addressed to the *praefectus urbi* Rufius Albinus which altogether forbade any pagan cult, and even prohibited visits to temples. It was Nicomachus Flavianus, the *praefectus praetorio Italiae*, to whom in June a severe law against apostates from the Christian religion was addressed. A week later Theodosius promulgated a special law against pagan cults in Egypt. It was significantly forwarded to the highest civil and military officials of the province because Theodosius correctly foresaw that the enforcement of the law would lead to disturbances. The destruction of the Serapeum of Alexandria, one of the most famous sanctuaries of the ancient world, was preceded and accompanied by bloody disorders.[2]

One can well imagine the growing indignation among the pagan senators in Italy. The fact that their leader Flavianus, because of his official position, was expected to enforce the new hateful legislation added insult to injury. The estrangement between Theodosius and the senate may have hastened the collapse of the Theodosian system in the West. At the court of Vienne the youthful Valentinian II ruled with the pagan Frank Arbogastes as *comes* at his side. Arbogast is the first of the Germanic protectors, such as Stilicho and Ricimer after him, who actually ruled while their emperors often remained mere figureheads,

---

[1] Cf. on the massacre of Thessalonica especially Dudden, *St. Ambrose*, ii. 381–92.
[2] The three laws are found in *Cod. Theod.* XVI. x. 10; XVI. vii. 4–5; XVI. x. 11. Cf. Seeck, *Regesten*, pp. 278 f.

until Odoacer in 476 put an end to the farce and had himself proclaimed King of Italy. Conflicts between Arbogast and Valentinian arose early and came to a head when a petition of the senate requesting the restoration of subsidies for the pagan cult was favoured by Arbogast, but rejected by Valentinian. On 15 May 392 Valentinian died, whether by his own hand or through assassination. Three months later the *magister scriniorum* Flavius Eugenius was raised to the throne by Arbogast.

Eugenius had taught rhetoric in Rome.[1] Like Ausonius who had also risen high in the hierarchy, he was a man of letters. Still it is most remarkable that someone of his background could reach the pinnacle of dignity. There can be little doubt that he became a middleman between Arbogast and the pagan aristocracy of Rome. He was nominally a Christian, but his sympathies lay with the pagan cause. Like Julian, he wore a 'philosopher's' beard[2] which probably contributed to rendering him suspect to the Christians. Eugenius first sought recognition from Theodosius and support from Ambrose, but failed in both endeavours. When he appointed Theodosius and himself consuls for 393, Theodosius ignored him and chose Abundantius as his colleague. This was probably shortly before he issued another stringent law against pagan activities in November 392. So nothing remained for Eugenius but to throw in his lot with the senate. As a compromise measure he turned over to the pagans the funds for the public cult as a personal gift.

By proclaiming his younger son Honorius Augustus of the West in January 393, Theodosius declared Eugenius a usurper. War thus became inevitable, and Eugenius marched into Italy. This was the signal for the pagan party to restore in earnest the ancient cults. While Symmachus, possibly sobered by his narrow escape in 388, kept more in the background, Virius Nicomachus Flavianus, aided by his son Nicomachus Flavianus the younger who became *praefectus urbi*, seized the leadership of Italy and of the pagan revival. The bonds between the two already related families were further strengthened by an alliance: Nicomachus the younger married a daughter of Symmachus.[3]

Until recently the main sources for our knowledge of the pagan revival were two poems written after the collapse of the

[1] Zosimus, iv. 54.
[2] *A New Document*, p. 226; A. Alföldi, *Die Kontorniaten* (Budapest, 1943), p. 65. A documented account of the first five months of Eugenius' reign is given in *A New Document*, pp. 225-8.   [3] Cf. Seeck, *Symmachus*, pp. li f., lix, n. 242; below, p. 212.

movement by two Christians: one the *Carmen adversus Flavianum*, preserved only in the *Codex Puteanus* of Prudentius' *In Symmachum*, written according to E. A. Lowe[1] in the first half of the sixth century; the other, the so-called *Carmen ad Senatorem* which is preserved under the name of Cyprian and directed against a formerly Christian senator who had been converted to Isis and Magna Mater. If we can believe the Anonymous, there seems to have been a veritable stampede by ostensibly Christian office seekers who succumbed to the proselytism of Flavianus and returned to the old religion. Processions in honour of Magna Mater and Isis could be seen once more in the streets of Rome. Other gods whose cult, according to the Anonymous, Flavianus tried to re-establish are Jupiter, Saturn, Mercury, Vulcan, Mithras, Sol, Liber, Trivia (that is Hecate), Sarapis and Anubis, Ceres and Proserpina. Presumably Symmachus' son was responsible for the restoration of the temple of Flora mentioned by the same author.[2]

Twenty years ago a remarkable confirmation of this partisan source came to light in Ostia. Not far from the Temple of Hercules which was probably built or rebuilt by Sulla (Fig. 3) fragments of a unique inscription were found (Fig. 4) a reconstruction of which is shown in Fig. 5:

'[Domini]s n[ostris Th]eodosio Arca[di]o et Eu[genio]
[pi]is felicibus [toto] orbe victoribus semper [Aug(ustis)]
[..] Numerius Proiect[us v(ir) c(larissimus) pra]ef(ectus)
     ann(onae) cellam Hercu[lis restituit]

The inscription is clearly dated in 393 or 394. Theodosius and Arcadius are recognized, but not Honorius, whom Theodosius had elevated in place of Eugenius. Numerius Proiectus may be identical with Symmachus' friend (*familiaris noster*) Proiectus mentioned by him in connexion with a mission in 380. As *praefectus annonae* he was subordinate to the *praefectus urbi* Nicomachus Flavianus the younger, and the restoration of this important sanctuary may have been inspired either by him or by his father. In any case it is an impressive document of the religious policy of Virius Nicomachus Flavianus and his followers.[3]

In a relief, also discovered near the temple, which at the time of Sulla had been dedicated to Hercules by a *haruspex* (Fig. 6), the

[1] *Cod. Lat. Antiqu.* v (1950), No. 571 b. Cf. also below, pp. 216, 217 (Add.).
[2] A detailed discussion of the *Carmen adversus Flavianum* (text in *Anthol. lat.* i (2nd ed.), 20–25) is given in *A New Document*, pp. 230–3; on the *Carmen ad Senatorem* cf. ibid., p. 232.
[3] This inscription formed the starting-point for my study of 1945: see *A New Document*, pp. 199–202, 234 f. For Proiectus cf. Symmachus, *Ep.* iii. 6. 4.

god appears issuing oracles like the Hercules of Tibur.[1] As the *Carmen adversus Flavianum* shows, Flavianus, who in Macrobius' *Saturnalia* is portrayed as an expert in the *scientia iuris auguralis* (1. xxiv. 17), revived the activity of the *haruspices*—he is called (v. 50) *Etruscis semper amicus*—and consulted the Sibylline books. St. Augustine says that Flavianus circulated an oracle which foretold the doom of Christianity as many years as the year has days after it (that is, Christianity) had begun its existence.[2] Putting the crucifixion in A.D. 29 and counting 365 years from that date, we come to the year 394 for this pagan *dies irae*. Theodosius had named both his sons consuls for this year; they were not recognized in Italy where Nicomachus Flavianus appears in dated inscriptions as *consul sine collega*. To the believers of the oracle it must have seemed particularly appropriate that Christianity was to be liquidated in a year named after the high priest of the pagan revival himself.

While the pagans made such attempts to restore the pagan religion with all its paraphernalia, Theodosius in the spring of 394 began his march against Italy. Arbogast, Eugenius, and Flavianus took their position on the river Frigidus (Vipacco), the Gorizia Gap, which also now is the most vulnerable spot in the natural defences of northern Italy. Before leaving Milan, the pagan leaders allegedly threatened that, upon their victorious return, they would transform the cathedral into stables and draft the clergy of Milan into the army.[3] Flavianus set up statues of Jupiter on the heights flanking the valley of the Frigidus, and standards bearing the picture of Hercules were carried before the army. The two gods who had been the patrons of Diocletian and Maximian a century before presided over the defeat of the last pagan army of the ancient world on 6 September 394. Flavianus had no wish to survive the cause with which he had identified himself all his life. He committed suicide, although Theodosius would have spared him.[4]

A bald account of the development of the pagan–Christian controversy in the second half of the fourth century does not do justice even to the religious aspects of this conflict. In addition,

---

[1] Cf. on this relief the excellent study of G. Becatti, 'Il culto di Ercole ad Ostia ed un nuovo rilievo votivo', *Bull. della Commissione Archeol. Comunale*, lxvii (1939), 37–60; R. Meiggs, *Roman Ostia* (Oxford, 1960), pp. 347 f.

[2] *De civ. dei*, xviii. 53. Cf. Rufinus, *Hist. eccl.* xi. 33.

[3] Paulinus, *Vita s. Ambrosii*, xxxi (Migne, P.L. xiv. 40).

[4] Cf. on the battle of the Frigidus and on the presence and significance of Jupiter and Hercules in the battle, *A New Document*, pp. 235–9.

evidence of a different nature illuminates the background of the controversy. In 1943 Prof. Alföldi in an important publication[1] called attention to a large group of coin-like monuments, the so-called contorniates (aptly called by Eckhel pseudomoneta) which seem to belong to this period, that is to the years from about 355–60[2] to 410. Emphatically pagan in content, they served in Alföldi's opinion as new year's gifts and, of course, as pagan propaganda. It is interesting that they continue to be produced after the catastrophe of 394. Among the subjects represented may be mentioned on the obverse: Alexander the Great and emperors of the past, especially Nero and Trajan; and on the reverse: scenes from the Alexander romance, the pagan religions, including the cults of Magna Mater, Attis, and Isis, classical mythology, Roman legends, the races and games in the circus. The fact that subjects connected with the circus appear so frequently among the representations[3] in contrast, for instance, to the rare but extremely interesting portrayals of Greek and especially Roman literary figures, such as Horace, Terence, Sallust, Apuleius, and Apollonius of Tyana,[4] gives us some idea of the recipients of the contorniates.

To understand better the aims of the leaders of the pagan revival we must study their individual religious affiliations. Fortunately there survives a relatively large number of inscriptions bearing information of this sort; the most important group of them is a number of altars dedicated to Magna Mater in her shrine near the Vatican, the *Phrygianum*, which became an important religious centre for the last pagans. There some of the most prominent pagans recorded for posterity that they had submitted to the bloody ritual of the *taurobolium*, the slaughtering of a bull above the head of the initiate who through this shower of blood, to quote one of them, was reborn for eternity (*in aeternum*

---

[1] *Die Kontorniaten. Ein verkanntes Propagandamittel der stadtrömischen heidnischen Aristokratie in ihrem Kampfe gegen das christliche Kaisertum* (Budapest, 1943). Pseudomoneta: Eckhel, *Doctrina nummorum veterum*, viii (2nd ed., 1828), 277–314. Alföldi seems to me to have demonstrated the thesis implied by his title, especially the propagandistic character of the contorniates; see also, for example, Piganiol, op. cit., p. 98, and *J. des Savants*, 1945, pp. 19–22; Grenier, *Rev. des Ét. Anc.* xlvi (1944), 374; Vogt, *Gnomon*, xxi (1949), 25–29. But cf. the interesting objections raised by J. M. C. Toynbee, *J.R.S.* xxxv (1945), 115–21.

[2] Alföldi has made it most probable that the creation of the contorniates is due to Memmius Vitrasius Orfitus, *praefectus urbi* 353–6 and 357–9, father-in-law of Symmachus (op. cit., pp. 49, 54 f.). On Orfitus' religious affiliations see *A New Document*, p. 212 and appended chart, No. (1).

[3] Hence J. M. C. Toynbee, loc. cit., p. 120, suggested that the contorniates 'may have been mementoes distributed to people at the beginning of every show'.

[4] Alföldi, *Die Kontorniaten*, pp. 88–90, 18, 71–78.

renatus).[1] The inscriptions which concern us here belong to the years 370 to 390. The series is, of course, not complete. In many of the surviving documents the dedicants have indicated their connexions with other cults, especially priesthoods, leaving once more the impression of a kind of religious propaganda. Fourteen years ago I collected on a prosopographical basis all the material then available in the form of a chart containing 23 names (19 men and 4 women), listing all their religious affiliations. We must limit ourselves here to the most striking observations. To begin with the old official priesthoods: 12 of the men are *pontifices maiores* or *Vestae*, 4 are *augures*, 8 *quindecim viri sacris faciundis*, 2 *septemviri epulonum*. To pass to the oriental cults: 15 are *tauroboliati*, 9 of the 19 men in the list are priests of Mithras, 3 of these in addition hold the charge of *pontifex Solis* (against 2 not affiliated with Mithras), 10 are linked with Hecate, 7 with Liber, 6 with Isis. The accumulation of priesthoods is evidence of the scarcity of people who were willing to shoulder the responsibility of these cults.

The most prominent among them are Vettius Agorius Praetextatus and his wife Fabia Aconia Paulina who died in the years 384 and 385 respectively. Their funeral monument is now kept in the Capitoline Museum (Figs. 7 and 8).[2] The *cursus honorum* of Praetextatus lists first his priesthoods and then—*in re publica vero*—his political offices; Fabia Paulina's religious affiliations follow. Both had been initiated in the mysteries of Eleusis, Lerna,

---

[1] Sextilius Agesilaus Aedesius in A.D. 376, *C.I.L.* vi. 510 = Dessau, *I.L.S.* 4152; *A New Document*, appended chart, No. (15). For the dedications to Magna Mater from the *Phrygianum* cf. above all *C.I.L.* vi. 497–504. For all details see the chart which cannot be repeated here. Two important new finds were made in 1949: cf. B. M. Apollonj-Ghetti, A. Ferrua, E. Josi, and E. Kirschbaum, *Esplorazioni sotto la Confessione di San Pietro in Vaticano*, i (Città del Vaticano, 1951), 14 f., figs. 2 and 3. The second of them is an altar dedicated by Alfenius Ceionius Iulianus Kamenius *taurobolio crioboloque percepto* on 19 July 374. It adds much to our knowledge of this man; cf. *A New Document*, p. 211, and chart, No. (11). His epitaph: Dessau, *I.L.S.* 1264 (A.D. 385). Two other inscriptions, very similar to each other, *C.I.L.* vi. 1675, cf. 31902 and 31940, belong to the period between A.D. 374 and 385. According to an altar dedicated by Ga . . . os, priest of Magna Mater, and published by O. Marucchi, *Notizie degli Scavi di Antichità* (1922), pp. 81–87 (cf. below, p. 213, note), the cult in the *Phrygianum* was resumed after an interruption of twenty-eight years. E. Josi related this information to the work on the basilica of Constantine, a period during which worshipping in the nearby sanctuary of Magna Mater would have ceased; see J. Carcopino, *Études d'histoire chrétienne* (1953), pp. 129–34, and especially M. Guarducci, *Cristo e San Pietro in un documento preconstantiniano della necropoli Vaticana* (Rome, 1953), pp. 65–69, 98 ff., nn. 162–70.

[2] *C.I.L.* vi. 1779 = Dessau, *I.L.S.* 1259 = *Anthol. lat.* ii. 1, ed. Buecheler, No. 111. The photographs are owed to the kindness of Carlo Pietrangeli, Director of the Capitoline Museums. The back of the monument, containing Paulina's poem (1–41), could not be photographed. Cf. *A New Document*, pp. 204–8, 242–4; chart, Nos. (7) and (23).

and Aegina, unquestionably during Praetextatus' proconsulship of Achaia, to which the emperor Julian had appointed him. Under Valentinian I he had protected these mysteries against the emperor's attempt to outlaw them. The prose part of the epitaph ends with the statement: 'They lived in harmony together forty years' ('hi coniuncti simul vixerunt ann. XL'). Both sides and the back of the altar contain touching poems in iambic senarii in which Praetextatus addresses his wife for the last time, and she in turn her husband.

For the religious affiliations of Praetextatus' successor in the leadership of the pagans, Virius Nicomachus Flavianus, the *Carmen adversus Flavianum* remains our principal source. It goes without saying that so biased a document has to be used with utmost discretion. Even so, the *Carmen* seems to indicate that Flavianus was involved with all the cults that had been favoured by Praetextatus. In the inscription in his honour found in the palace of the Symmachi on the Caelius only his pontificate is mentioned, and the new inscription from Leptis dated in 376, when Flavianus was *vicarius Africae*, and published in 1950 by Julien Guey does not yield new pertinent information.[1]

Among the men and women conspicuous in the fight for the pagan cause, one more family deserves special mention. They are the Ceionii who could boast among their ranks the emperor Julian.[2] Three of the most distinguished members of the family take part in the discussions of Macrobius' *Saturnalia*.[3] The readers of Ammianus Marcellinus will remember another famous bearer of the name Ceionius, C. Ceionius Rufius Volusianus, also called Lampadius. He was *praefectus praetorio Italiae* in 355 and made himself obnoxious as *praefectus urbi* in 365, 'a man', to quote Ammianus, 'who grew most indignant if he was not praised when he spat, because he also did this with more skill than anyone else'. Ammianus mentions as an example of his vanity his mania for inscribing his name on monuments erected by the

---

[1] *A New Document*, p. 230, chart No. (8). For the inscription from the Caelius cf. *C.I.L.* vi. 1782 = Dessau, *I.L.S.* 2947. For the inscription from Leptis see J. Guey, 'Flavius Nicomaque et Leptis Magna', *Rev. des Ét. Anc.* lii (1950), 77–89, and J. M. Reynolds and J. B. Ward Perkins, *The Inscriptions of Roman Tripolitania* (British School in Rome, without date), p. 134, No. 475.

[2] *A New Document*, pp. 212 f., and especially n. 36; cf. below, p. 217 (Add.).

[3] Publilius Ceionius Caecina Albinus, *consularis Numidiae c.* 365, and his son Caecina Decius Albinus, *praefectus urbi* 402, and Ceionius Rufius Albinus, *praefectus urbi* 389–91; cf. Seeck, *Symmachus*, pp. clxxv, clxxviii, clxxx–clxxxii; J. Sundwall, *Weströmische Studien* (Berlin, 1915), p. 44, Nos. 11–13.

emperors, and not as restorer of ancient buildings, but as their founder. His house on the Quirinal was once assailed by an angry crowd of people aroused by his confiscation of building material for which he had not paid an indemnity.[1] He was still alive in 371. In the list of leading pagans published by me in 1945 he was missing, but his wife Caecinia Lolliana, a son Ceionius Rufius Volusianus, and a daughter Sabina were represented.[2] Sabina, as *tauroboliata*, dedicated an altar to Attis and Magna Mater; she was also an initiate in the mysteries of Hecate. Caecinia Lolliana was a priestess of Isis, and her son in 390 underwent the *taurobolium* for the second time after twenty years in the sanctuary of the Vatican: 'iterato viginti annis expletis taurobolio suo.' One might certainly have conjectured that the head of the family had shared their religious views if he did not inspire them. The proof was discovered in 1941, but became known in America only after the War.

During the excavation of the triangular precinct dedicated to the Magna Mater and related deities which is situated close to the porta Laurentina in Ostia, a statue of Dionysos or Liber was discovered in the small sanctuary of Attis, which had already yielded important works of sculpture in the excavations of Visconti nearly a century ago (Fig. 9). On the base one reads the following inscription: 'Volusianus v(ir) c(larissimus) ex praefe<c>tis tauroboliatus d(ono) d(edit)' (Fig. 10).[3] The inscription is therefore later than 365, the year in which he held the *praefectura urbis*, but cannot be dated more precisely. It is, of course, closely related to the group of inscriptions from the Vatican sanctuary and demonstrates that the sacred precinct of Ostia was likewise prominent in the second half of the fourth century. On the other hand, the dedication of Volusianus Lampadius to Magna Mater reminds us of the inscription, previously discussed, of Numerius Proiectus which records the restoration of the temple of Hercules in Ostia. One may add in passing that Volusianus appears also repeatedly on columns which were found stored in the portico around the temple of the *Fabri Navales* (Fig. 11), some of which were used in the adjoining

[1] Ammianus Marcellinus, xxvii. iii. 5–10.
[2] *A New Document*, chart, Nos. (20), (17), and (21). Cf. especially *C.I.L.* vi. 512 = Dessau, *I.L.S.* 4154 and *C.I.L.* vi. 30966. Another son of Lampadius was executed in 371, convicted of *codicem noxiarum artium . . . descripsisse*, in spite of the intervention of his father (Ammianus Marcellinus, xxviii. i. 26).
[3] H. Bloch, *Notizie degli Scavi di Antichità* (*Atti della Accademia dei Lincei*) lxxviii (1953), 272 f. (with the earlier literature); Meiggs, *Roman Ostia*, p. 212.

Christian church. Four of them bear the inscription: *Volusiani v. c.* (Fig. 12) and one: *Ru. Bo.* = *Ru(fi) Bo(lusiani)*. These inscriptions are a fine confirmation from Ostia of the criticism raised by Ammianus Marcellinus against Volusianus.[1]

The interest of the whole circle of Symmachus in Ostia was already well known from his correspondence. He himself owned a *praedium Ostiense*, and in 398 he was invited to the *nuptiae Ostienses* of a son of one of his peers, named Sallustius.[2] The new excavations of Ostia have brought to light fascinating remains of elegant houses which must have belonged to well-to-do gentlemen. They were obviously built in the fourth century at a time of general decline of the city. These houses have been ably treated by Giovanni Becatti.[3] Two characteristic views are given here as examples, from the Domus of the Fortuna Annonaria (Fig. 13) and the Nymphaeum of the Erotes (Fig. 14).[4] Unfortunately the owners of all these houses are anonymous for us, just as anonymous as the magnificent statue in the Museum of Ostia which was found near the Baths of the Forum (Fig. 15). It is more than probable that we know the man represented, but are unable to say who he is. The fact that Ragonius Vincentius Celsus, *praefectus annonae* in the late eighties, did much to restore buildings in the area of the Forum, would make him a likely candidate, if the beard were not an argument against the identification with this Christian official and enemy of Symmachus.[5]

The description of Volusianus Lampadius by Ammianus Marcellinus warns us against an indiscriminate idealization of the largely pagan aristocracy in Rome. Even more significant are two long excursuses in which Ammianus subjects this aristocracy to scathing censure (XIV. vi; XXVIII. iv). He criticizes above all their vanity and arrogance and their lack of true culture. *Detestantes ut venena doctrinas*, some limit their reading to Juvenal

---

[1] H. Fuhrmann, *Epigraphica*, iii (1941), 107; Bloch, *Notizie*, 272 f.

[2] *Ostiense praedium*: Ep. i. 6. 2; ii. 52. 2 (A.D. 383); vi. 72. *Suburbanum viae Ostiensis*: vi. 66 (A.D. 398); cf. vi. 8. *Nuptiae Ostienses* of Sallust: vi. 35 (A.D. 398). See also Seeck, *Symmachus*, pp. lxiii f.; Meiggs, *Roman Ostia*, pp. 264, 213.

[3] G. Becatti, 'Case ostiensi del tardo Impero', *Bolletino d'Arte*, ii (1948), 102–28; iii (1948), 197–224.

[4] Domus della Fortuna Annonaria: Reg. V, Ins. ii. 8. Ninfeo degli Eroti: Reg. iv, Ins. iv. 1. Cf. G. Calza, G. Becatti, I. Gismondi, G. De Angelis D'Ossat, and H. Bloch, *Scavi di Ostia*, i (1953), 156–83, especially 158 f.

[5] Cf. on the statue R. De Chirico Calza, *Bull. della Commissione Archeol. Comunale*, lxix (1941), 113–28; *Museo Ostiense* (1947), pp. 13, 44; G. Becatti, loc. cit., 216. On Vincentius Ragonius Celsus see Becatti, ibid.; H. Bloch, *Studies Presented to David M. Robinson*, ii (Saint Louis, Missouri, 1953), 412 f. Cf. below, p. 217 (Add.).

and Marius Maximus, the author of biographies of emperors which were used and imitated by the compilers of the *Historia Augusta*.[1]

Ammianus speaks here with a chip on his shoulder, as he candidly admits. Apparently he, a *honestus advena*, an honourable stranger, was treated with haughtiness in the houses of some of these grandees. He resented this just as much as had Juvenal (from whom he may have borrowed some colours); and he resented even more the expulsion of foreigners from Rome when a food shortage was expected and the foreigners were ousted from the city, 'sectatoribus disciplinarum liberalium sine respiratione ulla extrusis' ('the representatives of the liberal arts who were few in number were ejected without a moment's notice'), while 3,000 dancing girls (we think of the well-known mosaic in the villa of Piazza Armerina) were allowed to remain with no questions asked.[2]

On the other hand, Ammianus speaks with great respect and affection of some of the leaders with whom we are concerned, especially Praetextatus and Symmachus. There can be little doubt that Ammianus, the Greek from Antioch who corresponded with a man of the stature of Libanius, could have stayed in the East if he had wanted to. Klingner justly pointed out that Ammianus' decision to go to Rome and to write his history under great difficulties in the Latin language shows the strange power of attraction which Rome, the *urbs venerabilis* in Ammianus' words, exercised even then.[3]

If Ammianus gives a rather unfavourable picture of what we may term the rank and file of the Roman aristocracy, its leaders have received glowing portrayals in a work which is perhaps the most outstanding document of the pagan revival: the *Saturnalia* of Macrobius, a book rarely studied for its own sake.[4] True, the

---
[1] Cf. W. Hartke, *Römische Kinderkaiser* (Berlin, 1951), p. 52; A. Alföldi, *A Conflict of Ideas in the Late Roman Empire* (1952), pp. 52 f. The passage quoted is taken from Ammianus Marcellinus XXVIII. iv. 14. Cf. XIV. vi. 18: 'et bybliothecis sepulcrorum ritu in perpetuum clausis' ('while the libraries are shut up forever like tombs').

[2] Ammianus Marcellinus, XIV. vi. 12, 19. Mosaic of Piazza Armerina: L. Bernabò Brea, *Musei e monumenti in Sicilia* (Novara, 1958), p. 144.

[3] Praetextatus: Ammianus Marcellinus XXII. vii. 6: *praeclarae indolis gravitatisque priscae senator*; in XXVII. ix. 8–10 Ammianus praises his conduct as *praefectus urbi* (A.D. 367–8), singling out his *integritas* and *probitas*, especially in handling the riots between the followers of Damasus and Ursinus. Flavianus: XXVIII. vi. 28. Klingner, loc. cit., p. 492. *Urbs venerabilis*: Ammianus Marcellinus XIV. vi. 5.

[4] It is a pleasure to report that a new critical edition of the *Saturnalia* is being prepared by James A. Willis of the University of London who recently has given an interesting account of the manuscript tradition of this work: 'De codicibus aliquot manuscriptis Macrobii

Saturnalia is a mine of antiquarian information wherever its author used sources not preserved to us. But both the setting of the dialogue and its major aims are also highly significant. The men who some time before 385 assemble on the eve of the *Saturnalia* and on the two days of the festival itself in the houses of Praetextatus, Nicomachus Flavianus, and Symmachus are the acknowledged leaders of the pagan opposition. Among the others are the *pontifex* Caecina Albinus, the friend and contemporary of Symmachus (who later was to hold on his knee his Christian granddaughter Paula, according to St. Jerome's testimony), his son Decius, and their more distant relative Rufius Albinus.[1] Macrobius himself belongs to the same class. Their learned retinue is best represented by Servius, the famous commentator of Virgil. His modesty in this gathering, awesome both for learning and for nobility (1. iv. 4), 'in hoc coetu non minus doctrina quam nobilitate reverendo', is especially emphasized.

What strikes the reader immediately is the *urbanitas* with which these grandees converse with each other, an *urbanitas* familiar from Cicero's dialogues. If we remember that at least two of the principal characters were dead when the work was written, Praetextatus and his successor Flavianus, the desire on the part of Macrobius to re-evoke in his dialogue an admired group of leading men becomes obvious, as obvious as is the work which inspired him—the commentator of the *Somnium Scipionis*—Cicero's *De re publica*. Just as Cicero had summoned from the past Scipio and his circle, so Macrobius brought to life the last pagans of Rome. To charge his work with a more dramatic meaning, Cicero makes it take place shortly before his hero's violent death, and in the *Somnium Scipionis* the imminent death and transfiguration of Scipio and the tragic destiny of the great statesman and of the Roman state will leave no reader unmoved. The contemporary sympathizers of Macrobius' pagans must have been equally conscious of the doom which had overtaken the two main leaders and their cause. That the connexion of the *Saturnalia* with *De re publica* is a deliberate one can be easily proved. Macrobius says so himself:

'Neque enim Cottae, Laelii, Scipiones amplissimis de rebus, quoad Romanae litterae erunt, in veterum libris disputabunt, Praetextatos

---

Saturnalia continentibus', *Rhein. Mus.* c (1957), 152–64. On the *Saturnalia* as a document of its time cf. Klingner, loc. cit., pp. 488–91; *A New Document*, pp. 206 f.

[1] For the Ceionii cf. above, p. 204, n. 3, St. Jerome, *Ep.* cvii. 1. The *terminus ante quem* for the fictitious date of the dialogue is the death of Praetextatus in 384.

at the End of the Fourth Century

vero, Flavianos, Albinos, Symmachos et Eustathios, quorum splendor similis et non inferior virtus est, eodem modo loqui aliquid licitum non erit.'[1] ('If men such as Cotta, Laelius, and Scipio for as long as Roman literature shall last will discuss the weightiest matter in the books of the ancient writers, men of similar stature and no less merit like Praetextatus, Flavianus, Albinus, Symmachus and Eustathius will most certainly be allowed to speak in the same way' (1. i. 4.)

The first book of the *Saturnalia* is particularly important because it gives Praetextatus the opportunity to deliver three discourses which, in addition to the information they convey, help to characterize the speaker. He traces back his *cognomen* to the episode reported by Aulus Gellius about the boy Papirius who earned the name Praetextatus as a reward for his discretion.[2] If Praetextatus himself believed in this derivation, it illustrates well the qualities for which he was noted: his diplomatic skill, mixed with *probitas* and *integritas*, which he displayed when made *praefectus urbi* in 367 in the midst of the bloody excesses which occurred between the followers of the two pretenders to the papal throne, Damasus and Ursinus. Both Ammianus and Macrobius emphasize his *gravitas* which, nevertheless, according to Ammianus, did not divert the love of his fellow citizens.[3] Macrobius (1. vii. 2) shows Praetextatus' equanimity in the face of provocation from the insolent intruder Euangelus. As the only one who possesses a unique knowledge of sacred matters (*sacrorum omnium unice conscius*), it is he who explains the origin of the *Saturnalia* (1. vii. 17 ff.). But his most important contribution is the demonstration that according to the *ratio divina* almost all gods *ad solem referunt*, are manifestations of Sol. It is a solar theology offered by the *pontifex Solis* in which Apollo, Minerva, Liber, Mars, Mercury, Salus and Aesculapius, Hercules, Sarapis, Adonis, Attis, Osiris, Horus, the Zodiac, Nemesis, Pan, Saturn, Jupiter, and Adad are identified with Sol.[4]

The restoration of the *Porticus Deorum Consentium* (cf. Fig. 2)[5] likewise may be explained in a similar vein. The monument appealed to Praetextatus because he saw in the twelve gods, to use

---

[1] The mention of (C. Aurelius) Cotta, cos. 75 B.C., indicates that Macrobius had also other dialogues in mind (*De oratore* and *De natura deorum*).

[2] *Saturn.* I. vi. 18–26; cf. Gellius, I. 23.

[3] Cf. above, p. 207, n. 3. Macrobius, *Saturn.* I. v. 4: Praetextatus speaks *morali ut adsolet gravitate*.

[4] I. xvii. 1–xxiv. 1. For a discussion of the discourse see *A New Document*, pp. 207–9.

[5] Cf. above, p. 195. For a connexion with Sallustius' Neoplatonic interpretation of the twelve gods cf. A. D. Nock, *Sallustius* (1926), pp. lvii, ciii.

the words of Fabia Paulina in the epitaph of her husband, the *numen multiplex* of the *one* god Sol. Her expression 'divumque numen multiplex doctus colis' describes most admirably the essence of Praetextatus' theology. His friends aptly praise him at the end of his discourse (1. xxiv. 1) as the only one fully aware of the secret nature of the gods—'adfirmantes hunc esse unum arcanae deorum naturae conscium'.

It is very significant that Praetextatus was a kind of predecessor of Boethius: he translated Themistius' paraphrase of Aristotle's *Prior* and *Posterior Analytics*, an achievement known to us from Boethius himself and alluded to by Fabia Paulina.[1]

The literary output of the circle around Symmachus deserves further scrutiny. Nicomachus Flavianus, apparently while *praefectus praetorio* of Italy, wrote *annales*, which he dedicated to Theodosius. He is called *historicus disertissimus* in the inscription from the Caelius. The work is believed to have been used by Ammianus Marcellinus. He also translated Philostratus' *Life of Apollonius of Tyana* into Latin. Thus in one work he preserved the Roman tradition, while in the other he popularized a pagan counterpart to Christ who, like Christ himself, wrought miracles.[2] For however little we notice even the existence of Christianity in the works of pagans of this time, whether because of contempt or of prudence,[3] these works often propagate the pagan cause. Macrobius' *Saturnalia* is a case in point: its main purpose is to present Virgil's *Aeneid*, we might be so bold as to say, as a pagan Bible. Servius' monumental commentary on the poem indirectly serves the same purpose.

It is well known how important a role the *Aeneid* plays in the *Historia Augusta*, a corpus which in my opinion was compiled in the period with which we are dealing, though hardly by one of the leaders themselves, as Hartke tried to prove by attributing it to the son of Nicomachus Flavianus, an hypothesis largely withdrawn in his book *Römische Kinderkaiser* (1951). It would be presumptuous to attempt to settle with a few words so difficult a problem as that of the authorship of the *Historia Augusta*. But when one remembers the dismal picture drawn by Ammianus Marcellinus of the intellectual pursuits of the Roman upper

---

[1] K. Praechter, *Die Philosophie des Altertums* in *Ueberwegs Grundriss* (12th ed.), i (1926), 648, 651.

[2] Cf. above, p. 202. Klingner, loc. cit. p. 497; Alföldi, *Die Kontorniaten*, pp. 59, 74; Hartke, op. cit., pp. 329, 333.

[3] Cf. A. Momigliano, above, p. 94.

class, one cannot help wondering whether the authors of the compilation did not have the shallow rank and file of this still largely pagan group in mind as their prospective readers, wishing to outdo Marius Maximus' collection of biographies of emperors, both in number and in those special qualities which this public appreciated particularly in the imitator of Suetonius.[1] As an instrument of pagan propaganda the *Historia Augusta* is not effective.

The voluminous correspondence of Symmachus which has disappointed so many readers can be evaluated with fairness only if we consider that it was heavily purged by his son when he edited it after his father's death, suppressing without doubt many of the most interesting letters which referred to the rebellion of 393 or 394 and would have compromised the family all the more because of its intimate ties with the chief culprit, Virius Nicomachus Flavianus. Even so, Symmachus is the author of the third *relatio* on the altar of Victoria which will always remain one of the most poignant documents of dying paganism.

Recently a spectacular new discovery by Augusto Campana has given us verses from the pen of one of Symmachus' correspondents. They were contained in an anonymous sylloge of epigrams, compiled presumably early in the fifth century, which was promptly edited by Franco Munari under the title *Epigrammata Bobiensia*, Rome, 1955.[2] Their author is Naucellius, a man who seems to have been a generation older than Symmachus and to whom seven letters of the third book are addressed. In one of them Symmachus mentions a 'carminum tuorum codicem'. Naucellius was a neighbour of Symmachus in Rome: both of them lived on the Caelius.[3] Of the sylloge which was discovered in Bobbio in the fifteenth century only to disappear again soon after, without leaving any traces, a humanist's copy survives in Cod. Vat. lat. 2836. It was in this manuscript that Campana rediscovered the collection.

The epigrams 2-9 are admittedly by Naucellius himself. They describe his villa near Spoleto; in one of them the bath of the

---

[1] Cf. S. Mazzarino, *Aspetti sociali del quarto secolo* (Rome, 1951), p. 367. Cf. above, pp. 206 f.
[2] Munari's volume (ii) will be followed by volume i, in which Augusto Campana will present the text history of the collection. Cf. among reviews especially O. Weinreich, *Gnomon*, xxxi (1959), 239-50; H. Dahlmann, *Gymnasium*, lxiii (1956), 558 ff.; cf. below, p. 218 (Add.).
[3] On Naucellius see Seeck, *Symmachus*, p. ccxxvi; W. Kroll, in Pauly-Wissowa, *Realencyclopädie* xvi. 2, 1898; Munari, op. cit., pp. 22 ff.; Weinreich, loc. cit., p. 240.

villa addresses the *hospes*, warning him that it is too small to serve more than a few people at a time. The subjects of two of the epigrams are portraits of himself. About thirty pieces are translations from the *Anthologia Palatina,* some of them composed in competition with Ausonius, obviously to show that one could safely adhere more closely to the original than Ausonius had done.[1] One poem (48) is addressed to the baths of Nonius Atticus Maximus, consul in 397, one (65) is a translation by Anicius Probinus, consul in 395 with his brother Olybrius. Both brothers were Christians, but were much interested in the literary efforts of the pagan circles.[2] Arusianus Messius, *vir clarissimus,* dedicated to them his still preserved *Exempla elocutionum ex Vergilio, Sallustio, Terentio, Cicerone digesta per litteras* in which he quotes also Symmachus.[3] Thus Arusianus also seems to have been close to Symmachus. Certainly the *Epigrammata Bobiensia* cast an interesting light on the classicistic tendencies of the circle of Symmachus.

This taste did not manifest itself in literature alone. There survive works of art of this period which have induced archaeologists to speak of a Theodosian Renaissance,[4] in view of the overwhelmingly pagan character of these works not a felicitous term. The work which shows classical inspiration in its purest form is the famous ivory diptych with the inscriptions NICOMACHORVM and SYMMACHORVM now in the Cluny Museum in Paris and the Victoria and Albert Museum in London (Fig. 16), respectively. The classical bearing of the two priestesses is striking. One of them is shown with the attributes of the cults of Ceres and Magna Mater (torches; pine tree and cymbals); the other with those of Liber and Jupiter (ivy wreath and oak tree). The occasion for the creation of the diptych was presumably the wedding of Symmachus' daughter and Nicomachus' son which took place probably in 393-4.[5]

[1] Munari, op. cit., pp. 36-38; Weinreich, loc. cit., p. 244.
[2] Cf. Munari, op. cit., pp. 21, 28; A. Campana, *Annali della Scuola Normale Superiore di Pisa,* xxvii (1958), 121; J. Sundwall, op. cit., p. 103, no. 308; p. 121, no. 386.
[3] Edid. Keil in *Gramm. Lat.* vii (1880), 437-514; cf. Munari, op. cit., p. 28, n. 3.
[4] Cf. T. Dohrn, *Mitteil. d. deutsch. archäol. Inst.* ii (1948), 126 f., also for the earlier literature; and in general A. Rumpf, *Stilphasen der spätantiken Kunst* (Cologne, 1955).
[5] Cf. above, p. 199, n. 3. That the diptych was created on the occasion of one of the two weddings between members of the two houses, either in 393-4 or in 401, still seems the most likely explanation of this work of art. R. Delbrück opposed this interpretation in *Die Consulardiptychen* (1929), pp. 209 ff., pl. 54 and lately in *Bonner Jahrb.* clii (1952), 174. Cf. also *A New Document,* p. 229; Alföldi, *Die Kontorniaten,* pp. 42, 63, 68; W. F. Volbach, *Elfenbeinarbeiten der Spätantike und des frühen Mittelalters* (Römisch-germanisches Zentralmuseum zu Mainz, Katalog vii)(Mainz, 1952), p. 39, No. 55, pl. 14. For the symbols of

Another diptych, closely related in subject-matter though not of equal quality, now in Liverpool, depicts Aesculapius and Salus, both divinities linked by Praetextatus with Sol in his discourse in Macrobius.[1] Some of the most outstanding works of this group, such as the Corbridge Lanx and the Mildenhall treasure, were found in England.[2] Their essentially pagan character can hardly be disputed, even if comparable figures and a similar style occur in works executed for Christians, e.g. the famous *missorium* of Theodosius in Madrid or the bridal casket of Proiecta in the British Museum.[3]

If we had to stop our account here, we would have to dismiss the last pagan revival of the West as one of the many unsuccessful fights for lost causes which abound in the history of mankind. Although we might add that this controversy occurred at a particularly important juncture of history, still its significance would be strictly academic. But the last Romans did not leave the stage of history without having made a lasting contribution. In their effort to protect the Roman tradition, they devoted special attention to the preservation of Latin literature.

Rufius Albinus in Macrobius' *Saturnalia* expresses at one point very well the passionate interest of this circle in safeguarding their ancient heritage (III. xiv. 2): 'Vetustas quidem nobis semper, si sapimus, adoranda est.' Conversely, Servius in the same work criticizes his age for not showing enough interest in early Latin literature when he says (VI. ix. 9): 'Nam quia saeculum nostrum ab Ennio et omni bibliotheca vetere descivit, multa ignoramus, quae non laterent, si veterum lectio nobis esset familiaris' ('for because our age shies away from Ennius and all ancient literature, we ignore much that would not be concealed from us, if we were more accustomed to reading ancient authors').

Ammianus Marcellinus here becomes unwittingly a very

Magna Mater see the altar of Ulpius Egnatius Faventinus of A.D. 376 (*C.I.L.* vi. 504 = Dessau, *I.L.S.* 4153; cf. *A New Document*, chart, No. (14)) in the drawing published by C. Pietrangeli, *Bull. della Comm. Archeol. Comunale*, lxviii (1940), 237 f., and the altar of the priest Ga . . . os discussed above, p. 203, n. 1.

[1] Delbrück, *Consulardiptychen*, p. 215, pl. 55; *Bonner Jahrb.* clii (1952), 174; Volbach, op. cit., no. 57. For the discourse of Praetextatus cf. above, p. 209.

[2] Corbridge Lanx: Haverfield, *J.R.S.* iv (1914), pl. 1; T. Dohrn, 'Spätantikes Silber aus Britannien', *Mitteil. d. deutsch. archäol. Inst.* ii (1948), 116 f.; Rumpf, op. cit., p. 21. Mildenhall treasure: Dohrn, loc. cit., pp. 67 ff.; T. D. Kendrick, *The Mildenhall Treasure. A Provisional Handbook* (London, Brit. Mus., 1947).

[3] Missorium of Theodosius: Delbrück, *Spätantike Kaiserporträts* (1933), p. 200, pl. 94; Dohrn, loc. cit., p. 93; Rumpf, op. cit., pp. 20–25. Casket of Proiecta: O. M. Dalton, *Catalogue of Early Christian Antiquities* . . . (London, Brit. Mus., 1901), No. 304, pls. 13 ff.; Dohrn, loc. cit., *passim*.

weighty witness indeed. His criticism of the upper class for restricting their reading to Juvenal and Marius Maximus will be recalled.[1] It is certainly not by accident that in two manuscripts of Juvenal, the Laurentianus and the Leidensis, a *subscriptio* is found saying: 'Legi ego Niceus apud Serbium magistrum Romae et emendavi'. This is generally interpreted to mean that Niceus, a pupil of Servius, emended a manuscript of Juvenal under his master's supervision. From this emended manuscript many of our manuscripts are ultimately descended.[2] Marius Maximus served as an important source to the compilers of the *Historia Augusta*. Ammianus Marcellinus himself continued the great work of Tacitus, which in the intervening two and a half centuries had exercised remarkably little influence upon literature. Syme justly calls Ammianus 'the heir of Tacitus, in every sense'.[3]

As in the case of Juvenal there exist other *subscriptiones*, almost always copied from earlier manuscripts, which constitute invaluable evidence of the work of salvaging carried out by the élite of the pagan, though later Christianized, aristocracy and by their learned aides whose co-operation is clearly shown in the *Saturnalia*. It will suffice to present here only a few examples.[4]

In the famous cod. Laurentianus 68, 2 which contains Apuleius' *Metamorphoses* and the last books of Tacitus' *Annals* as well as what survives of the *Histories*, the following *subscriptio* is found at the end of book 9 of the *Metamorphoses*:[5] 'Ego Sallustius legi et emendavi Romae felix Olybrio et Probino v. c. cos. in foro Martis controversiam declamans oratori Endelechio. Rursus Constantinopoli recognovi Caesario et Attico cos.' The two years are 395 and 397, respectively. Sallustius is a member of the family close to Symmachus and mentioned by him precisely in those years.[6] That Apuleius' work enjoyed some popularity then is demonstrated by the contorniates.[7] The last book must have appealed to the worshippers of Isis. Marrou has shown that both the Forum of Augustus—which is the one meant here—and the Forum of

---

[1] Above, pp. 207, 211.
[2] U. Knoche, *Die römische Satire* (2nd ed., Göttingen, 1957), p. 95; W. V. Clausen, *Persi et Iuvenalis saturae* (Oxford, 1959), pp. x–xii.
[3] R. Syme, *Tacitus* (Oxford, 1958), p. 503, n. 8.
[4] The only complete treatment of the *subscriptiones* still is Otto Jahn's admirable 'Über die Subscriptionen in den Handschriften römischer Classiker', *Berichte der Sächs. Gesellsch. der Wissensch.* (1851), pp. 327–72.
[5] H. I. Marrou, 'La Vie intellectuelle au Forum de Trajan et au Forum d'Auguste', *Mél. de l'École française*, ii (1932), 93 ff. Jahn, loc. cit., p. 331.
[6] Cf. above, p. 206.
[7] Alföldi, *Die Kontorniaten*, p. 90 and pl. XVIII. 9. Cf. above, p. 202.

Trajan were used for school purposes in this period. The Forum of Augustus is mentioned also in a *subscriptio* of the cod. Arondellianus Q of Martial dated in 401 which begins: 'emendavi ego Torquatus Gennadius in foro divi Augusti Martis'.[1] This is Fl. Gennadius Felix Torquatus to whom Claudian dedicated one of his poems.[2] The *protector domesticus* Fl. Iulius Tryphonianus Sabinus corrected his manuscript of Persius in Barcelona and Tolosa in 402 in his thirtieth year, while on military service: 'legi prout potui sine magistro emendans.'[3]

For Praetextatus' activity in this field we have the testimony of his wife in the poem addressed to him where she claims that he improved works written in either language *legendo*.[4] That no trace of his efforts survives may serve as a warning against the belief that we possess more than a fraction of the evidence. Most scribes of later periods did not copy the *subscriptiones* which they found in their models.

It is fitting that we conclude with the most famous set of *subscriptiones* that has been preserved, the *subscriptiones* to the books of the first decade of Livy:[5]

1. Nicomachus Flavianus v. c. III praefect. urbis emendavi apud Hennam.
2. Nicomachus Dexter v. c. emendavi ad exemplum parentis mei Clementiani.
3. Victorianus v. c. emendabam domnis Symmachis.

No. 3 is found at the end of all books of the first decade, No. 1 at the end of 6, 7, and 8, No. 2 at the end of 3, 4, and 5.

Nicomachus Flavianus, the son of Virius Nicomachus Flavianus, held the prefecture of the city for the first time in 393–4. In the inscription set by his son Nicomachus Dexter to his grandfather in 431, his father is called *praef. urbi saepius*,[6] whereas in the private *subscriptio* the younger Flavianus did not hesitate to count the title received by Eugenius. The work was carried out in a

---

[1] *M. Valerii Martialis epigrammaton libri* ed. L. Friedländer, i (Leipzig, 1886), 69; W. M Lindsay, *The Ancient Editions of Martial with Collations of the Berlin and Edinburgh Manuscripts* (Oxford, 1903), p. 43. Not included by Marrou in his article (above, p. 214, n. 5).

[2] *Carm. min.* xix (43). On Gennadius Torquatus, proconsul of Achaia shortly before 395, cf. Groag, op. cit., pp. 64 f.

[3] Jahn, loc. cit., pp. 331 f.; *Persius*, ed. W. Clausen (Oxford, 1956), p. viii.

[4] Dessau, *I.L.S.* 1259, 8–12; *A New Document*, p. 205 and n. 23; Jahn. loc. cit., p. 341

[5] Jahn, loc. cit., pp. 335 ff.; Tite-Live, *Histoire Romaine* i (ed. J. Bayet; Paris, 1954), pp. xcii–c; Gius. Billanovich, *J. of the Warburg and Courtauld Institutes*, xiv (1951), 199.

[6] *C.I.L.* vi. 1783 = Dessau, *I.L.S.* 2948.

villa of the Nicomachi near Enna. It might be good to remember that the grandiose villa del Casale near Piazza Armerina would fit this description.

The *emendatio* of Livy was by necessity a co-operative undertaking, and Dexter helped his father with the first decade. Victorianus is known to have edited the elder Flavianus' Latin translation of Philostratus' Life of Apollonius of Tyana.[1] Here we see him at work for the Symmachi. Symmachus himself mentions in 401 the *munus totius Liviani operis* in which he was then engaged.[2] Whether they succeeded in this ambitious project, covering the whole work of Livy, remains extremely doubtful. But by a rare coincidence we are in a position to judge what this edition meant for the text of the first decade. For in the celebrated Verona palimpsest there survives a manuscript of this part of Livy's work which was written just about the time of the *recensio* by the Symmachi and Nicomachi.[3] It is, in spite of its venerable age, of very limited value for the constitution of the text.

The tradition established by the circle of Symmachus, and this is another great merit of these men, did not break off with the collapse of their religious aspirations. The *subscriptiones* last almost until the middle of the sixth century, and it is significant that the work was carried on at a time of increasing barbarization, and especially by the families of this circle. Vettius Agorius Basilius Mavortius, obviously a relative and probably a descendant of Vettius Agorius Praetextatus, bestowed his loving care both on Horace and, curiously, on Prudentius' antipagan poem *In Symmachum* after 527, the year in which he held the consulship, 150 years after Praetextatus' death.[4] Macrobius' commentary on the *Somnium Scipionis* received the attention of the great-grandson of the Symmachus who had been one of the main participants in the symposion of the *Saturnalia*: 'Aurelius Memmius Symmachus v. c. emendabam vel disting. meum Ravennae cum Macrobio Plotino Eudoxio v. c.', the latter unquestionably a descendant of the author Macrobius.[5] But this very Symmachus, consul in 485, is the father-in-law of Boethius,[6] whose efforts were directed

---

[1] Sidon. Apoll. *Ep.* viii. 3. Ensslin in Pauly–Wissowa, *Realencyclopädie* viii. 2 A (1958), 2072 f., No. 5. Cf. above, p. 210.

[2] *Ep.* ix. 13. Jahn, loc. cit., p. 338; Bayet, op. cit., pp. xcii f.

[3] E. A. Lowe, *Cod. Lat. Antiqu.* iv (Oxford, 1947), No. 499.

[4] Jahn, loc. cit., p. 353; Klingner, loc. cit., p. 522; Lowe, *Cod. Lat. Antiqu.* v (1950), No. 571a; J. Sundwall, *Abhandlungen zur Geschichte des ausgehenden Römertums* (Helsinki, 1919), pp. 130, 139.   [5] Cf. Jahn, loc. cit., p. 347; J. Sundwall, op. cit., pp. 114 f.

[6] Seeck, *Symmachus*, p. xl; Sundwall, op. cit., pp. 101–5, 159–62.

toward similar aims. Boethius, already a Christian, though imbued with a profound knowledge of ancient philosophy, found a tragic death at the hands of the executioner. The significance of his premature disappearance for the intellectual development of the Middle Ages cannot be adequately estimated. He truly deserves the title of the last Roman. Yet in another sense this honour belongs to Virius Nicomachus Flavianus who, when he saw that the Rome for which he had lived was coming to an end, refused to compromise with the new order, and chose instead the death of Cato. Yet in dying he left in his own family and among his friends men who were prepared to rescue in a crumbling world what was most precious of the ancient heritage.

ADDENDA

During the three years which have elapsed since this lecture was delivered, scholarship in this field has been very active. As it was not possible—except for a few special cases—to take into consideration in the foregoing paper these new investigations, perhaps some of them may be mentioned here.

In the most important recent work on Roman religion, Kurt Latte's *Römische Religionsgeschichte* (München, 1960), the problems with which this paper is concerned are treated on pp. 366–71.

p. 200 (above): The so-called *Carmen adversus Flavianum* has been studied anew by Giacomo Manganaro, 'La reazione pagana a Roma nel 408–9 d. C. e il poemetto anonimo "contra paganos" ', *Giornale ital. di filologia*, xiii (1960), 210–24. He dates it after 400 because of alleged borrowings from Claudian, first observed by Th. Birt in 1892. While this *terminus post quem* would not necessarily affect the usual interpretation of the poem, he tries to show that it actually reflects the pagan reaction at the time of Alaric's first siege of Rome in 408/9, and that it is specifically directed against Gabinius Barbarius Pompeianus, *praefectus urbi* 408/9. In spite of the persuasive aspects of some of Manganaro's arguments, it seems doubtful that his thesis will stand up under serious scrutiny.

p. 204: On the Ceionii cf. also the interesting article by A. Chastagnol, 'Le sénateur Volusien et la conversion d'une famille de l'aristocratie romaine du Bas-Empire', *Rev. des Ét. Anc.* lviii (1956), 240–53. The stemma on p. 249 incorporates without dissent the family-tree of Lampadius first given in *A New Document*, p. 212, n. 36.

p. 206, n. 5: To the statue of Ostia should be compared the portrait statue of Virius Audentius Aemilianus, *v. c., consularis Campaniae*, found in Puteoli with its inscribed base and now in the Antiquario Flegreo in Pozzuoli. Mario Napoli, who published

218   *The Pagan Revival in the West*

it in *Boll. d'arte*, xliv (1959), 107–13, correctly dates it about 370, a few decades before the statue of Ostia.

p. 211: The *Epigrammata Bobiensia* have been the subject of a monograph by W. Speyer, *Naucellius und sein Kreis. Studien zu den Epigrammata Bobiensia, Zetemata*, xxi (München, 1959). The main result, that Naucellius was not the compiler of the collection, as Munari had assumed in his excellent editio princeps, seems now generally accepted (also above in the text). See especially the thorough and critical review of Speyer's book by W. Schmid, *Gnomon*, xxxii (1960), 340–60.

Sources of photographs

The following sources of illustrations are herewith gratefully acknowledged:

Figs. 1, 7, 8: Musei Capitolini, Rome.
Figs. 2, 3, 9, 13, 14: Fototeca Unione Roma.
Figs. 4, 15: Gabinetto Fotografico Nazionale, Rome.
Figs. 6, 10–12: Soprintendenza alle Antichità, Roma III (Ostia).
Fig. 16: By courtesy of Victoria and Albert Museum, London.
Fig. 5 is reproduced from *Harvard Theological Review*, xxxviii (1945), 201.

FIG. 1. Constantius II. Palazzo dei Conservatori, Rome

FIG. 2. Porticus Deorum Consentium. Forum Romanum, Rome

FIG. 3. Temple of Hercules. Ostia

FIG. 4. Inscription of Numerius Proiectus. Ostia

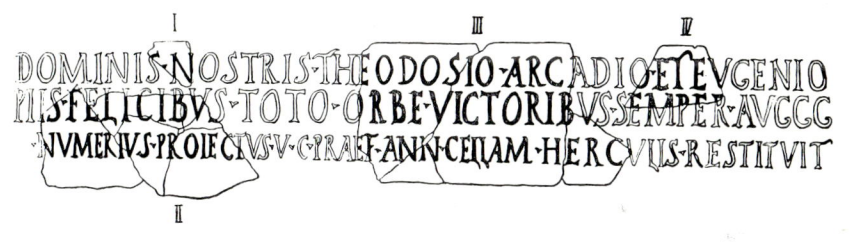

FIG. 5. Inscription of Numerius Proiectus. Reconstruction

FIG. 6. Relief of the haruspex C. Fulvius Salvis. Ostia.

7. Front   8a. Left side   8b. Right side

FIGS. 7–8. Funeral monument of Praetextatus and his wife. Museo Capitolino, Rome

Fig. 9. Temple of Attis. Ostia

Fig. 10. Statue of Liber dedicated by Volusianus Lampadius. Ostia

FIG. 11. Columns stored near the temple of the Fabri Navales. Ostia

FIG. 12. Inscription of Volusianus. Ostia

Fig. 13. Domus of the Fortuna Annonaria. Ostia

Fig. 14. Nymphaeum of the Erotes. Ostia

Fig. 15. Statue. Museum, Ostia

Fig. 16. Diptych of the Symmachi and Nicomachi, right half. By courtesy of the Victoria and Albert Museum, London

Index

Ablabius, *praefectus praetorio*, 29, 51.
Abraxas, 104.
Actus Silvestri, 45.
Aeneas of Gaza, 138, 163-4.
  Theophrastus, 148.
Aesculapius, diptych, 213.
Alamanni, 58.
Alaric I, 10.
Albinus, Caecina, 208.
Albinus, Rufius, 198, 208, 213.
Alexandria, School of, 131 ff.
Alfaric, P., 148.
Alföldi, A., 4, 196, 202.
Altar of Victory, 21, 33, 194, 196, 211.
Altheim, F., 4, 40.
Amantius of Aquileia, 66.
Ambrose, St., 8, 10, 31, 32, 60, 66, 122, 157-65, 195-9.
  De Bono Mortis, 165.
  De Isaac, 165.
  De Jacob, 165.
Ammianus Marcellinus, 71, 81, 89, 94, 95, 97, 98, 99, 103, 107, 108, 109, 110, 111, 114, 115, 116, 120, 194, 204-6, 207, 209, 210, 213-14.
Ammonius, Alexandrian philosopher, 132, 134, 137-8.
Amous of Nitria, 144.
Anastasia, half-sister of Constantine the Great, 47.
Anonymus Valesianus (*Origo Constantini Imperatoris*), 87, 88.
Antaura (Neoplatonic name of female demon), 121.
Anthologia Palatina, 212.
Apuleius, *Metamorphoses*, 214.
Arbetio, *magister peditum*, 28.
Arbogast the Frank, 25, 198-9, 201.
Arcadius, 26, 200.
Argenteus, Codex, 74 f.
Arnobius, *Adversus nationes*, 58, 151-7, 165.
Artemis of Ephesus, 121.
Arykanda, inscription of, 39,
Asmus, R., 127.
Athanasius, St., *Life of St. Anthony*, 11.
Athens, School of, 132.
Attila, 75, 76.
Augustine, St., 13, 14, 95, 99, 129, 143, 145, 196, 201.
  Civitas Dei, 2, 10, 87, 99, 104, 163.
  De anima et eius origine, 146.
  De opera Monachorum, 12.

De sancta Virginitate, 12.
  Regula ad servos Dei, 12.
Augustus, 41, 102.
Ausonius, 195, 212.
Avianus, Festus, 98.

Bagaudae, revolt of, 13.
Baronio, Cesare, 92.
Bartholomew, St., apocryphal Gospel of, 123.
Basil, St., 11, 122.
Bavarians, 68.
Baynes, N. H., 4.
Becatti, G., 206.
Bernard of Clairvaux, St., 193.
Besa, shrine of (at Abydos), 108-9.
Biondo, Flavio, 3.
Boethius, 210, 216-17.
Burckhardt, J., 16.
Burgundians, 71.

Caecilius of Calacte, 82.
Campana, A., 211.
Caracalla, 102.
Carmen ad Senatorem, 200.
Carmen adversus Flavianum, 200, 201, 204, 217.
Cassian, John, St., 12.
Cassiodorus, 12, 98.
Ceionii, family of, 204-6, 208, 217.
Celsus, anti-Christian polemicist, 147.
Chalcidius, *In Timaeum*, 163.
Chaldaean Oracles, The, 139.
Charlemagne, 1, 2, 5.
Chronica Gallica, 71.
Chronica urbis Romae, 86, 97.
Chronographer of 354, 84, 86, 97.
Chrysostom, St. John, 8, 14, 19, 26, 31, 106, 116, 149.
Cicero, *Somnium Scipionis*, 208.
Circumcelliones, revolt of, 13, 18-19.
Claudius Gothicus, 7, 44, 152.
Clement of Alexandria, 83, 90.
Commodus, 103.
Constans, 47, 48, 51, 193-4.
Constantia, half-sister of Constantine the Great, 47.
Constantine the Great, 1, 7, 15, 24, 33, 36, 79, 80, 85, 105, 106, 109-25, 193.
Constantine Caesar, 47, 51.
Constantinople, Council of (381), 56.
Constantius II, 27, 29, 47, 48, 51, 103, 108, 109, 115, 194.

Corbridge Lanx, 213.
Crispus Caesar, 47–48, 49.
Cyprian, St., 122.

Dalmatius, half-brother of Constantine the Great, 46, 51.
Dalmatius Caesar, 51.
Damascius, *Life of Isidore*, 135.
Damasus I, Pope, 31–32, 209.
Damigeron, 118, 119.
Datianus, consul in A.D. 358, 29.
Dee, John, 120.
Defixiones, 119–20.
Dexter, *see* Nicomachus.
Diehl, C., 4.
Diocletian, 7, 26, 35.
Dörries, H., 41.
Domitian, 103.
Domitianus, *praefectus praetorio Orientis*, 29.
Donatists, 18, 54.
Dopsch, A., 5, 6.
Dorotheus of Antioch, 74.

Eleusius, Bishop of Cyzicus, 22.
Eliade, M., 2.
Elpidius, *praefectus praetorio Orientis*, 29.
Enchiridion Leonis Papae, 123.
Epiphanius, St., Bishop of Salamis, 118.
Epigrammata Bobiensia, *see* Naucellius.
Eugenius, 33, 199–201, 215.
Eugippius, *vita Severini*, 15.
Eunapius, *Lives of the Sophists*, 81, 95, 98, 99.
Eupraxius, 97.
Eusebius, Bishop of Caesarea:
  Chronicle, 84, 85.
  Ecclesiastical History, 79, 80, 89–92.
  Life of Constantine the Great, 36, 40, 43–45, 93.
  Preparation for the Gospel, 80.
Eutropius, *Breviarium*, 86.
Evagrius, translator of Athanasius' *Life of St. Anthony*, 92.
Evoptius, Bishop of Ptolemais, 140.
Exsuperantissimus, cult of, 38.

Fausta, wife of Constantine the Great, 46–48.
Faustus Reiensis, 145.
Festus (Rufius?), *Breviarium*, 86, 95, 98.
Firmicus Maternus, 117.
Flavianus, *see* Nicomachus.
Florus, *Epitome*, 2.
Fravitta the Goth, 25.
Frigidus, battle of, 201.
Fritigil, Queen of the Marcomanni, 60, 66, 68.
Frumentius, Bishop of Axum, 60, 61.

Gabinius Barbarius Pompeianus, 217.
Galen, 103.
Galerius, 46, 47.
Gallienus, 26.
Geffcken, J., 145.
Gellius, Aulus, 209.
Gennadius Felix Torquatus, 215.
Generid the Goth, 25.
Gepids, 75, 76.
Germanicus, 103, 119.
Gibbon, E., 1, 3, 6, 9, 16, 107.
Goēteia, 101, 106, 108.
Gothic Calendar, 73.
Gratian, Emperor, 195, 196.
Gratian, *comes rei militaris*, 28.
Grégoire, H., 39, 40.
Gregory the Great, Pope, 19, 20.
Gregory Nazianzus, St., *Oration IV*, 25.
Gregory of Nyssa, St., 146; *De hominis opificio*, 164.
Gregory Thaumaturgus, 122.
Guey, J., 204.
Guicciardini, Francesco, 89.

Hadot, P., 165.
Hannibalianus, half-brother of Constantine the Great, 46, 51.
Harnack, A., 6.
Hartke, W., 210.
Haruspices, 105, 110, 200.
Hecate, 112, 115.
Hegesippus, 89.
Helena, 43, 45, 50.
Hermias, Alexandrian philosopher, 134.
Heruls, 68.
Hierocles, 134, 138, 148.
Hilarian, bishop, *De cursu temporum*, 85.
Hilarius, 111–12.
Hildebert of Lavardin, 2.
Hippolytus of Rome, 83, 84.
Historia Augusta, 81, 89, 94, 95, 96, 98, 207, 210, 211, 214.
Holl, K., 92.
Honorius, 199, 200.
Hypatia, 126, 133, 134, 135, 140.

Iamblichus of Chalcis, 115, 117, 132, 136, 139, 162.
Iliberris, Council of, 21.
Isidorus, Athenian philosopher, 135.

James, St., Gospel of, 123.
Jerome, St., 11, 20, 208.
  Chronicon, 85, 86.
Joannes Philoponus, 137, 140, 148, 150.
John of Ephesus, 19.
John the Grammarian, *see* Joannes Philoponus.

Index

John of Jerusalem, 149.
John, St., Gospel of, 74, 122, 123.
Jordanes, *Getica*, 70, 73.
Josephus, Flavius, 91.
Jovian, 195.
Julian the Apostate, 24, 30, 52, 95, 96, 110, 115, 195, 204.
Julius Africanus, 83, 84, 85.
Justinian, 1, 15, 136.
Juvenal, 206, 214.

Kingsley, C., 127, 129.
Klingner, F., 207.
Kraft, H., 41, 44.

Lacombrade, C., 128, 130.
Lactantius, *De mortibus persecutorum*, 39, 40, 44, 45, 47, 79, 80, 82, 88.
Laodicea, Synod of, 107.
Latte, K., 217.
Lemerle, P., 128.
Leontius, 32.
Libanius, *Orations*, 28, 29, 30, 31, 32, 116, 120.
Licinius, 46-47.
Lithica, 117, 119.
Livy, 215-16.
Lolliana, Caecinia, 205.
Lombards, 68.
Louÿs, P., 127.
Lowe, E. A., 200.
Lucian, *The Cock*, 164.
Luke, St., Gospel of, 74.

Macrobius Plotinus Eudoxius, 216.
Machiavelli, Niccolò, 3, 89.
Macrobius:
   Commentarii in Somnium Scipionis, 157, 165, 208, 216.
   Saturnalia, 157, 201, 204, 207-10, 213, 214.
Magdeburg centuriators, 92.
Mamertus, Claudius, 145.
Manganaro, G., 217.
Marbod, Bishop of Rennes, 119.
Marcomanni, 60, 68.
Marinus, *Vita Procli*, 139.
Marius Maximus, 207, 211, 214.
Mark, St., Gospel of, 74.
Martial, 215.
Marx, K., 4.
Marxist theory, 2.
Matthew, St., Gospel of, 69, 74.
Maurists, 92.
Mavortius, Vettius Agorius Basilius, 216.
Maximinus, *praefectus praetorio Galliarum*, 28.
Maximus, tutor to Emperor Julian, 32, 115, 117.

Maximus, usurper, 197.
Maximus, Nonius Atticus, 212.
Messius, Arusianus, *Exempla*, 212.
Methodius of Olympus, 146.
Mildenhall Treasure, 213.
Missorium of Theodosius, 213.
Monasticism, 11, 12.
Montaigne, Michel de, 165.
Montesquieu, Charles Louis, 3.
Munari, F., 211.
Museum of Alexandria, 133.

Naucellius and the *Epigrammata Bobiensia*, 211-12, 218.
Nazarius, *Panegyricus*, 95.
Nemesius of Emesa, *On the Nature of Man*, 146, 162-3.
Niceta, Bishop of Remesiana, 64-65.
Niceus, pupil of Servius, 214.
Nicomachi, diptych, 212.
Nicomachus Dexter, 215, 216.
Nicomachus Flavianus, 33, 98, 197-201, 204, 208-11, 215-17.
Nicomachus Flavianus the younger, 199, 200, 210-11, 215.
Numerius Proiectus, 200, 205.

Odoacer, 199.
Olympius, philosopher, 32.
Opus Imperfectum in Mattheum, 69.
Origo gentis Romanae, 96, 97.
Orosius, *Historiae*, 13, 67, 70, 71, 87, 88, 99.
Ostrogoths, 72-75.
Otto III, 2.

Palladius, bishop, 63-64.
Pamprepius, Neoplatonist philosopher, 32.
Paruta, Paolo, 3.
Patricius, 111-12.
Paul, St., 84, 123.
Paulina, Fabia Aconia, 203-4, 209, 210.
Paulinus of Nola, 65, 66.
Paulus Tartareus, 109.
Péguy, C., 126.
Persius, 215.
Peter, St., 104, 110.
Philippus, Flavius, consul A.D. 348, 29.
Philostratus, *Life of Apollonius of Tyana*, 93, 103, 131, 210, 216.
Phrygianum, shrine of Magna Mater, 202.
Piazza Armerina, villa, 216.
Piganiol, A., 44.
Pirenne, H., 5, 6.
Plato:
   Phaedo, 156-7, 162, 163.
   Republic, 162.
   Timaeus, 162, 163.

Plotinus, 132, 136, 165.
   Enneads, 162, 165.
Polybius, 2.
Porphyry, 84, 131, 132, 136, 139, 162.
   Against the Christians, 156.
   Isagoge, 140.
   On the Return of the Soul, 156, 165.
   Philosophy of the Oracles, 140.
Porticus Deorum Consentium, 195, 209.
Praechter, F., 140.
Praetextatus, Vettius Agorius, 97, 195–7, 203–4, 207–10, 215, 216.
Probinus, Anicius, 212.
Procopius of Caesarea, 89.
Procopius of Gaza, *Refutation*, 148.
Proiecta, Casket of, 213.
Prudentius, *In Symmachum*, 200, 216.
Pseudo-Philo, *Liber antiquitatum biblicarum*, 88.

Ragonius Vincentius Celsus, 206.
Rechiarius, Ruler of the Sueves, 71.
Reitzenstein, R., 92.
Romulus Augustulus, 1.
Rostovtzeff, M., 5, 6.
Rugi, 76.

Sabas, St., 57.
Sabians, 136, 138.
Sabina, daughter of C. Ceionius Rufius Volusianus, 205.
Sabinus, Fl. Iulius Tryphonianus, 215.
Saffrey, H. D., 135.
Sallustius, 214.
Salus, diptych, 213.
Salvianus, *De gubernatione Dei*, 13, 14, 75.
Schwartz, E., 85, 90.
Serapeum of Alexandria, 198.
Servius, 208, 210, 213–14.
Severus of Antioch, 30.
Simon Magus, 154.
Solignac, A., 165.
Souda, 133, 134.
Sozomen, 91.
Staerman, E. M., 4.
Stettner, W., 162.
Sublime, On the, 82.
subscriptiones, 214–16.
Sueves, 71, 78.
Suidas, *see Souda*.
Sulpicius Severus, *Vita Martini*, 19, 85, 87.
Symmachi, diptych, 212.
Symmachus, Aurelius Memmius, 216.
Symmachus, Q. Aurelius, 9, 95, 97, 157, 199, 200, 206–12, 214, 216.
   Relatio III, 21, 157, 196–7, 211.
Synesius of Cyrene, 14, 127–31, 135, 138.
   Commentary on Aristotle, 140.
   De Insomniis, 130, 147.
   Dion, 131, 144–5.
   Hymns, 130, 141.
   Letter 105, 141, 142, 145.
Syrianus, Athenian philosopher, 135.

Tacitus, *Annals*, 214.
Taormina, L., 165.
Tatian, consul A.D. 391, 30, 197.
Taurobolium, 202, 205.
Taurus, Flavius Palladius Rutilius, consul A.D. 361, 29.
Tertullian, *De anima*, 163.
Testamentum Salomonis, 119.
Themistius, 30, 32, 210.
Theodorus, 111, 112, 114.
Theodosius, 10, 32, 81, 97, 114, 120, 195–201, 212–13.
Theon, father of Hypatia, 133, 134, 139.
   On Omens, 139.
Theophilus, patriarch, 141, 149.
Theurgia, 101, 106, 108, 115.
Tiberius, 102, 105.
Tiberius Constantine, 30.
Tillemont, Le Nain de, 92.
Toynbee, A., 1, 128.
Treu, K., 128, 144.
Troeltsch, E., 6.

Ulfila, 'Apostle of the Goths', 58, 63, 69, 74.
Ursinus, papal pretender, 209.

Valens, 26, 86, 95, 110, 111.
Valentinian I, 26, 110, 111, 195, 204.
Valentinian II, 196, 198–9.
Valerian, edict of, 21.
Vandals, 69–70.
Varro, 99.
Veneficium, 102.
Venenum, 102.
Victor, Aurelius, *Caesares*, 26, 81, 86, 94, 96, 98.
Victorianus, editor of *Life of Apollonius of Tyana*, 215–16.
Victorinus, Marius, 145.
Victricius of Rouen, 66.
Virius Audentius Aemilianus, 217–18.
Visigoths, 58, 63, 69, 71, 74.
Voltaire, F.-M. A. de, 3.
Volusianus, C. Ceionius Rufius (Lampadius), 204–6, 217.

Wilamowitz-Möllendorf, U. v., 144.

Zacharias of Mytilene, 30.
Zacharias Scholasticus:
   Ammonius, 148.
   Life of Severus of Antioch, 136–7.
Zonaras, 49.
Zosimus, 49.

PRINTED IN GREAT BRITAIN
AT THE UNIVERSITY PRESS, OXFORD
BY VIVIAN RIDLER
PRINTER TO THE UNIVERSITY